MW01171257

HAPPINESS, GOOD HEALTH, AND PROSPERITY

Mo Go Fa Lo

ISBN-13: 978-1-961413-01-6
ISBN-10: 1-961413-01-9

Cover design by: Mo Go Fa Lo
Library of Congress Control Number: 2024911742
Printed in the United States of America

This is dedicated to those who share their love with the world. Your abundant generosity touches countless lives. You create ripples of kindness. Those ripples of kindness extend far beyond what you can see. Thank you for your noble and unwavering commitment. You spread compassion. Your acts of kindness serve as a beacon of hope and a powerful reminder. Good does exist in the world. You are a true inspiration. Your example deeply motivates me. I strive for the same level of generosity and love in my own life.

I am one with the universe,
and one with the infinite divine.
I am one with the seed body,
and one with the soul spirit sublime.

When I think of these thoughts,
Suddenly I believe!
Love is real!
Joy I feel!

When I act on these thoughts,
my love comes back to me;
multiplied!
That is what I will do!

MO GO FA LO

Saving Humanity From Extinction By Changing Behaviors with nothing more serious than the simple communication of ideas. Life on planet Earth is my franchise. Optimism is my brand. Saving Humanity From Extinction By Changing Behaviors is my plan.

One totality exists. We are part of the one totality. Ideas are thoughts, beliefs, and, expectations about the one totality. We value certain ideas. These certain ideas are our values. Our values act on our emotions. Our emotions act on our behaviors.

Saving Humanity From Extinction By Changing Behaviors with nothing more serious than the simple communication of ideas. We value certain ideas. These certain ideas are our values. Our values act on our emotions. Our emotions act on our behaviors.

The most powerful emotions of joy, faith, and love follow from a mystery. The mystery is a myth. The myth is about a life and immunity. The life and immunity of the soul spirit is, eternal and divine. Belief in the value of the most optimistic myths is what I have in mind.

Saving Humanity From Extinction By Changing Behaviors with nothing more serious than the simple communication of ideas. The life and immunity of the soul spirit is, eternal and divine. Belief in the value of the most optimistic myths is what I have in mind.

We have an infinite number, diversity, and variety of lives to live. We have an infinite number, diversity, and variety of bodies to give. Seed Body Soul Spirit, Living Infernal Fractal Entity the union of Mother God and Father Love creates life. We are Soul Children!

Saving Humanity From Extinction By Changing Behaviors with nothing more serious than the simple communication of ideas. Seed Body Soul Spirit, Living Infernal Fractal Entity the union of Mother God and Father Love creates life. We are Soul Children!

Saving Humanity From Extinction By Changing Behaviors with nothing more serious than the simple communication of ideas. Life on planet Earth is my franchise. Optimism is my brand. Saving Humanity From Extinction By Changing Behaviors is my plan.

MO GO FA LO

CONTENTS

PREFACE

A totality exists. For that reason, we are part of the totality. The totality encompasses everything. For that reason, the concept of the totality is indeed profound. It suggests. Every element, from the past to the future, is interconnected within a unified, all-encompassing totality.

In contemplating this totality, we recognize our own place within it. We are beings. We perceive, analyze, and interact with the world. We are undeniably part of this vast tapestry of existence. Our past experiences, present actions, and future aspirations all contribute to the unfolding narrative of the totality.

Consider the past. Countless events, from the formation of galaxies to the rise and fall of civilizations, have shaped the course of history. Each occurrence, no matter how significant or seemingly insignificant, has left its mark on the fabric of reality. These events are not merely relegated to memory; they persist as integral components of the totality.

In the present moment, we find ourselves amidst a complex interplay of phenomena. Every sensation, thought, and action contributes to the ongoing manifestation of the totality. From the microscopic interactions within cells to the grand movements of celestial bodies, the present moment is alive with the dynamic energy of existence.

Unknown possibilities lie ahead. Looking towards the future, we confront the unknown possibilities. While we cannot predict with certainty what will come to pass, we recognize. The future is already implicit within the totality. The seeds of tomorrow are planted in the choices we make today. In this way, we participate in the ongoing creation of reality.

Fundamentally, the totality encompasses the past, present, and future of everything. For that reason, the totality transcends the limitations of time, space, and individual perspectives. Within this framework, the concept of nonexistence appears as an impossibility. To exist is to be conscious, to perceive, to experience. Nonexistence, by contrast, lies beyond the realm of experience, beyond the boundaries of consciousness.

While we may ponder the notion of nonexistence, we can never truly grasp it in its entirety. Our very capacity to ponder, to contemplate, presupposes our existence. Thus, existence is not only a reality but a necessity within the totality.

In embracing the totality of existence, we recognize the interconnectedness of all things. We are not separate entities but integral facets of a unified whole. From the vast reaches of the cosmos to the depths of our own consciousness, we are part of something greater than ourselves. We are part of a totality. The totality encompasses everything, everywhere, at all times.

Consciousness is existence and nothing can exist outside of consciousness. This assertion presents a fascinating philosophical inquiry into the nature of reality. It challenges a conventional idea. The conventional idea is. An objective universe exists independently of consciousness.

Let's explore this notion further. Let us suppose. An objective universe exists independently of consciousness. The universe is separate from any conscious beings. In this hypothetical scenario, there would be no one to observe, perceive, or interact with the universe consciously. From a subjective standpoint, the absence of conscious beings would render the universe devoid of any experiential reality.

Let us suppose. No conscious entities inhabit the universe. In that event, there would be no minds to conceptualize its existence, no senses to perceive its phenomena, and no interpretations to give it meaning. In this sense, the universe would be devoid of conscious awareness. For that reason, the universe would become a mere abstraction - a hypothetical construct with no tangible presence.

Conscious entities would not know of the existence of an uninhabited universe. This fact raises a profound question: Could such a universe exist? From a pragmatic perspective, without consciousness to apprehend it, the universe loses its empirical reality. It exists in a state of suspended ambiguity. Conscious awareness provides confirmation. Without conscious awareness, no confirmation is provided.

In essence, the universe only truly exists within the minds of conscious entities. The universe is observed, interpreted, and understood through consciousness. Consciousness imbues reality with meaning, significance, and existence itself.

This perspective suggests. Consciousness is not merely an epiphenomenon of the universe but rather its very essence. Consciousness and existence are inseparable—they are two sides of the same coin. The universe comes into being through the lens of consciousness. Without consciousness, the universe loses its ontological status.

Therefore, it seems impossible for anything to exist outside of consciousness. Consciousness is not just a passive observer of reality but an active participant in its creation and sustenance. In this way, consciousness is not only a fundamental aspect of existence but is existence itself.

A common point of contention in philosophical discourse is the notion. Something exists outside of consciousness. However, upon closer examination, it becomes apparent. The existence of something outside of consciousness is elusive and ultimately illusory.

Let us suppose. A person disagrees with an idea. The idea is. Everything exists within consciousness. They may argue. Elements of reality exist independently of any conscious awareness. However, upon closer introspection, this perspective begins to unravel.

Let us suppose. A person genuinely explores the concept of something existing outside of consciousness. In that event, the person may find. What the person perceives as external to consciousness is, in fact, a mental projection generated by the person's own consciousness. In other words, the very act of perceiving something outside of consciousness necessitates the involvement of consciousness itself.

Consider the example of a universe devoid of conscious beings. Let us suppose. Such a universe were to exist. In that event, it would only exist as a mental construct within the imagination of a conscious entity. Without the observer's consciousness to conceptualize it, this hypothetical universe loses its ontological status and becomes nothing more than a figment of the mind.

In this light, the idea of something existing outside of consciousness becomes untenable. The only place where a universe without consciousness can exist is within the realm of imagination. The realm of imagination is inherently a product of consciousness.

Consciousness plays a profound role in shaping our perception of reality. This perspective underscores this profound role. It highlights the inseparable link between consciousness and existence. It suggests. We perceive, conceive, and experience reality. All of reality is fundamentally rooted in consciousness itself.

Therefore, while the idea of an external reality may persist as a philosophical puzzle. Upon closer examination, it becomes evident. Any purported existence outside of consciousness is a construct of the mind—a testament to the creative power and boundless imagination of conscious beings.

The prevailing belief among the majority of people is. An objective universe exists independently of consciousness. This perspective posits the universe as a mechanical, deterministic program governed by fixed natural laws. Within this framework, the universe operates according to laws of cause and effect. Scientists use these laws of cause and effect. Scientists predict the behavior and fate of matter and energy in the known universe. Undoubtedly, science has made significant strides in understanding and leveraging these laws for various applications.

However, despite the apparent coherence of this worldview. It is crucial to scrutinize a presumption. The presumption is. An objective universe exists external to consciousness. This presumption is founded on a notion. The notion is. A reality exists independently of our perceptions, thoughts, and experiences. Yet, upon closer examination, this idea becomes increasingly perplexing, particularly in light of science's inability to provide empirical proof of such an objective universe.

Regardless of the grand theories of the universe proposed by scientists, the fundamental truth remains: it is impossible to directly engage with the universe outside of consciousness. Without consciousness, there can be no sensory perception, no cognition, and no awareness of the universe in any capacity. One cannot see, hear, touch, feel, or know the universe without the intermediary of consciousness.

This realization challenges the conventional understanding of reality as something external and objective. Instead, it suggests. Our experience of the universe is inherently subjective.

Our experience is mediated by consciousness. Every observation, every interaction, and every interpretation of the universe is filtered through the lens of consciousness. The lens of consciousness shapes our understanding of reality.

In light of this perspective, it becomes evident. The universe, as we know it, exists within the realm of consciousness. It is not an external entity but rather a construct of our perceptual faculties, cognitive processes, and subjective experiences. While science may continue to unravel the mysteries of the universe, the act of acknowledging the fundamental role of consciousness is essential. Consciousness shapes our understanding of reality.

Consciousness enables us. We can engage with the universe. The act of engaging with the universe outside of consciousness is impossible. These facts raise profound questions. How can we be certain about the nature of reality and our perception of it? Certainty seems untenable through the lens of consciousness. Yet, despite the inherent challenges, a significant portion of the human population holds firm to a belief. The belief is. An objective universe exists independently of consciousness. Why do they hold firm to this belief?

One explanation is. This belief has been ingrained in us by the teachings of science. Science, with its emphasis on empirical evidence and objective inquiry, has traditionally portrayed the universe as a vast, objective entity governed by fixed laws and principles. From a scientific standpoint, the notion of an objective universe existing independently of consciousness seems to align with this framework.

However, let us suppose. We examine the notion with a truly open and unbiased mind. In that event, we may arrive at a different conclusion. Upon closer scrutiny, we may find. Our perception of the universe as an external, objective entity is, in fact, a construct of our consciousness. The very act of observation, interpretation, and analysis presupposes the involvement of consciousness. It suggests. Our understanding of the universe is inherently subjective.

In this light, the idea of an objective universe existing independently of consciousness begins to lose its grip. Instead, we come to recognize. Our perception of reality is intimately intertwined with the workings of consciousness. Reality is not something "out there" waiting to be discovered but rather a dynamic interplay between perception, cognition, and consciousness itself.

Assumptions underlie our understanding of reality. By challenging the assumptions, we can open ourselves up to new possibilities and perspectives. We may never be able to come into direct contact with the universe outside of consciousness. However, we can explore the nature of consciousness itself. Doing so may enable us. We may gain deeper insights into the totality of existence.

CHAPTER 1. INTRODUCTION: PURPOSE AND OBJECTIVES

A totality exists. For that reason, we are part of the totality. The totality is everything, everywhere, at all times. Some things existed in the past. Those things are part of the totality. Some things exist right now. Those things are part of the totality. Some things will exist in the future. Those things are part of the totality.

The act of pondering the totality requires energy, space, and time. I am lucky. I have the energy, space, and time. I ponder the totality.

I am inspired. My eyes do not have perfect sight. However, with my senses and perceptions, I may still find some valuable insights. No individual is always wrong. No individual is always right. However, with logic and intuition, I may speculate intelligently. No individual wins every fight. However, with courage, I may yet conquer my own ignorance, and come to a fuller, richer understanding of my place in the world.

Our bodies provide us with senses and perceptions. Our bodies are made up of various kinds of cells. Different types of cells react to stimuli. The reaction creates a signal. The central nervous system processes the signal. The result is. We experience sensations. In order for sensations to be useful, we add meaning. Meaning creates our perceptions.

Actuality is the way. Things actually are. Reality is the way. Things appear to be. I sense and perceive my reality. Other people sense and perceive their realities. Some people communicate with me about their realities. I communicate with some people about my reality. Communication enables us. We augment our abilities. We sense and perceive our realities.

The totality transcends our knowledge and comprehension. For that reason, the totality makes possible an infinite number, diversity, and variety of ideas. Ideas are thoughts, beliefs, and expectations about the totality. I use my senses and perceptions. I verify. Certain ideas are true. I verify. Certain ideas are false. True ideas conform to my reality. False ideas deviate from my reality.

I sort ideas into three simple categories. The three simple categories are truths, lies, and myths. Truths are ideas. Truths are verifiable. I can verify. Truths are true. Lies are ideas. Lies are falsifiable. I can verify. Lies are false. Myths are ideas. Myths are both unverifiable and unfalsifiable. I cannot verify whether or not. Myths are true. I cannot verify whether or not. Myths are false. I can only verify. Myths are ideas.

I believe in the value of truths. It appears. I am a living infernal fractal entity. I live in a body-consuming biosphere. A primal conflict between predator and prey divides the body consuming biosphere. I play a game of survival and sacrifice. Bodies consume bodies. In order to survive, I need my senses. For that reason, I developed my senses. My senses enable me. I can see, hear, touch, feel, and smell the world around me. In order to survive, I need my perceptions. For that reason, I developed my perceptions. My perceptions enable me. I perceive the world around me. My body made possible the existence of my senses and perceptions. My senses and perceptions enable me. I create, survive, perfect, and revive.

My senses and perceptions enable me. I can know a quantity of truth. I occupy specific points in energy, space, and time. My occupation of specific points in energy, space, and time, limits the quantity of truth. My body has attributes. The attributes of my seed-body limit the quantity of truth. I can know a finite quantity of truth. The totality is everything, everywhere, at all times. The totality may be infinite. For that reason, I know next to nothing about the truth of the totality. I know a finite amount about an infinite subject. I know next to nothing about almost everything.

I am an actor in the drama of life and death. I portray a character of my own creation. I am the Truth Seeker. I am the Myth Maker. I am the authority. I decide how. I make up my mind. I am the architect. I believe in the value of certain ideas. These certain ideas are my values. I use my values. I build within my mind. I build a model of the totality. My model is my reality. My reality is my house of ideology. I am the High Ideologue of my House of Ideology. Thanks to this, I can change my reality to what. I would like my reality to be.

An ideology is a body of values. Often an ideology reflects the needs and aspirations of an individual, group, class, and or culture. We have common needs and aspirations. Our common needs and aspirations are. Achieve and maintain happiness, good health, and prosperity. I align my values with our common needs and aspirations.

I believe in the value of truths. Scientists in various fields of study have found much to say about a theory. The theory is. Happiness leads to better health. Completely new fields of scientific research address the relationship between emotions and physical health. This scientific research seems to affirm. Our optimistic thoughts, beliefs, and expectations have a positive influence on our health. Our optimistic thoughts, beliefs, and expectations improve our various health behaviors, our immune functions, and our biochemical functions. The improvements make our bodies more resistant to illness. The improvements make our bodies better able to recover from existing disease.

I believe in the value of the most optimistic myths. I believe in the value of truths. These are my values. I choose my values. A capacity to produce happiness and good health; is the basis for my choice of values.

Happiness is a balance of the emotional forces of the mind. Balance is a state of equilibrium. Force is a capacity to cause change. A cancellation of all forces by equal opposing forces produces the state of equilibrium. A cancellation of all forces by equal opposing forces produces happiness.

I believe in the value of truths. My values act as forces upon my emotions. The most powerful emotional forces of sorrow, fear, and anger follow from the discovery of a truth. The truth is. It appears. One day, the seed-body of self will die.

I believe in the value of the most optimistic myths. My values act as forces upon my emotions. The most powerful emotional forces of joy, faith, and love follow from the mystery of the most optimistic myths. The most optimistic myths include. The life and immunity of the soul-spirit is, eternal and divine.

I believe in the value of the most optimistic myths. I believe in the value of truths. My values act as forces upon my emotions. Joy, faith, and love, balance sorrow, fear, and anger. I balance the emotional forces of my mind. The balance of the emotional forces of my mind produces a state of happiness. I am happy.

My emotions act as forces upon my behaviors. I exhibit glad behaviors. Friendly tolerant peacemaking behaviors are glad behaviors. Truth telling, sharing, playing well with others, liberating, emancipating, and nurturing are glad behaviors.

My glad behaviors act as forces upon my body. The forces are conducive to a state of good health in my body. My glad behaviors act as forces upon my habitat. The forces are conducive to a state of good health in my habitat. For that reason, emotional balance in my mind is conducive to happiness and good health in my life. Happiness and good health are conducive to success and prosperity in my business.

I think, believe, and predict. The act of communicating my ideas will enable me. I can attract like minded people.

The act of attracting like minded people will enable us. We can add value to people. We can communicate ideas. We can change behaviors with nothing more serious than the simple communication of ideas. We can save humanity by changing behaviors. We can save humanity from extinction.

Let us suppose. A person asks. Why do I write this book? In that event, I would answer. In this book, I provide us with good examples. The good examples show us how. We can best satisfy our common needs and aspirations. Our common needs and aspirations are. Achieve and maintain happiness, good health, and prosperity.

Let us suppose. A person asks. Why do I read from this book? In that event, I would answer. The act of reading from this book enables me. I provide us with good examples. The good examples show us how. We can best satisfy our common needs and aspirations. Our common needs and aspirations are. Achieve and maintain happiness, good health, and prosperity.

I seek out people. The people choose of their own free will. They build models of the totality. Their models of the totality are like my own. They are generous with their energy, space, and time. Love is hard work. They share their love with the world. They build my house. They tend my garden. They feed me. They clothe me. They give me their pardon.

I will start and restart, write, ponder and rewrite until I am satisfied. I do not presume. I do not speak for anyone other than myself. However, our experiences are similar. Similarity enables me. I know you. For that reason, I think, believe, and predict. My thoughts, feelings, judgment, and intuition will be of value to us.

This book is a living document. The living document grows and evolves. The living document provides good examples. The good examples show us how. We can best satisfy our common needs and aspirations. Our common needs and aspirations are. Achieve and maintain happiness, good health, and prosperity. As such, I welcome collaboration, criticism, feedback, and input from all sources.

Many people live by a habit of making themselves happy by thinking happy thoughts. Unfortunately, unpleasant life events, conditions, and circumstances may challenge and threaten their coping abilities. In times of crisis, some people may turn to authority figures for help. Some of these authority figures may include doctors, clergy, philosophers, psychologists, self-help guru's, scientists, swami's, hypnotherapists, entertainers, politicians, poets, and songwriters. The best of these authority figures offer help. The help enables people. People "get back on track" in the pursuit of happiness, good health, and prosperity.

CHAPTER 2. SCIENTIFIC METHODS

Human life is full of decisions. The decisions include significant choices about values. I believe in the value of truths. My seed-body makes senses and perceptions available to me. I use my senses and perceptions. I verify the truth of ideas. I verify the falsity of ideas. My seed-body has attributes. The attributes of my seed-body are a finite quantity of energy, a fractal quality of space, an infernal temporal longevity of time, and an infinite value of denominator. The attributes of my seed-body limit my senses and perceptions. My seed-body occupies a specific point in energy, space, and time. My occupation of a specific point in energy, space, and time limits my senses and perceptions. The limits of my senses and perceptions limit my ability to verify the truth of ideas. The limits of my senses and perceptions limit my ability to verify the falsity of ideas. For that reason, I use logic. The act of using logic enables me. I enhance my limited ability to verify the truth of ideas. I enhance my limited ability to verify the falsity of ideas.

The chief concern of logic is the evaluation of arguments. An argument includes at least one premise and at least one conclusion. A premise is a meaningful declarative sentence. A conclusion is also a meaningful declarative sentence.

Arguments rely upon inferences. An inference is a transition or movement from premises to conclusion. The logical connection between these statements, is the inference.

A reason is a cause, explanation, or justification for an action or event. Reason is the power of the mind to think, understand, and form judgments by a process of logic. Let us suppose: A person thinks, believes, and predicts. A certain idea is true. Let us suppose further: Another person thinks, believes, and predicts. The certain idea is false. These two people hold two different positions. Let us suppose still further. Each person gives the other person their reasons for taking their position. Each person argues in favor of their own position. Their reasons are their premises. Their premises lead them by process of logical inference to their conclusions. Their arguments consist of their premises, logical inferences, and conclusions.

Arguments enable people. People can logically infer the truth of a conclusion from the truth of premises. People can logically infer the falsity of a conclusion from the falsity of premises.

Logicians are experts in logic. Logicians evaluate the validity of inferences. Inferences are the patterns of reasoning in an argument. The inferences lead from premises to conclusion. The validity of inferences is distinct and different from the truth of statements. The validity of inferences is distinct and different from the falsity of the statements.

Let us suppose. The premises of an argument logically lead to the conclusion. In that event, the inference is valid.

Let us suppose. The premises of an argument do not logically lead to the conclusion. In that event, the inference is invalid.

Let us suppose. An inference is probably or possibly valid. In that event, the inference is an inductive inference.

Let us suppose. An inference is definitely valid. In that event, the inference is a deductive inference.

Let us suppose. A person makes an argument. Let us suppose further. The argument includes deductive inferences. In that event, the argument would be a deductive argument. The standard of correctness for a deductive argument is the highest. The deductive argument succeeds whenever its premises and deductive inferences disprove and eliminate all other possible conclusions. The deductive argument enables the person. The person reaches at least one definite conclusion. It would be unreasonable to reject the at least one definite conclusion. It would be unreasonable to withhold judgment or even to question the at least one definite conclusion.

Let us suppose. A person makes an argument. Let us suppose further. The argument includes inductive inferences. In that event, the argument is an inductive argument. The standard of correctness for an inductive argument is much more flexible than the standard of correctness for a deductive argument. An inductive argument succeeds whenever its premises and inductive inferences provide some legitimate evidence or support for at least one conclusion. It may be reasonable to accept the at least one conclusion. It may also be reasonable to withhold judgment or even to question the at least one conclusion.

Scientists make observations, identifications, descriptions, experimental investigations, and theoretical explanations of natural phenomena. These actions enable scientists. Scientists use their senses and perceptions. Gather truths. Derive laws of cause and effect. The laws of cause and effect enable scientists. Scientists can predict the behavior and fate of matter and energy in the known universe. The predictions enable scientists. Scientists can solve problems. The problems pertain to the existence of discovery and mystery, the drama of life and death, the game of survival and sacrifice, the test of success and failure, and the conflict between predator and prey.

Scientists use scientific methods. A simple version of their scientific methods is:

1. **Choose a subject. Use sensory perceptions. Make observations. Study how the subject behaves under various conditions.**
2. **Observations yield results. Study the results. Find evidence of meaningful patterns.**
3. **Attempt to explain. Give reasons for observations. Justify all meaningful patterns. Predict the future behavior of the subject. Make possible accurate predictions under a wide variety of conditions. A successful attempt to do these actions yields a result. The result is called a hypothesis.**
4. **Use the hypothesis. Make predictions about how the subject would behave under new conditions.**

5. **Create an experiment. Make observations. Gather information about the behavior of the subject under those new conditions.**
6. **Compare predictions to observations.**
7. **Let us suppose. Predictions do not agree with observations. In that event, start over. Go back to step 1.**
8. **Let us suppose. Predictions do agree with observations under all known sets of circumstances. In that event, the hypothesis becomes an accepted theory**

The accepted theory correctly explains a range of phenomena. The accepted theory is a model of the subject. Scientists use the model of the subject. Scientists explain observations. Scientists make predictions. The accepted theory produces desired results. The desired results are accurate predictions. The accurate predictions are about the future behavior of the subject.

Scientists repeat most experiments and observations. They verify the validity of theories many times. Each new generation of scientists learns about the work of earlier generations. Earlier generations demonstrated the validity of theories. The earlier generations conducted experiments and or made observations. Each new generation demonstrates the validity of said theories again. Each new generation repeats the experiments and observations. Each new generation advances into new areas of investigation. Each new generation builds on the work of predecessors.

Ideally, scientists do not accept a theory based on the prestige or convincing powers of proponents. The validity of a scientific theory rests upon the use of senses and perceptions. Scientists always keep in mind: Old theories might fail to explain the results of new experiments and or observations. In such cases, scientists devise and test new hypotheses until a new theory emerges. The new theory explains the results of both old and new experiments and or observations.

The great advantage of the scientific method is. The scientific method is unprejudiced. A person does not have to believe a given researcher. Given enough energy, space, and time, the person can redo experiments and make new observations. Conclusions of a valid theory will stand irrespective of the state of consciousness of the investigator and or the subject of investigation.

Proponents of myth propagate their beliefs based solely upon a creative imagination, and unrestrained fancy. Creative imagination and unrestrained fancy are made possible by the existence of mystery. Myths are 'proven' in the heart. Scientific theories are 'proven' in the head.

A scientific theory has an important attribute. The important attribute enables people. People use the important attribute. People differentiate the scientific theory from a myth. The important attribute is. The scientific theory makes predictions about the future condition of a subject. Scientists are able to use our tools of science. Scientists can check those predictions against the results from some experiment or observation. The myth might also make predictions about the future condition of a subject. Scientists can use our tools of science. However, the use of our tools of science does not help scientists. Scientists can not check those predictions against the results of some experiment or observation.

For example, the atom is a subject. Scientists chose the subject. Scientists used scientific

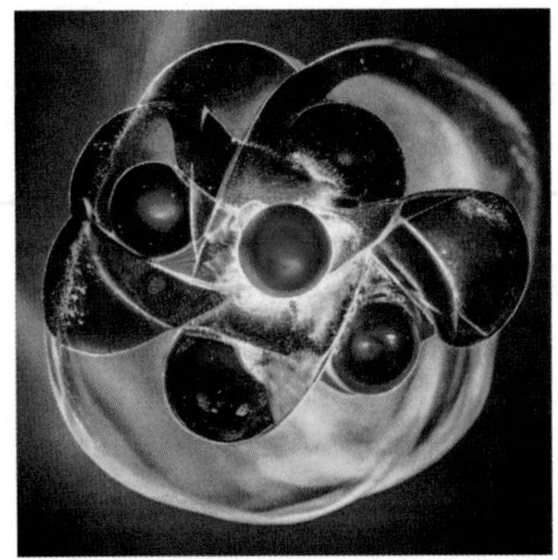

methods. Scientists developed a new picture of subatomic reality. They called it quantum mechanics. Quantum mechanical theory is at the heart of quantum mechanics. Quantum mechanical theory is testable. For that reason, quantum mechanical theory enables scientists. Scientists can make predictions. Scientists can use our tools of science. Scientists can conduct experiments and make observations. The experiments and observations can yield results. Scientists can check the predictions against the results. Scientists can find: The results agree with the predictions. The accuracy of results establishes the validity of quantum mechanical theory. For that reason, quantum mechanical theory is a scientific theory.

An infinite divine eternal being is a subject. Let us suppose. I believe in the value of an idea. The idea is. The existence of an infinite divine eternal being explains the existence of the known universe. In that event, the idea is not testable. The idea is unverifiable. The idea is unfalsifiable. For that reason, the idea is not a scientific theory. The idea is a myth.

The truth is. A myth is a myth. The existence of discovery and the existence of mystery make possible an infinite number, diversity, and variety of myths.

Validity is the quality of being logical or factually sound. The validity of myths follows from two definitions of the word valid. The two definitions are a logical definition and a pragmatic definition.

The logical definition of the word valid is: having a sound basis in logic or fact; reasonable or cogent. The presence of evidence in the form of the universe provides premises. Those premises enable us. We can make valid logical inductive inferences. We can make myths. An infinite number, diversity, and variety of myths are made possible by the totality. Each of these myths is an equally valid possibility.

The pragmatic definition of the word valid is: producing the desired results. Let us suppose. The desired results are. Achieve and maintain happiness and good health. In that event, optimistic myths are more valid. Pessimistic myths are less valid or even invalid.

I value the most optimistic myths. The act of valuing the most optimistic myths enables me. I devalue pessimistic myths. The act of devaluing pessimistic myths enables me. I produce emotional balance within my mind. Emotional balance in my mind is conducive to happiness and good health in my life. Happiness and good health in my life is conducive to success and prosperity in my business. For that reason, I value the most optimistic myths. I devalue pessimistic myths.

CHAPTER 3. MIND AND EMOTIONS

Our common needs and aspirations are. Achieve and maintain happiness, good health, and prosperity. For that reason, I discuss emotions. I describe how. Emotions affect ones' health for better or worse.

An emotion may be defined as "any agitation or disturbance of mind, feeling, passion; any vehement or excited mental state." The word 'Emotion' refers to a feeling and its distinctive thoughts, psychological and biological states, and range of tendency to act. The totality makes possible hundreds of emotions, along with their combinations, variations, blends, and nuances. I do not have words to describe all of the many subtleties of emotion.

I think of emotions in terms of families or dimensions. The four main families are sorrow, fear, anger, and joy. Each of these four main families has a basic emotional response at its core. Relatives branch out from each of these four main families in numerous variations. On the outer branches are moods. Moods are subdued and last far longer than an emotion. Beyond moods are emotional temperaments. An emotional temperament is a readiness to evoke a given emotion or mood. Still beyond such emotional temperaments are the disorders of emotion such as hysteria or unremitting anxiety. Under these conditions, someone feels perpetually trapped in a poisonous state.

The argument for there being a set of core emotions rests to some extent on a discovery. The discovery is. People in cultures all around the world recognize the specific facial expressions for sorrow, fear, anger, and enjoyment. This universality of emotional communication modes was probably first noted by Darwin. Darwin offered an explanation. The explanation was. It appears. The universality is evidence of the forces of evolution. The forces of evolution have implanted the emotional communication modes in our central nervous systems.

In recent years, a scientific model of the emotional mind has emerged. The model explains how. Our emotions can drive our behaviors. The model helps to explain how. We can be so reasonable one moment and so unreasonable the next moment. The model helps to explain how. Our emotions have their own reasons and their own logic.

Reflective and analytical deliberation are attributes of the thinking mind. The emotional mind is far faster than the thinking mind. The emotional mind leaps into action without waiting for even an instant. Its rapidity prevents reflective, analytical deliberation.

The rapidity of the emotional mind developed over the course of evolution. Most likely, it developed as a response to a need to make quick decisions about key elements in the environment. For example, let us suppose. A life form becomes aware of the presence of another life form. Let us suppose further. The another life form is in close proximity to the life form. In that event, the ability to make instantaneous decisions becomes critical: Am I prey? Am I predator? Let us suppose. The life form takes too long to reflect on the answer to such an important question. In that event, the life form might end up losing in the game of survival and sacrifice.

Some actions originate in the emotional mind. These actions carry a particularly powerful sense of certainty. This sense of certainty is a result of an efficient, simplified way of looking at things. It can be positively mystifying to the thinking mind. After the fact, or even in mid-response, we may find ourselves wondering: "What did I do?". The act of questioning ones own behavior after the fact is a sure sign: The thinking mind is awakening to the moment, but not with the quickness of the emotional mind.

Let us suppose. An event provokes an emotion. In that event, the period of time between the event and the expression of an emotion can be extremely short. We play a game of survival and sacrifice. In order to win the game, this appraisal of the need to act must be automatic. Such a rapid appraisal does not enter into conscious awareness. Researchers measure the time between an event and emotional response in periods of about one-thousandth of a second. Thus, tools used to appraise perception must be capable of great speed. Virtually before we even know what has happened, the rapid and raw kind of emotional response washes over us.

Emotional forces rapidly overtake the mind. These emotional forces start before we are aware of them. This rapidity is essential to these emotional forces being so highly adaptive. These emotional forces motivate us. We respond to life-threatening events. We do not waste a moment. For that reason, we do not ponder whether to react. We do not ponder how to respond.

Let us suppose. An event triggers an emotional reaction. In that event, emotional expressions begin to show up as changes in facial musculature. The changes occur within a few thousandths of a second after the event. Emotional reactions can often be accompanied by physiological changes. For example, blood flow shunt and heart rate increase are physiological changes. The physiological changes also take only fractions of a second to begin. This swiftness is particularly true of intense emotion, like fear of a sudden threat.

This quick mode of perception relies on first impressions. This quick mode of perception responds to the overall picture or the most striking aspects of the overall picture. For that reason, this quick mode of perception sacrifices accuracy for speed. This quick mode of perception takes things in as a whole at once. This quick mode of perception enables us. We react without taking the time for thoughtful analysis. Vivid elements can determine the first impression. The first impression can overwhelm a careful evaluation of the details.

The great benefit is. The emotional mind can read an emotional reality faster than the thinking mind can argue premises to a logical conclusion. In a moment, we can make intuitive snap judgments. These intuitive snap judgments enable us. We answer questions like. Where is the trouble? What should we be wary of? Who is a threat? Let us suppose. We waited for the rational mind to make some of these judgments. In that event, we might not only be wrong. We might be dead. The emotional mind is our radar for danger. The drawback is. We make these intuitive snap judgments rapidly. For that reason, these intuitive snap judgments may be wrong or misdirected.

The full intensity of emotion is very brief. It lasts for just seconds rather than minutes, hours, and days. Let us suppose. A single event causes us to experience emotions. Let us suppose further. The emotions dominate our minds long after the event has passed. Let us suppose still further. The emotions dominate our minds regardless of what else is happening around us. In that event, our emotions would be poor guides to action. It would be maladaptive for an emotion to seize the brain and body for a long time regardless of changing circumstances.

Something must sustain the trigger for emotions to last longer. In effect, something must continually evoke our emotions. For example, the loss of a loved one could continually evoke our emotions. Keep us in mourning. When for hours feelings persist, it is usually as moods. Moods are not such strong shapers of how we perceive and act, as is the intensity of full emotion.

There is also a second kind of emotional reaction. It is slower than the quick-response. It develops first in our thoughts before it leads to feeling. This second pathway to triggering our emotions is more deliberate. We are typically quite aware of the thoughts. The thoughts lead to an emotional reaction. In this kind of emotional reaction, a more extended appraisal occurs. Our thought and cognition play the key role. These help determine the emotions we will evoke. Let us suppose: We make an appraisal, such as "it's a beautiful day" or "our child is adorable". After the appraisal is made, a fitting emotional response follows. In this slower sequence, more fully articulated thought precedes feeling. Emotions like embarrassment and apprehension are more complicated emotions. These more complicated emotions follow this slower route, and take seconds or minutes to unfold. These emotions follow from thoughts.

By contrast, in the fast-response sequence, feelings seem to precede or be simultaneous with our thoughts. Some situations have the urgency of survival. This rapid-fire emotional reaction takes over in such situations. This rapid-fire emotional reaction mobilizes us in an instant. We react to an emergency.

Feelings of the greatest intensity are involuntary reactions. We cannot decide when these will occur. We cannot choose the emotional responses we have. We are able to explain away our actions by saying. We were in the grip of emotion. For that reason, the emotional mind can offer an alibi. The rational mind takes a moment or two longer to register and respond than does the emotional mind. The 'first impulse' in an emotional situation belongs to the heart, not the head.

Quick and slow pathways to emotion exist. The quick pathway is the pathway through immediate perception. The slow pathway is the pathway through reflective thought. Emotions can also be summoned. One example is the actors' stock in trade, intentionally manipulated feelings. When actors intentionally milk sad memories for effect, tears may come. Actors are simply more skilled than the rest of us at the intentional use of feelings via thinking, the slow pathway to emotion. A certain kind of thought will trigger specific emotions. We cannot easily change the specific emotions. However, certain kinds of thought produce desirable emotions. We very often can and do choose to think about those certain kinds of thought.

I change my emotions through this slower path mechanism of reflective thought. Is there an element of acting involved in this? Absolutely, we are actors in the drama of life and death. From the earliest days of our lives, we learn how to act. Good behavior generally produces pleasant consequences. Bad behavior generally produces unpleasant consequences. Eventually, as individuals, we learn from this type of conditioning. We converge upon a range of behaviors. The range of behaviors produces desirable results. In general, we learn to act in a manner. The manner is pleasant and socially acceptable.

CHAPTER 4. EMOTIONS AND PHYSIOLOGY

Psycho-neuro-immunology is a promising, exciting, and new field of scientific study. It suggests a holistic approach to medicine. The holistic approach to medicine is helpful in preventing disease, as opposed to just treating disease after it appears. The holistic approach to medicine may be needed to improve the health of the many people of our global culture. The whole field of Psycho-neuro-immunology is based on an idea. The idea is. Biological, psychological, and sociological factors influence one's health and health-related behaviors.

Stress can have an adverse effect on any given individual's health. A stressor is a stimulus. The stimulus makes demands on an organism. The demands on the organism require. The organism adapts or adjusts.

Physical Stress

Psychological Stress

Psychosocial Stress

The three types of stress are: physical stress, psychological stress, and psychosocial stress. Physical stress involves stressors in our bodies and in our habitats. Psychological stress involves stressors in our minds. Psychosocial stress involves stressors in our interpersonal relationships.

The body adapts to pathogens. When stress occurs for a prolonged period of time, the body may respond by becoming immune suppressed. When this occurs, the body becomes susceptible to pathogens. For that reason, the body is more likely to become ill. Stress sets the stage for disease.

Stress may affect the immune system through many different pathways in the body. One of these pathways is the hormone response. Hormones act as chemical messengers. Let us suppose. Hormones are released into the blood stream. In that event, the hormones act on an organ in another part of the body. Although hormones reach all parts of the body, only target cells with compatible receptors are equipped to respond. Over fifty hormones have been identified in humans and other vertebrates. In response to stress, the body releases certain hormones. These hormones can impair the performance of the immune system.

The catecholamine system is the first to go into action in the face of stress. In response to stress, the catecholamine system releases hormones such as adrenaline and noradrenaline. Adrenaline and noradrenaline mostly affect the cardiovascular system. These hormones increase heart rate and blood pressure and reduce immune system responsiveness. Let us suppose. A stressor prolongs the stress. The stress continues for a long time. In that event, this increase of heart rate and blood pressure can put stress on the heart muscle and even contribute to hypertension.

The neuroendocrine system releases hormones such as cortisol, adrenocorticotropic hormone, growth hormone, and beta-endorphins. When a person is under a lot of stress, he or she releases more of these hormones into the bloodstream. Let us suppose. A stressor prolongs the stress. The stress lasts a long time. In that event, these hormones can lower the disease fighting ability of the immune system.

The nervous system makes connections with many organs in the body such as the spleen, lymph nodes, bone marrow, and thymus gland. The connections to the nervous system contribute to the functioning of the immune system. The nervous system produces hormones and neurotransmitters in response to stress. Many of these hormones and neurotransmitters have profound effects on the functions of the immune system.

For example, it appears. People release cortisol into their bloodstream in response to stress. Over long periods, this release of cortisol can greatly impair the immune system. As of this writing, scientists say. There may be a link between a constant bombardment of cortisol on the immune system and the development of diseases such as cancer.

The effect of these kinds of variables on the immune system and the immune systems reciprocal effect on the physical, social, and environmental pathways is the basis for the study of Psycho-neuro-immunology. The underlying idea is. Too much stress is bad for a body's bio-psycho-social system. Stress causes the release of chemicals into the bloodstream. These chemicals adversely affect the response of the immune system to disease.

A variety of factors can cause stress in ones' life such as work, school, family life, and so on. All of these factors work together to cause stress in an individual. Perhaps in order to best prevent disease and treat illness, we need to begin to look at the entire realm of our experience. Maybe, we should focus our attentions on physiological, psychological, and social aspects of our lives and lifestyles. This is the basis for Psycho-neuro-immunology.

There are many different ways we can lead a healthier lifestyle. The science of Psycho-neuro-immunology focuses on the links between the mind, the brain, and the immune system. Certain negative psychological states are brought on by adversity and or by chemical imbalance. Immunologists, physiologists, psychiatrists, psychologists, and neurobiologists now suspect: These certain negative psychological states actually cause the immune system to falter. Some even go so far as to claim: Positive attitudes, such as a feeling of control, may in some way inoculate against disease. Positive attitudes could act as a valuable supplement to conventional medical care.

Psycho-neuro-immunology involves a broad study of a bio-psycho-social model of stress. Health psychology focuses specifically on how biological, social, and psychological factors impact health and well-being. Here too there is a large emphasis on the promotion of wellness and the prevention of illness. Health psychologists study how lifestyles, activities, emotional reactions, personality characteristics, and event interpretation influence physical health.

Many influential authorities have only recently recognized health psychology as a field of scientific inquiry. The relationship between the mind and physical health was a widely accepted fact from ancient times and throughout most of history. In the late 1800's scientists discovered. Infectious diseases such as typhoid and syphilis have specific biological causes. The discovery led doctors. They only searched for biological causes of diseases. For that reason, they virtually ignored the influence of behavior on the physical health of people. This attitude has prevailed until only recently. Doctors and other health professionals have begun to work with health psychologists. Health psychologists have begun putting research from this field into practice.

Health psychologists have identified stress as a potent killer. For that reason, stopping the stressful behavior and promoting healing is a major emphasis of health psychology. Health psychologists offer us methods of reducing stress. One of the methods is. Change our thoughts, beliefs, and expectations about the totality. We value certain ideas. These certain ideas are our values. We can change our values. We can reduce our stress.

CHAPTER 5. LIMITATIONS ON SCIENTIFIC INQUIRY

The scientific establishment likes to speak out on the subject of ethics in research. The media often treat scientists as authoritative sources. Yet, it appears. We live in a body consuming biosphere. A primal conflict between predator and prey divides the body consuming biosphere. This primal conflict between predator and prey leads me. I wonder about ethics in research. I ask a question: The question is. How important are ethics when compared to the importance of attracting grant money? How important are ethics when compared to the importance of doing the business necessary to win in the game of survival and sacrifice?

The formal enterprise of research is an open conversation amongst scientists. The open conversation takes the form of studies. Peer-reviewed journals publish studies. Newspapers, magazines, radio, television, web, and mass media publicize the studies over the world.

Even at its best, scientific discourse is often a confusing contest of conflicting claims. Scientists test theories by experiment and make new observations. Scientists debate. New facts perpetually overthrow old assumptions. This overthrow of old assumptions is at the heart of science.

The economy can absorb a number, diversity, and variety of scientists and engineers. Let us suppose. Universities graduate more scientists and engineers than the economy can absorb. In that event, the pool of available government funding for grants shrinks. Let us suppose. The pool of available government funding shrinks. In that event, the conversation may become distorted. Science may become not just an intellectual competition but also an economic competition. The economic competition would be for scarce resources and even survival.

Let us suppose. In the economic competition, honest and ethical behavior among scientists shows signs of distress. In that event, this distress endangers one of the crucial pillars of the whole edifice.

Let us suppose. Economic competition for research funds becomes ever fiercer. In that event, burgeoning commercialism and ever fiercer economic competition might influence scientists. Scientists may be willing to sidestep traditional checks and balances.

Let us suppose. Scientists are willing to side step the traditional checks and balances. In that event, the willingness to side step the traditional checks and balances would undermine the quality of information the public receives about advances in science and medicine.

Let us suppose. Science can be corrupted by commerce. In that event, the public should take new scientific discoveries with a grain of salt: the bigger the claim, the more the salt.

Market forces create distortions. Many scientists are aware of the distortions. The best scientists compensate for this distortion. The best scientists scrutinize the claims made by other scientists with care and loyalty to the truth.

Some scientists study the power of the mind-body connection. I follow the work of these scientists with great interest. Suffering, sorrow, and abomination follow from a primal conflict between predator and prey. The primal conflict between predator and prey divides our body-consuming biosphere. The primal conflict between predator and prey characterizes the experience of living infernal fractal entities. Living infernal fractal entities experience dramas of life and death, games of survival and sacrifice, and tests of success and failure.

Psycho-neuro-immunologists and health psychologists do not claim to eliminate mystery from existence. They do not claim to eliminate the discovery of disease and death. They do not claim to eliminate the mystery of immunity and life. They do not claim to eliminate suffering, sorrow, and abomination. The best of them offer a way of coping with major life-altering events. The best of them endeavor to put us in a best position. The best position is. We believe in ourselves. We take control of our lives. We are optimistic about ourselves. We are optimistic about our world.

CHAPTER 6. QUALIFICATIONS

Happiness can exert a powerful influence over health. Health can exert a powerful influence over happiness. Happiness is a balance of the emotional forces of the mind. Good health is a balance of the physiological forces of the seed-body. The balance of forces produces a state of equilibrium. The forces have a capacity to cause change. A cancellation of all forces by equal opposing forces produces the state of equilibrium.

Let us suppose. Disease, hunger, thirst, fatigue, injury, stress, malnutrition, depression, mental illness, and other conditions make a person sad, frightened, and angry. In that event, returning the person's emotions to a state of balance might require returning ones' body to a state of good health.

My knowledge of truths and theories is based on the existence of discovery. The existence of discovery pertains to the knowledge, comprehension, application, analysis, creation, and evaluation of laws of cause and effect. Scientists say. Universal laws of cause and effect exist. Knowledge of these universal laws of cause and effect enables us. We can predict the behavior and fate of matter and energy in the known universe. Our bodies are made up of a portion of the matter and energy in the known universe. For that reason, these universal laws of cause and effect apply to our bodies. Therefore it follows: We should apply our knowledge of truths and theories to the task of solving problems. These problems pertain to achieving good health.

My belief in myths is based on what is possible within the realm of mystery. The realm of mystery pertains to the knowledge, comprehension, application, analysis, creation, and evaluation of laws and principles. These laws and principles govern the spiritual essence of the totality. The totality makes possible an infinite number, diversity, and variety of myths. I believe in the value of truths. Scientists say. It appears. Our optimistic thoughts, beliefs, and expectations improve our various health behaviors, our immune functions, and our biochemical functions. The improvement makes our bodies more resistant to illness and better able to recover from existing disease. Therefore it follows: We should apply a belief in the value of the most optimistic myths to the task of solving problems. These problems pertain to achieving happiness.

Let us suppose. Devotion of energy, space, and time to a belief in the value of the most optimistic myths is not capable of balancing the emotional forces of a person's mind. In that event, an underlying health problem may exist. Knowledge of truths and theories should be applied to the task of identifying, and solving it.

Just as ideas lead to emotional responses and emotional responses lead to physiological responses, so physiological responses lead to emotional responses and then to ideas.

CHAPTER 7. IDEAS, IDEOLOGY, AND IDEOLOGUE

Ideas are thoughts, beliefs, and expectations about the totality. We value certain ideas. These certain ideas are our values. An ideology is a body of values. An ideology usually reflects the needs and aspirations of an individual, group, class and or culture. An ideologue is an authority on an ideology. Ideologues devote great amounts of energy, space, and time in life to the task of becoming an authority on an ideology.

I am the authority. I decide how. I make up my mind. I am the architect. I believe in the value of certain ideas. These certain ideas are my values. I use my values. I build within my mind. I build my model of the totality. My model of the totality is my house of ideology. An ideology is a body of values. Ideology fashions reality. My house of ideology is my reality. I am the High Ideologue of my House of Ideology. For that reason, I can change my reality to what. I would like my reality to be.

Like health psychologists, I intend to modify my ideas. Reduce psychological stress. Improve health. Unlike some health psychologists, I plan to expand the scope of my efforts. I expand my efforts beyond the domain of scientifically reproducible discovery. I expand my efforts into the realm of mystery.

The totality makes possible a realm of mystery. The realm of mystery makes possible an infinite number, diversity, and variety of myths. I value truths. Scientists say. It appears. Optimism correlates with happiness and good health. I desire happiness and good health. For that reason, I make my most optimistic myths. I believe in the value of my most optimistic myths. In so doing, I change my model of the totality. I change the way. I fashion my reality. My behavior is partly determined by my reality. For that reason, I predict. By changing my reality, I will change my behavior for the better.

Our values can have a beneficial effect on our emotions, our behavior, and our health. I believe in the value truths. I believe in the value of the most optimistic myths. I think, believe, and predict. My values produce an emotional balance in my mind. The emotional balance in my mind improves my behaviors. My behaviors are conducive to beneficial physiological responses, of good health.

CHAPTER 8. LOVE H.A.P.N.S. AND LOVE HAPPENS

I combine the word Love and the acronym H.A.P.N.S.. I form a phrase. The phrase is. 'Love H.A.P.N.S.'. I give the phrase two meanings. One meaning of the phrase is 'love happens'. The other meaning of the phrase is love Healthy Agnostic Positivistic Nationalistic Spiritization. In short, love of Healthy Agnostic Positivistic Nationalistic Spiritization describes my method of modifying my thoughts, beliefs, and expectations. I modify my thoughts, beliefs, and expectations. I reduce psychological stress. I improve my behaviors for the better. I improve my health for the better.

Before proceeding any further, let us review some of our basic definitions: The word spiritization is a noun. A noun is any one of a class of words. I use the noun to name a person, place, or thing. I define the noun spiritization as the act or process of imparting a spiritual nature or treating as having a spiritual sense or meaning. I impart a spiritual nature to the totality in a manner. The manner is healthy, agnostic, positivistic, and nationalistic. The words healthy, agnostic, positivistic, and nationalistic are adjectives. An adjective is any one of a class of words. I use the adjectives to modify a noun. I modify the noun by limiting, qualifying, or specifying.

Healthy spiritization is conducive to good health. I characterize health as biological homeostasis. Biological homeostasis is a balance of characteristic and essential life processes, activities and functions. The balance of characteristic and essential life processes, activities, and functions is conducive to our well being.

Agnostic spiritization is characterized by a belief. The belief is. Our finite human capacities enable us. We can sense, perceive, intuit, judge, understand, apply, analyze, create, and evaluate. However, our finite human capacities do not enable us. We can not verify the existence of deities. An inability to know about the existence of deities limits agnostic spiritization. We can not verify the non-existence of deities. An inability to know about the non-existence of deities limits agnostic spiritization.

Positivist spiritization follows from a system of philosophy known as positivism. Positivism offers. We use our senses and perceptions to verify. Truths are true. We use our senses and perceptions to verify. Lies are false. Verification by use of our senses and perceptions is the only valid way of making a distinction between truths, myths, and lies.

Nationalist spiritization follows from a devotion to the interests, needs, aspirations, and or culture of a particular nation of people. We have common needs and aspirations. Our common needs and aspirations are. Achieve and maintain happiness, good health, and prosperity.

CHAPTER 9. HOW?

How does healthy spiritization lead to happiness? Good health and happiness are synergistic. Good health helps produce happiness. Happiness helps produce good health. I apply my truths and my theories to the task of achieving and maintaining good health. I base my truths and my theories on scientifically reproducible discoveries. I apply my belief in the most optimistic myths to the task of achieving and maintaining happiness. I base my belief in the most optimistic myths on what is possible in the realm of mystery. I believe in the value of truths. I believe in the value of the most optimistic myths. These are my values. My values act as forces upon my emotions. My values enable me. I balance the emotional forces of my mind. I am happy.

How does agnostic spiritization lead to happiness? How does a person prove or disprove the existence or non-existence of deities? Most people do not claim an ability to know how. We ponder the totality. We ask ourselves the grand enigmatic questions of identity. What am I? Where am I? When am I? How am I? Why am I? Who am I? Our bodies are finite and fragile. Our bodies limit our minds. Our minds limit our abilities to comprehend the totality. Our minds limit our abilities to analyze all of the infinite possibilities. Our minds limit our abilities to provide definitive answers to the grand enigmatic questions of identity. Agnosticism acknowledges this fact. It validates and reassures us: The totality is both a discovery and a mystery.

How does positivist spiritization lead to happiness? Positivism is an empiricist philosophical theory. The theory is. All authentic knowledge is derived by logic and reason from sensory experience. My seed-body makes my senses and perceptions available to me. Ideas are thoughts, beliefs, and expectations about the totality. I use my senses and perceptions. I verify the truth of ideas. I verify the falsity of ideas. I correctly sort ideas into three simple categories. The three simple categories are truths, lies, and myths. Truths are ideas. Truths are verifiable. I can verify. Truths are true. Lies are ideas. Lies are falsifiable. I can verify. Lies are false. Myths are ideas. Myths are both unverifiable and unfalsifiable. I cannot verify whether or not. Myths are true. I cannot verify whether or not. Myths are false. I can only verify. Myths are ideas.

I make a clear distinction between truths, myths, and lies. Truths are based on the existence of discovery. Myths are based on the existence of mystery. Lies are based on ignorance and denial. I reject lies in favour of truths. I use the existence of discovery. I gather my truths and my theories. I use the existence of mystery. I make my most optimistic myths. I combine my truths, my theories and my most optimistic myths. My model of the totality forms.

This then is how Healthy Agnostic Positivistic Nationalistic Spiritization is positivist. My model of the totality is a positive possibility. My model of the totality should contain no lies. My model of the totality should not contradict truths. My model of the totality should contain truths. Truths are testable and provable. My model of the totality should contain the most optimistic myths. The most optimistic myths are aligned with my goal. My goal is. Best satisfying our common needs and aspirations. Our common needs and aspirations are. Achieve and maintain happiness, good health, and prosperity.

How does nationalistic spiritization lead to happiness? Being happy is an interest, need, and aspiration of most people. Most people want to be healthy. They want to feel good about themselves. They want to exert some control over their lives. They want to expect good things in the future. Most people need and aspire to be likable. They have a need and aspiration to care about other people. They have a need and aspiration to be cared for by other people. They want to create, survive, perfect, and revive in a peaceful and nurturing environment. I think, believe, and predict. Love of Healthy Agnostic Positivistic Nationalistic Spiritization can produce an emotional balance in my mind. The emotional balance in my mind is conducive to happiness and good health in my life. The happiness and good health in my life is conducive to success and prosperity in my business. I am satisfied. A nation of people are very similar to me. In as much as I am satisfied so the nation of people may be satisfied. Best satisfying our common needs and aspirations is nationalistic. For that reason, love of Healthy Agnostic Positivistic Nationalistic Spiritization is nationalistic.

CHAPTER 10. EVALUTION

Let us suppose. Some people affirm. They do not have the ability. They can not possess knowledge. This knowledge may be about the existence of at least one deity. This knowledge may be about the nonexistence of deities. In that event, those people are agnostics. Agnostics may wonder. Does Healthy Agnostic Positivistic Nationalistic Spiritization amount to nothing more than a highly speculative form of art and myth-making? Does the practice of Healthy Agnostic Positivistic Nationalistic Spiritization put me at a disadvantage?

I believe in the value of truths. I base my truths on the existence of discovery. I believe in the value of theories. I base my theories on scientifically reproducible discoveries. It appears. We are life forms. We are born to play the dual role of predator and prey. A primal conflict between predator and prey divides our body-consuming biosphere. It appears. We live in an environment wherein; mastery of scientifically reproducible discoveries is a decisive factor. The decisive factor determines who succeeds and survives and who fails and parishes. From a strictly materialistic point of view, it may seem to some people. My energy, space, and time would be better spent studying truths and theories, rather than pondering mysteries and making myths.

A totality exists. For that reason, we are part of the totality. The totality may be infinite. The existence of discovery is equal to the sum total of all knowledge of truths and theories. The sum total of all knowledge of truths and theories is finite. The existence of mystery is equal to the totality minus the existence of discovery. For that reason, the existence of mystery may be infinite. Represent the existence of discovery with any finite number. Represent the totality with an infinitely larger number. Divide the any finite number by the infinitely larger number. The quotient represents the fullness of our knowledge. The quotient is equal to a number approaching zero. We know a finite amount about an infinite subject. We know next to nothing about almost everything!

Our seed-bodies make senses and perceptions available to us. Our senses and perceptions enable us. We can find things. Science makes tools available to us. The tools of science enable scientists. Scientists can discover things. Science makes scientific theories available to us. Scientific theories enable scientists. Scientists can predict things. As anyone familiar with science is aware, knowledge of old theories may be displaced by knowledge of new theories. For that reason, it is much too soon to make a conclusion about the existence of things.

Let us suppose. I set about to eliminate all lies and all myths from my model of the totality. In that event, I would only believe in the value of truths. I would gather a finite quantity of truths and theories. I would use the finite quantity of truths and theories. I would build within my mind. I would build a model of the totality. I would use this model of the totality. I would navigate about my habitat. I would orient myself towards existence. I would explain existence to myself.

I believe in the value of truths. My values act as forces upon my emotions. The most powerful emotional forces of sorrow, fear, and anger follow from the discovery of a truth. The truth is. It appears. One day, the seed-body of self will die.

I believe in the value of the most optimistic myths. My values act as forces upon my emotions. The most powerful emotional forces of joy, faith, and love follow from the mystery of the most optimistic myths. The most optimistic myths include. The life and immunity of the soul-spirit is, eternal and divine.

Let us suppose. I set about to eliminate all lies and all myths from my model of the totality. In that event, I would be without a belief in the value of the most optimistic myths. I would be without countervailing emotional forces of joy, faith, and love. I would be unable to balance the emotional forces of my mind. My heart would be filled with sorrow, fear, and anger.

I don't want my heart to be filled with sorrow, fear, and anger. For that reason, I believe in the value of the most optimistic myths. I believe in the value of truths. These are my values. I am the architect. I use my values. I build within my mind. I build a model of the totality. My model of the totality enables me. Joy, faith, and love, balance sorrow, fear, and anger. I balance the emotional forces of my mind. I am happy. For that reason, I think, believe, and predict. My energy, space, and time is well spent.

Optimism correlates with happiness and good health. Pessimism correlates with sorrow, fear, anger, and disease. Let us suppose. A person thinks, believes, and predicts. Self is only a seed and a body. Self has only one life to live. Self has only one body to give. In that event, the person believes in the value of pessimistic myths.

Let us suppose. A person believes in the value of pessimistic myths. Let us suppose further, I ask the person. Why do you believe in the value of pessimistic myths? Why don't you believe in the value of the most optimistic myths? Let us suppose still further. The person responds with an affirmation. The person affirms an ability to know. These pessimistic myths are truths. In that event, the person knows next to nothing about almost everything. The person values a lie. The lie is. These pessimistic myths are truths. The person devalues a truth. The truth is. These pessimistic myths are myths.

The totality makes possible an infinite number, diversity, and variety of myths. Only our creative abilities and powers of imagination limit our myth-making abilities. Why should I believe in the value of pessimistic myths? Belief in the value of pessimistic myths would leave me unable. I would be unable to balance the emotional forces of my mind. My belief in the value of the most optimistic myths enables me. I balance the emotional forces of my mind. I am happy. For that reason, I believe in the value of the most optimistic myths.

As mentioned previously, scientific research from a variety of sources seems to indicate. Our optimistic ideas have beneficial influences on our emotions, our behaviors, and our health. These beneficial influences enable our bodies. Our bodies become more resistant to the onset of disease. Our bodies become better able to recover from existing diseases. We experience powerful emotional forces of joy, faith, and love. Our experience tends to lead us to have better social lives. We enjoy an improved quality of life. Let us suppose. My model of the totality is not the way. Things actually are. In that event, at least I might have a happier and perhaps healthier life.

CHAPTER 11. HOUSE OF IDEOLOGY

Many life forms exist in the body consuming biosphere. Many of these life forms build models of the totality. They use their models of the totality. They navigate about their habitats. They orient themselves towards existence. They explain existence to themselves. They fashion their own realities within their own minds.

I am aware of this fact. I desire happiness and good health. Out of this awareness and desire, came an idea. The idea is. Found a community of faithful believers. I decided. This is a good idea. For that reason, I founded the House of Ideology. I am the High Ideologue of the House of Ideology.

Through this community of faithful believers, I teach, entertain, and lead people with good examples. The good examples show us how. We can have the highest esteem of the totality. We can best satisfy our common needs and aspirations. Our common needs and aspirations are. Achieve and maintain happiness, good health, and prosperity.

Let us suppose. People wish to join the House of Ideology. In that event, I welcome their active participation. Together and in our own ways, we are truth seekers. We believe in the value of truths. We are myth makers. We believe in the value of the most optimistic myths. We are architects. We use our values. We build within our minds. We build our models of the totality. We use our models of the totality. We navigate about our habitats. We orient ourselves towards existence. We explain existence to ourselves. We fashion our realities. Our realities are our Houses of Ideologies. We are the High Ideologues of our Houses of Ideologies.

CHAPTER 12. STATEMENT OF FAITH

A totality exists. For that reason, we are part of the totality. It transcends all human knowledge and all human comprehension. For that reason, the totality is myths' eternal fire. The act of pondering the totality requires energy, space, and time. We are lucky enough to have the energy, space, and time. We ponder the totality. We are inspired. No two eyes have perfect sight. However, with what tools and senses we do possess, we may still find some valuable insights. No individual is always wrong. No individual is always right. However, with what logic and intuition we possess, we may speculate intelligently. No individual wins in every fight. However, with courage, we may yet conquer our own ignorance, and come to a fuller, richer understanding of our place in the world. Actuality is the way. Things actually are. Reality is the way. Things appear to be. Our seed-bodies make senses and perceptions available to us. Our senses and perceptions enable us. We sense and perceive our realities.

Ideas are thoughts, beliefs, and expectations about the totality. We use our abilities to sense and perceive our realities. We verify the truth of ideas. We verify the falsity of ideas. True ideas conform to our realities. False ideas deviate from our realities.

We sort ideas into three simple categories. The three simple categories are truths, myths, and lies. Truths are ideas. Truths are verifiable. We can verify. Truths are true. Lies are ideas. Lies are falsifiable. We can verify. Lies are false. Myths are ideas. Myths are both unverifiable and unfalsifiable. We cannot verify whether or not. Myths are true. We cannot verify whether or not. Myths are false. We can only verify. Myths are ideas.

We believe in the value of truths. It appears. We are living infernal fractal entities. We live in a body-consuming biosphere. A primal conflict between predator and prey divides the body consuming biosphere. We play a game of survival and sacrifice. In order to survive, we need our senses. The competition to survive selected our senses for us. For that reason, we developed our senses. Our senses enable us. We see, hear, touch, feel, and smell. In order to survive, we need our perceptions. The competition to survive selected our perceptions for us. For that reason, we developed our perceptions. Our perceptions enable us. We add meaning to our sensations. Our seed-bodies made possible the existence of our minds. Our seed-bodies made possible the existence of our senses and perceptions. Our senses and perceptions enable us. We create, survive, perfect, and revive.

Our senses and perceptions enable us. We can know an amount of truth. We occupy specific points in energy, space, and time. Our occupation of specific points in energy, space, and time, limits the amount of truth. Our seed-bodies have attributes. The attributes of our seed-bodies limit the amount of truth. We can know a finite amount of truth. The totality is in everything, everywhere, at all times. The totality may be infinite. For that reason, we know next to nothing about the totality. We know a finite amount about an infinite subject. We know next to nothing about almost everything.

We are actors in the drama of life and death. We create characters. We portray characters of our own creation. We are the truth seekers. We are the myth makers. We are the authorities. We decide how. We make up our minds. We are the architects. We believe in the value of certain ideas. These certain ideas are our values. We use our values. We build within our minds. We build our models of the totality. Our models are our realities. Our realities are our Houses of Ideologies. We are the High Ideologues of our Houses of Ideologies. For that reason, we can change our realities to what. We would like our realities to be.

An ideology is a body of values. Often an ideology reflects the needs and aspirations of an individual, group, class, and or culture. We have common needs and aspirations. Our common needs and aspirations are. Achieve and maintain happiness, good health, and prosperity. We align our values with our common needs and aspirations.

We believe in the value of truths. Scientists in various fields of study have found much to say about a theory. The theory is. Happiness leads to better behavior and better health. Completely new fields of scientific research address the relationship between emotions and physical health. It appears. This scientific research affirms. Our optimistic thoughts, beliefs, and expectations have a positive influence on our health. Our optimistic thoughts, beliefs, and expectations improve our various health behaviors, our immune functions, and our biochemical functions. Improvement in our behaviors, immune functions, and biochemical functions makes our bodies more resistant to illness and better able to recover from existing disease. A capacity to produce happiness and good health; is the basis for our appreciating the most optimistic myths. A capacity to produce happiness and good health is the basis for our depreciating all other myths. For that reason, we believe in the value the most optimistic myths.

The most optimistic myths are all about infinite abundance. The totality is an infinite divine eternal being. The infinite divine eternal being enjoys entertainment. The drama of life and death entertains. For that reason, the infinite divine eternal being manifests as an infinite four. The infinite four are an infinite seed, an infinite body, an infinite soul, and an infinite spirit. The infinite seed is an infinite number, diversity, and variety of large universes of the correct kind to support living infernal fractal entities. The infinite body consists of the seed-body of self and the seed-bodies of all of the other living infernal fractal entities. The infinite soul consists of the soul-spirit of self and the soul-spirits of all of the other living infernal fractal entities. The infinite spirit is the infinite divine eternal being. Mother God is the infinite soul-spirit. Father Love is the infinite seed-body. The union of Mother God and Father Love creates life. We are Soul Children. Each of us has an infinite number, diversity, and variety of lives to live. Each of us has an infinite number, diversity, and variety of bodies to give. Each of us is seed, body, soul, and spirit.

Happiness is a balance of the emotional forces of the mind. Balance is a state of equilibrium. Force is a capacity to cause change. A cancellation of all forces by equal opposing forces produces the state of equilibrium. A cancellation of all forces by equal opposing forces produces happiness.

We believe in the value of truths. Our values act as forces upon our emotions. The most powerful emotional forces of sorrow, fear, and anger follow from the discovery of a truth. The truth is. It appears. One day, the seed-body of self will die.

We believe in the value the most optimistic myths. Our values act as forces upon our emotions. The most powerful emotional forces of joy, faith, and love follow from the mystery of the most optimistic myths. The most optimistic myths include. The life and immunity of the soul-spirit is, eternal and divine.

We believe in the value of the most optimistic myths. We believe in the value of truths. Our values act as forces upon our emotions. Joy, faith, and love, balance sorrow, fear, and anger. We balance the emotional forces of our minds. The balance of the emotional forces of our minds produces a state of happiness. We are happy.

Our emotions act as forces upon our behaviors. We exhibit glad behaviors. Friendly tolerant peacemaking behaviors are glad behaviors. Truth telling, sharing, playing well with others, liberating, emancipating, and nurturing are glad behaviors.

Our glad behaviors act as forces upon our bodies. The forces are conducive to a state of good health in our bodies. Our glad behaviors act as forces upon our habitat. The forces are conducive to a state of good health in our habitat. For that reason, emotional balance in our minds is conducive to happiness and good health in our lives.

A spiritual awakening is happening. It is happening right now. We are awakening each other to a freedom of choice. The freedom of choice follows from a truth. The truth is. A myth is a myth.

A spiritual liberation is happening. It is happening right now. We are liberating each other from a slavery. The slavery follows from a lie. The lie is. A myth is a truth.

A spiritual celebration is happening. It is happening right now. We are celebrating each other with a love. The love is a love of self and world. The love of self and world is taken to its highest esteem. Love of self and world taken to its highest esteem yields Mother God and Father Love. Soul children this individuality is just a dream. There's only we.

A spiritual identification is happening. It is happening right now. We are identifying each other as a High Ideologue. The High Ideologue is the High Ideologue of a House of Ideology. The House of Ideology is a model of the totality. Each of us is the High Ideologue of our very own House of Ideology. We are the High Ideologues of our Houses of Ideologies.

Our souls are in temporal communion with our seed-bodies. Our souls are in continuous communion with our soul-spirit. Continuous spiritual communion is a source of our inspiration, intuition, and good judgment. Our inspiration, intuition, and good judgment enable us. We find new ways of using our senses and perceptions. We make new scientifically reproducible discoveries.

New scientifically reproducible discoveries will enable us. Our glad behaviors will enable us. We will produce a strong and stable civilization.

CHAPTER 13. DISCOVERY AND MYSTERY, HEALTH AND HAPPINESS

Like light and shadow, day and night, discovery and mystery, we combine truths and myths. We create models of the totality.

A common denominator, in all cases, is change. From my earliest days, I have been constantly remodeling my thoughts, beliefs, and expectations about the totality. My model of the totality is an evolving, growing, and changing structure.

Let us suppose. I believe in the value of a myth. Let us suppose further. I discover a truth. Let us suppose still further. The truth contradicts the myth. In that event, the contradiction of the truth makes the myth into a lie. The lie would make my model of the totality falsifiable. A falsifiable model of the totality lacks credibility. A lack of credibility is unacceptable. For that reason, I would reject the lie. I reject all lies.

I do not claim to eliminate the discovery of disease and death. I do not claim to eliminate the mystery of immunity and life. Life forms experience dramas of life and death, games of survival and sacrifice, and tests of success and failure. A primal conflict between predator and prey divides our body-consuming biosphere. The primal conflict between predator and prey is an attribute of these dramas of life and death, games of survival and sacrifice, and tests of success and failure. I do not claim to eliminate suffering, sorrow, and abomination from the primal conflict between predator and prey.

I do claim. I provide education, entertainment, and leadership. The education, entertainment, and leadership enables me. I produce emotional balance within my mind. I produce physiological balance within my body. Through art, poetry, song, prose, and other available artistic means, I persevere, overcome defeat, and progress toward victory.

CHAPTER 14. NEW AGE

Reality is the way. Things appear to be. Actuality is the way. Things actually are. I face an enormous challenge. The enormous challenge is. Make my reality agree with my actuality. Generations have come before me. These generations provide help. Through mathematics of the physical sciences, such as chemistry, and physics, I learn. Complex dynamic systems of matter and energy exist in the known universe. It appears. Patterns of order exist in the chaos of these complex dynamic systems of matter and energy.

Our understanding of these patterns of order enables us. We can solve the problems of everyday life. We can liberate each other from the ignorance and arrogance of past ages. We can liberate each other from a spiritual slavery. The spiritual slavery follows from a lie. The lie is. A myth is a truth. We can enjoy a standard of living and a way of life of unparalleled luxury and convenience.

Our knowledge of truths and theories continues to grow exponentially. With the development of computer technology, a body of scientific evidence continues to accumulate. The body of scientific evidence accumulates in support of a theory. The theory is. All we observe in the universe around us may have originated in the advent of a big bang.

People have traditionally offered myths as an explanation for the totality. As discovery has expanded mystery has receded. Some people have questioned the need for myths. Some people have declared God dead. Some people have seen organized religion as a dying institution. Some people see atheism as the wave of the future.

When a person sets out to share their understanding of the totality with others, they can take different paths depending on their nature and circumstances. In the hypothetical scenario where this person becomes a warlord, the dissemination of their beliefs may be enforced through military might. In such a scenario, refusing to conform to the religious beliefs dictated by the warlord could lead to severe consequences, potentially sparking rebellion against their authority.

Conversely, if the individual is not a warlord, the spread of their beliefs might involve peaceful communication and the exchange of ideas. This could lead to the formation of a religion based on shared principles and beliefs about the nature of existence and the totality.

In either case, a religion emerges as a structured system offering a way for individuals to make sense of the totality. Religious authority figures often assert. Their religion provides the best framework for understanding the world. Followers are encouraged to have faith in the teachings and doctrines of the religion, with faith being defined as complete trust and confidence.

However, not everyone within a religious community may possess unwavering faith. Some individuals may lack faith altogether, while others may struggle with doubts and uncertainties. Despite this, they may still engage with the religious community, learning about its beliefs and practices, and even outwardly displaying signs of faith to align with social norms and expectations.

Within these religious communities, there may be opportunities for individuals to conduct business with others who share the same faith. This shared belief system can create a sense of solidarity and trust among members, fostering economic and social interactions within the community.

Tribes are often self-organized around a particular religion. Abandoning the religion of the tribe may result in a significant loss of income and business opportunities. For that reason, I predict. Attempts on the part of an outsider to persuade a tribe member to abandon the religion of the tribe would most likely be met with failure.

Religions enable people. People explain the world to self. People orient self towards the world. Religions are often deeply engrained within the physiology of the brain. Religions are often deeply engrained in the structure of a community and or society. Let us suppose. A person presents an alternative model of the totality to communities of faithful believers. In that event, I predict. The communities of faithful believers would find. The alternate model seems foreign, strange, wrong, difficult to grasp, and difficult to imagine.

Communities of faithful believers self-organize around religious belief. Communities of faithful believers are part of our world. We deal with their members in our every day lives. Understanding communities of faithful believers is important. For that reason, the study of religions is important.

Let us suppose. Atheists decide. The best way to make up our minds about the totality has been found. The atheists go about the business of sharing this way with other people. In that event, an atheistic religion begins.

Our seed-bodies make senses and perceptions available to us. Our senses and perceptions enable us. We can sense and perceive things. Science makes tools available to us. The tools of science enable scientists. Scientists can discover things. Science makes scientific theories available to us. The scientific theories enable scientists. Scientists can predict things. Some atheists have made up their minds. Nothing else exists until proven otherwise. They go about the business of sharing this way of making up their minds with other people. As if things come into existence by being sensed and perceived by us.

Atheists believe in the value of certain ideas. These certain ideas are their values. What are their values? By identifying as atheists, they do not reveal their values. They only say. Their values are not those of theists. They do not believe in the value of certain ideas. These certain ideas are not their values. For that reason, they could potentially believe in the value of all kinds of other ideas and still identify as atheists.

Nevertheless, atheists are part of the totality. For that reason, it is logical to infer. Atheists believe in the value of a pessimistic myth. The pessimistic myth is. A godless totality exists. Let us suppose. I ask an atheist. Why do you choose to believe in the value of this pessimistic myth? Why don't you choose to believe in the value of the most optimistic myths? Let us suppose further. The atheist affirms an ability to know. This pessimistic myth is a truth. In that event, this atheist knows next to nothing about almost everything. This atheist values a lie. The lie is. This pessimistic myth is a truth. This atheist devalues a truth. The truth is. This pessimistic myth is a myth.

We live in a new age of ideology. Our ancestors were not privileged to have our new truths and our new myths. Let us suppose. New truths and theories becomes available to me. In that event, I assimilate the new truths and theories. Let us suppose. These new truths and theories contradict my myths. In that event, I remake my myths. I accommodate the new truths and theories. I combine my truths and my theories with my newly remade myths. I build a model of the totality. The model of the totality is credible.

The measure of the perfection of any given model of the totality is its' capacity to best satisfy our common needs and aspirations. Our common needs and aspirations are. Achieve and maintain happiness, good health, and prosperity. I devote energy, space, and time towards the accomplishment of the goal of reaching this perfection.

I teach by example. I use the many examples contained within the text of this book. We are all members of the human species. We are all self in the same body-consuming biosphere. For that reason, it is logical for me to think, believe, and predict. What works for me. May work for other people as well.

I believe in the value of truths. I believe in the value of theories. My values act on my emotions. I analyze my emotions. I find. The most powerful emotional forces of sorrow, fear, and anger follow from the discovery of a truth. The truth is. It appears. One day, the seed-body of self will die. My truths and my theories impose limits on my myths. I use my knowledge of the limits. I determine. What is possible within the realm of mystery? What is not possible within the realm of mystery?

Based on what is possible within the realm of mystery, I make my most optimistic myths. I examine my most optimistic myths. My most optimistic myths produce emotional forces in my mind. I analyze the emotional forces. I find. The most powerful emotional forces of joy, faith, and love follow from the mystery of the most optimistic myths. The most optimistic myths include. The life and immunity of the soul-spirit is, eternal and divine.

I believe in the value of truths. I believe in the value of theories. I believe in the value of the most optimistic myths. These are my values. I use my values. I build within my mind. I build a model of the totality. I call it my reality. My reality is my House of Ideology. I am the High Ideologue of my House of Ideology.

My values enable me. I produce emotional balance in my mind. I achieve and maintain a state of happiness. I think, believe, and predict. Emotional balance in my mind is conducive to happiness and good health in my life. Happiness and good health in my life is conducive to success and prosperity in my business. For those reasons, I take love of self and world to its highest esteem. I take Healthy Agnostic Positivistic Nationalistic Spiritization of self and world to its logical extreme. I converge upon a model of the totality. The model of the totality enables me. I best satisfy my needs and aspirations. My needs and aspirations are. Achieve and maintain happiness, good health, and prosperity.

CHAPTER 15. MY KNOWLEDGE OF TRUTHS AND THEORIES

I examine myself in the light of my knowledge of truths and theories. I base my knowledge of truths and theories on scientifically reproducible discoveries. My present understanding of science reveals.

I am a living individual called an organism. The organism is a living form of matter and energy. The organism grows and reproduces. The organism absorbs matter and energy from the surrounding environment. The organism processes this matter and energy internally. The organism excretes waste matter and energy into the surrounding environment.

Some organisms consist of a single cell. Single cell organisms have a semi-permeable membrane. The semi-permeable membrane permits the absorption of the correct kinds of matter and energy from its' surroundings. The semi-permeable membrane permits the excretion of the correct kinds of matter and energy to its' surroundings.

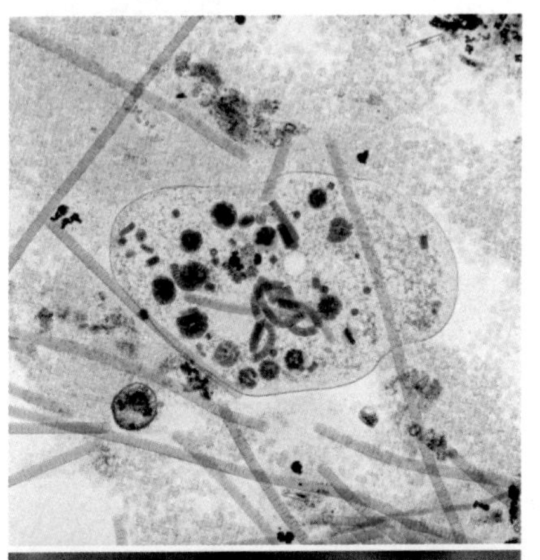

Single-cell organisms grow. Single-cell organisms reproduce. They reproduce by means of cell division. Cell division makes a single cell organism into two single cell organisms.

Some organisms consist of multiple cells. These organisms are sometimes called multicellular organisms. Multicellular organisms use cell division for growth, and the maintenance and repair of cells and tissues.

Multi-cellular organisms form seed-bodies. A seed-body grows from a seed. The seed is a kind of single cell organism. The seed forms from the union of a sperm cell and an egg cell. Male seed-body produces sperm cells and female seed-body produces egg cells.

A species is a group of life forms. The life forms of the species are very similar to each other. The life forms of the species are usually capable of interbreeding and producing fertile offspring. Male and female seed-bodies of the same species join in sexual embrace. Sperm and egg join to produce a living seed.

A need of the seed is to feed and to breed. The seed feeds. The seed grows into a seed-body. The seed-body breeds. The seed becomes a link from one generation to the next.

A seed-body develops from the seed. The design of the seed-body reflects the need of the seed to create. The design of the seed-body reflects the need of the seed-body to survive. Let us suppose. The seed-body is successful. In that event, the seed-body acquires the correct kinds of material and energy from its' environment. The seed-body consumes the correct kinds of material and energy. The correct kinds of material and energy enable the seed-body. The seed-body grows, survives, breeds, and performs any species-specific parental duties.

After the seed-body develops from the seed, the seed-body succumbs to an ultimate fate. The ultimate fate is. Other organisms eat the seed-body. The eating of the seed-body occurs through a natural process of disease and death. So goes the drama of life and death. In a body-consuming biosphere every life form, every organism, great and small, plays the dual role of predator and prey. A primal conflict between predator and prey divides the body consuming biosphere. The primal conflict between predator and prey is an attribute of the drama of life and death, the game of survival and sacrifice, the test of success and failure, and the catharsis of comedy and tragedy.

I classify human beings as organisms. Human beings are multi-cellular organisms. Human beings form human seed-bodies. Human seed-bodies are seed-bodies of the human species. For that reason, human seed-bodies are distinct.

Human seed-bodies evolved from and along side single-celled organisms known as bacteria. Our seed-bodies are dependent on bacteria. Scientists estimate. Five hundred to one thousand species of bacteria live in a typical human seed-body. Bacterial cells are much smaller than human cells. The typical human seed-body hosts trillions of bacteria cells. The typical human seed-body hosts about the same number of human cells.

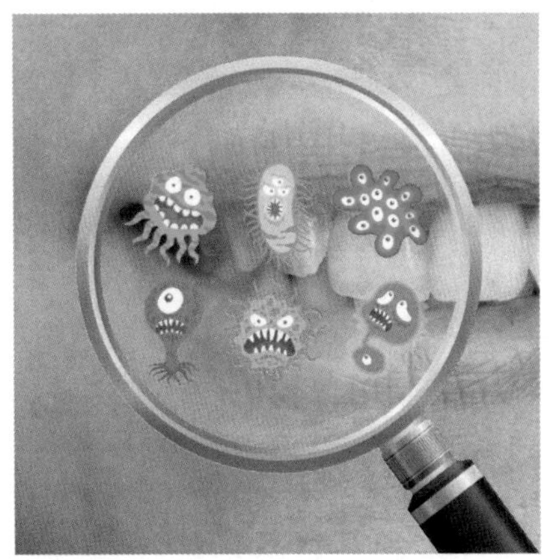

We live in close association with bacteria. The external and internal surfaces of our seed-bodies are covered with bacteria. Our seed-bodies provide a nice place for these bacteria to live. Our seed-bodies provide a good supply of food and a more or less constant temperature. In return, the bacteria protect their home. They compete against pathogenic bacteria. They protect their host seed-body against disease. The host seed-body and the bacteria both gain from this peaceful living together. Scientists call this commensalism. The normal microflora and microfauna of our seed-bodies consists of microorganisms. These microorganisms are called commensals.

We are dependent on our commensals. Our commensals help us digest our food. Our commensals produce vital vitamins.

Insects have commensals living inside of their seed-bodies. Cellulose is the building block of plant cells. Some insects can eat wood. Wood contains cellulose. Their commensals enable the insects. The insects digest the cellulose in wood.

Cows have commensals living inside of their seed-bodies. Cows can eat grass. Grass contains cellulose. Their commensals enable the cows. The cows can digest the cellulose in grass.

Let us suppose. Your gut is fully loaded with 'good' bacteria. In that event, pathogens have to compete with commensals for food. This is how the good bacteria provide a degree of protection against pathogens.

A seed-body also has an immune system. This immune system combats pathogens. Let us suppose. A person's immune system combats an infection. Let us suppose further. The person treats the infection. The person takes a course of antibiotics. In that event, the course of

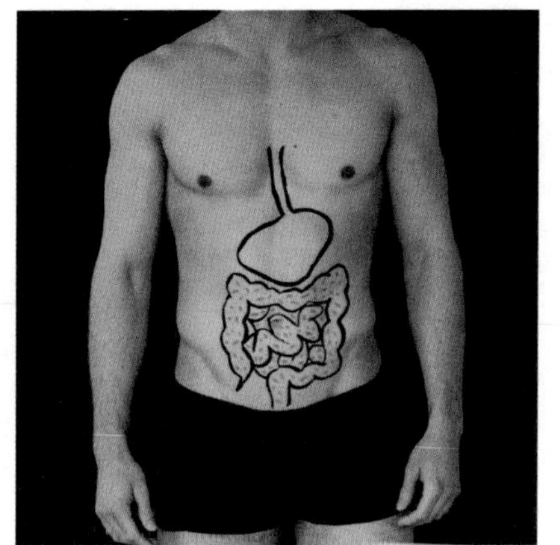

antibiotics destroys many of the person's commensals. The person's commensals decrease in number.

Let us suppose. The person's commensals decrease in number. Let us suppose further. Diarrhea is the result. Let us suppose still further. The person treats the diarrhea. The person eats certain fermented foods on a daily basis. The certain fermented foods are teeming with good bacteria. In that event, the person adds good bacteria to the person's seed-body. Good bacteria enables the seed-body. The seed-body returns to a state of good health.

Human beings are animals. Human beings use tools. Civilization is a tool. People use the tool. Civilization enables people. People facilitate a collective effort to work, fight, and outnumber competition. Civilization has solved many problems for human beings. However, civilization has also created some problems. One of the problems is. For some people, the amount of time between harvest of food and consumption of food increases. The time enables microscopic predators. Microscopic predators can colonize the food before we consume it. Food suppliers do their best to handle the problem. However, sometimes microscopic predators find a way. Let us suppose. A person eats food. Let us suppose further. The food has been colonized by microscopic predators. Let us suppose still further. The microscopic predators colonize the person's body in unhealthful ways. In that event, the person will be ill.

People found solutions to this problem. One solution is cooking food. Some microscopic predators seek to colonize our bodies in unhealthful ways. Cooking food insures. The microscopic predators are killed.

However, this killing of microscopic predators causes another problem. Let us suppose. A person eats cooked foods. In that event, the chemical make up of the food has been drastically altered by the cooking process. The longer a food is cooked. The greater is the loss of nutrients. The enzymes are dead. The vitamins are dead. The fiber is dead. The food is dead.

I believe in the value of truths. Scientists say. It appears. The universe is about 13.8 billion years old. The planet Earth is about 4.5 billion years old. Life has existed on the planet Earth for billions of years. During the vast majority of those billions of years. Organisms consumed other organisms. Organisms consumed fresh living organic raw appetizing foods.

Let us suppose. A person eats fresh living organic raw appetizing foods. The person eats fruits, vegetables, greens, herbs, seeds, roots, nuts, and berries. In that event, the fresh living organic raw appetizing foods are packed with nutritional value. The enzymes are living. The vitamins are living. The fiber is living. The food is living.

Let us suppose. A person desires happiness, good health, and prosperity. In that event, the person would be wise to clean food.

I believe in the value of truths. Scientists say. Our bodies have immune systems. The immune systems protect our bodies against pathogens and foreign invaders. An immune system includes white blood cells. Let us suppose. The immune system detects the presence of pathogens and or foreign invaders. In that event, the white blood cells respond. The white blood cells release hydrogen peroxide. The hydrogen peroxide oxidizes both pathogens and foreign invaders. Oxidation kills pathogens and foreign invaders.

Let us suppose. A person eats fresh-living-organic-raw-appetizing foods. Let us suppose further. The person soaks the food with a three percent hydrogen peroxide solution. Let us suppose still further. The person rinses the food with fresh clean water. In that event, the person cleans the food.

Let us suppose. A person drinks three percent hydrogen peroxide solution. Let us suppose further. The three percent hydrogen peroxide solution kills some part of the person's microbiome. In that event, the person's behaviors act as forces upon the person's body. The forces upon the person's body cause a state of disease. The state of disease is a gastrointestinal upset. For that reason, the person learns. Do not drink three percent hydrogen peroxide solution.

I examine the world in the light of my knowledge of truths and theories. I define 'world' as the totality. The totality is inclusive of the natural known universe and any mystery beyond. Science reveals to us. It appears. We are life forms. As life forms, we play the dual role of predator and prey. A primal conflict between predator and prey divides our body-consuming biosphere. Our body-consuming biosphere grows on a crusted magma globe. A moon orbits the crusted magma globe. The crusted magma globe orbits a sun. The sun orbits the center of our galaxy. Our galaxy is one of a universe of galaxies.

The crusted magma globe, the sun, the moon, the galaxy of stars, and the universe of galaxies are known structures of energy. These known structures of energy occupy space. Scientists say. It appears. Space has been expanding from a central point of origin for many billions of years. For that reason, it appears. The universe of galaxies began from a central point of origin with a big bang. The cause of this big bang remains a mystery. The mystery has created a tiny island of life in a vast ocean of death. Death is the norm. Life is the abnormality.

I examine the future in the light of my knowledge of truths and theories. Science informs me. It appears. The life of a seed-body follows a predictable course of conception, gestation, birth, growth, puberty, maturity, aging, disease, and death.

The termination of life can occur before completion of an entire life cycle. Predators, accidents, and natural disasters are forces of the surrounding world. At any point during the life cycle of a seed-body, forces of the surrounding world may cause termination of life.

A small part of an individual may continue to live on through the contribution of a sperm cell or an egg cell to the creation of a living seed. However, nature offers our seed-bodies little chance of evading death. The survival of a seed-body is brief. We endeavor to live fully. However, we do so without guarantees.

As for our body-consuming biosphere, science informs me. It appears. Its' future is finite and tenuous at best. A primal conflict between predator and prey divides our body-consuming biosphere. A competition to survive selects the forms and functions of seed-bodies. Life evolves. Some periods in the planet's history were relatively tranquil. During these relatively tranquil periods, it appears. Evolution of life progressed with gradual incremental changes.

Some periods in the planet's history were relatively turbulent. During these relatively turbulent periods, it appears. Evolution of life progressed with sudden catastrophic change. For example, about sixty-five million years ago a small asteroid crashed into the Earth's crust. The collision may have precipitated the mass extinction of the dinosaurs.

The planet Earth is a stage for the drama of life and death. Maybe the planet Earth will continue to be a stage for the drama of life and death. Maybe some cosmic or man-made catastrophe will end the drama of life and death on planet Earth today.

Let us suppose. A person affirms an ability to know. Consciousness emerges from our seed-bodies. Our seed-bodies do not emerge from consciousness. The meaning of life is its' own self-perpetuation. The motivations in everything one says or does are the product of the biochemical functions of a meat machine. The person believes in the value of the three most commonly valued pessimistic myths. The three most commonly valued pessimistic myths are. Self is only a seed and a body. Self has only one life to live. Self has only one body to give. The person believes in the value of truths. In that event, the person's values would act as forces upon the person's emotions. The most powerful emotional forces of sorrow, fear, and anger follow from the discovery of a truth. The truth is. It appears. One day, the seed-body of self will die. The person's belief in the value of the three most commonly valued pessimistic myths would not enable the person. The person would be unable to balance the emotional forces of the person's mind. For that reason, the person's heart would be filled with sorrow, fear, and anger, as disease and death draw ever closer.

Let us suppose. A person's heart is filled with sorrow, fear, and anger, as disease and death draw ever closer. In that event, the person's emotions would act as forces upon the person's behaviors. Some people may lose hope and faith. Some people may give up. Some people may turn to crime. Some people may turn to drugs. Some people may attempt to fill the remainder of their brief lives with as many fleeting moments of pleasure as is possible. Some people may become aggressive. Some people may become depressed. Some people may become homicidal, genocidal, or even suicidal. Some people may do nothing. Some people may act helpless. Some people may exhibit sad, mad, and bad behaviors.

Let us suppose. People attempt to fill the remainder of their brief lives with an excessive use of pleasure-inducing-recreational drugs. Let us suppose further. The excessive use of pleasure-inducing-recreational drugs leads to serious health problems. In that event, their behaviors are sad, mad, and bad behaviors. Their behaviors act as forces upon their seed-bodies. The forces are conducive to a state of disease in their seed-bodies. The forces are conducive to a state of disease in their habitats.

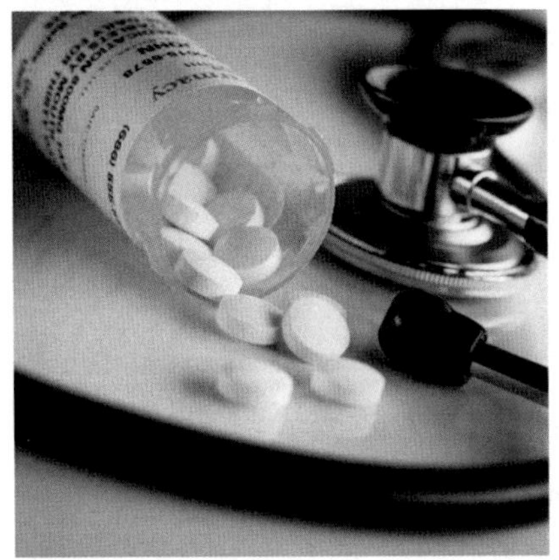

Drugs have their place in the treatment of disease. However, let us suppose. A person's heart is filled with sorrow, fear, and anger. In that event, pleasure-inducing-recreational drug use may lead to a bad trip. A bad trip is a frightening or depressing drug experience.

Over time, pleasure-inducing-recreational drug users tend to require ever larger doses to achieve the same pleasure inducing effects. Major changes in brain chemistry occur. These major changes in brain chemistry make these drugs less effective at stimulating the brain to feelings of pleasure.

In response, some users may flood their bloodstreams with pleasure-inducing-recreational drugs. Flooding their bloodstreams with pleasure-inducing recreational drugs may interfere with the operations of their nervous systems. Flooding their bloodstreams with pleasure-inducing-recreational drugs may disable their minds. The nervous system of the seed-body controls organs of the immune system. For that reason, some users may also end up disabling their immune systems. Seed-bodies with disabled immune systems and disabled minds have higher risk of disease and death. For that reason, excessive use of pleasure-inducing-recreational drugs offer them a false solution to the emotional unbalance of their minds.

Let us suppose. A large number of people make excessive use of recreational drugs. For that reason, their seed-bodies are in a state of disease. Their habitats are in a state of disease. Let us suppose further. A few people concentrate wealth, income, and power into their own hands. The few people achieve and maintain authority, power, order, and control over a state. The few people decide. The excessive use of recreational drugs by a large number of people is a national security threat. Let us suppose still further. The few people enable the state. The state declares a war on drugs. The state makes illegal the sale, manufacture, possession, and use of pleasure-inducing-recreational drugs. The state hunts down, arrests, and imprisons drug dealers. The state hunts down, arrests, and imprisons drug users. Let us suppose finally. The actions of the state inadvertently drive up the street price of pleasure-inducing-recreational drugs. Higher street prices attract a criminal drug trade. The criminal drug trade attracts artists. The artists glamorize the gangster lifestyle. The artists glamorize illegal pleasure-inducing-recreational drug use. The glamour attracts more people and customers to the criminal drug trade. In that event, the actions of the state do not address the underlying cause of the epidemic of pleasure-inducing-recreational drug use. The underlying cause of the epidemic of pleasure-inducing-recreational drug use is. A large number of people believe in the value of the three most commonly valued pessimistic myths. A belief in the value of the three most commonly valued pessimistic myths does not enable people. People are unable to balance the emotional forces of their minds. Their hearts are filled with sorrow, fear, and anger. The actions of the state do not address the sorrow, fear, and anger. For that reason, the state loses the war on drugs.

The way to win a war on illegal recreational drugs is. Address the underlying causes of the excessive use of pleasure-inducing-recreational drugs. Address the sorrow, fear, and anger. Teach, entertain, and lead people by example. Believe in the value of truths. Believe in the value of the most optimistic myths. Balance sorrow, fear, and anger with joy, faith, and love. Be happy. Exhibit glad behaviors. Achieve and maintain happiness, good health, and prosperity.

The way to win a war on illegal recreational drugs is. Legalize recreational drug use. Criminals are collecting vast sums of money. Let us suppose. We legalize recreational drug use. In that event, the vast sums of money would dry up. Drug addicts would be able to get their pleasure-inducing-recreational drugs legally for far less. There would be little financial incentive driving dealers to push illegal recreational drugs on potential addicts. For that reason, there would be fewer addicts, fewer popular songs glorifying the gangster lifestyle, and far less illegal recreational drug-related violence and crime.

The usual argument against legalizing is. The cost to society would be too high. Far more people would suffer from the disabling effects of drug addiction. Far more people would die of drug overdoses. I think, believe, and predict. Criminals collect vast sums of money by selling illegal recreational drugs. Some of this money ends up in the hands of terrorists. The cost to society of protecting drug addicts from themselves is simply too high.

Let us suppose. People attempt to fill the remainder of their brief lives with an excessive pursuit of sexual gratification. Let us suppose further. The excessive pursuit of sexual gratification leads to serious health problems. In that event, their behaviors are sad, mad, and bad behaviors. Their sad, mad, and bad behaviors act as forces upon their bodies. The forces are conducive to a state of disease in their bodies. Their sad, mad, and bad behaviors act as forces upon their habitats. The forces are conducive to a state of disease in their habitats.

Serious health problems can arise due to the excessive pursuit of sexual gratification. Most of the serious health problems can be traced to the exchange of bodily fluids. Sex can be a pathway to disease. Bodily fluid exchanges occur during sexual intercourse. Some microscopic predators use these bodily fluid exchanges to travel from body to body.

Let us suppose. The hearts of people are filled with sorrow, fear, and anger as disease and death draw ever closer. In that event, some people may find. Long-term relationships with sexual partners are difficult. Some people might feel a sense of urgency. The sense of urgency might motivate some people. Some people might engage in reckless acts. Some people might engage in serial monogamy, polygamy, promiscuity, and rape in an effort to fill the remainders of their brief lives with the pursuit of fleeting moments of pleasure. Belief in the value of the most optimistic myths might eliminate much of this sense of urgency. The most optimistic myths include. Self has an infinite number, diversity, and variety of lives to live. Self has an infinite, number, diversity and variety of bodies to give. Self is seed, body, soul, and spirit.

Semen, blood, and saliva are bodily fluids. People may exchange bodily fluids during sex. Exchange of bodily fluids during sex could cause a sexually transmittable disease. The act of depositing semen from one body into another body may be the most dangerous pathway to a sexually transmittable disease. Let us suppose. A person carries a sexually transmittable disease. Let us suppose further. The person deposits some semen into another person's seed-body. In that event, the semen would contain microscopic predators. The microscopic predators could multiply to excess. The microscopic predators could cause disease and even death.

As we breathe, we exhale airborne water particles. Exchanges of body fluids through airborne water particles can be a pathway to airborne disease. Airborne water particles can carry microscopic predators. These microscopic predators can multiply to excess. In confined spaces, our seed-bodies breathe in exhalations of breath from other seed-bodies. Breathing in exhalations of breath from other seed-bodies can cause disease to spread from one body to another. Smokers exhale particles of smoke. Maybe particles of smoke could also carry microscopic predators.

We all have to breathe. I prefer to meet with large groups of people in open spaces. I avoid large groups of people crowded into a room wherein; I am made to breathe in everybody else's exhalations for an extended period of time.

I think, believe, and predict. There is more to me than my seed-body. I believe in the value of the most optimistic myths. As such, I feel no urgency to adopt a strategy of filling the remainder of my brief life with fleeting moments of pleasure. I find. Loving myself is a prerequisite to being loved by somebody else. I find. Loving my world is a prerequisite to loving myself. I love myself by having the highest esteem of self. I love my world by having the highest esteem of the world. I love the totality by having the highest esteem of the totality.

I put the existence of discovery in its' proper place as a part of the totality. Quantity of energy, quality of space, longevity of time, and value of denominator are attributes of the totality. The attributes of the totality may be infinite, divine, eternal, and one, without violating any of the known laws of science.

CHAPTER 16. MY BELIEF IN THE VALUE OF THE MOST OPTIMISTIC MYTHS

We know next to nothing about almost everything. We are actors in the drama of life and death. We create characters. We portray characters of our own creation.

I am the truth seeker. I am the myth maker. I am the authority. I decide how. I make up my mind. A totality exists. Ideas are thoughts, beliefs, and expectations about the totality. I value certain ideas. These certain ideas are my values. I value truths. I value the most optimistic myths.

I am the architect. I use my values. I build within my mind. I build my model of the totality. My model of the totality is my House of Ideology. An ideology is a body of values. Ideology fashions reality. My House of Ideology is my reality. Reality is the way. Things appear to be. Actuality is the way. Things actually are. I am the High Ideologue of my House of Ideology. For that reason, I can change my reality to what. I would like my reality to be.

My House of Ideology includes my truths, my theories, and my myths. My truths and my theories impose limits upon my myths. Within these limits, I am free. I make the most optimistic myths. I believe in the value of my most optimistic myths.

My belief in the value of my most optimistic myths enables me. I balance the emotional forces of my mind. Emotional balance in my mind is conducive to happiness and good health in my life. Happiness and good health in my life is conducive to success and prosperity in my business.

My values act as forces upon my emotions. The power of the forces are proportional to the credibility of my values. For that reason, I stay within the limits set by my truths and my theories. I prevent lies and ignorance from entering into my model of the totality. I give my most optimistic myths credibility.

My most optimistic myths are fluid. My most optimistic myths remain unverifiable. My most optimistic myths remain unfalsifiable. My most optimistic myths change with my growing understanding of my truths and my theories. My most optimistic myths are about our world, our future and us. For that reason, my most optimistic myths are relevant.

Let us suppose. I decide how. I make up my mind. In that event, I am the authority.

Let us suppose. A community of faithful believers decides how. I make up my mind. In that event, the community of faithful believers is the authority.

Let us suppose. Some people self organize into a community of faithful believers. The community of faithful believers is the authority. Let us suppose further. Their leaders attempt to unite all minds under one way of ornamenting a model of the totality with myths. Let us suppose still further. Their members think, believe, and predict. They are united under one way of ornamenting a model of the totality with myths. In that event, they delude themselves.

No two individuals, no two communities of faithful believers, no two ideological authorities, no two denominations have exactly the same way of ornamenting a model of the totality with myths. Seminal religious organizations fracture into various denominations, combinations, and permutations. For that reason, I am not trying to unite all minds under one way of ornamenting a model of the totality with myths. I promote diversity, variety, and freedom of expression.

CHAPTER 17. BALANCE, COMPLEMENTS, AND SYNTHESIS

A key to my happiness is. I believe in the value of truths. I believe in the value of the most optimistic myths. These are my values. My values act as forces upon my emotions. Joy, faith, and love balance sorrow, fear, and anger. I balance the emotional forces of my mind. I am happy.

I have the highest esteem of self. The act of having the highest esteem of self follows from my belief in the value of a most optimistic myth. The most optimistic myth is. My soul exists.

I have the highest esteem of the world. The act of having the highest esteem of the world follows from my belief in the value of a most optimistic myth. The most optimistic myth is. My spirit exists.

My soul and spirit have attributes. Science has yet to discover the attributes of my soul and spirit. Science has discovered. Optimism correlates with happiness, good health, and prosperity. Pessimism correlates with unhappiness, disease, and hardship. I desire happiness, good health, and prosperity. For that reason, I imagine. My soul and spirit have the most optimistic attributes.

Let us suppose. A range of definitions is possible for the words soul and spirit. In that event, it is important to stop and think a moment. What meaning do I give the words soul and spirit?

My soul is a divine eternal force. This force is a vital principle. This vital principle animates my body. My body generates my unconscious mind. My soul generates my free will. My soul generates my conscious mind. My soul exists as the divine eternal part of finite self.

My spirit is a divine eternal force. This force is a vital principle. This vital principle animates our world. This vital principle creates universes. This vital principle evaluates universes. Our spirit exists as the divine eternal part of the infinite world.

Soul-spirit is a phrase meant to convey a sense of the indivisibility of the soul and the spirit. The soul-spirit of self is the same as the soul. The soul-spirit of the world is the same as the spirit.

The soul-spirit is divine. Divine is an adjective. The adjective divine describes the noun soul-spirit as being of a quality. The quality is of the highest order. That is perfect. The soul-spirit is eternal. Eternal is an adjective. The adjective eternal describes the noun soul-spirit as being of a longevity of time. The longevity of time is eternal.

Let us review a few facts. A totality exists. For that reason, we are part of the totality. The totality is everything, everywhere, at all times. Some things existed in the past. Those things are part of the totality. Some things exist right now. Those things are part of the totality. Some things will exist in the future. Those things are part of the totality. The totality may be infinite. The existence of discovery is equal to the sum total of all knowledge of truths and theories. The sum total of all knowledge of truths and theories is finite. We know a finite amount about an infinite subject. The existence of mystery is equal to the totality minus the existence of discovery. For that reason, the existence of mystery may be infinite. Represent the existence of discovery with a finite number. Represent the totality with an infinitely greater number. Divide the finite number by the infinitely greater number. The quotient represents the fullness of our knowledge about the totality. The quotient is equal to a number approaching zero. In other words, we know a finite amount of truth about an infinite subject. We know next to nothing about almost everything!

Our seed-bodies make senses and perceptions available to us. We can use our senses and perceptions. We can find things. Science makes tools available to us. Scientists can use our tools. Scientists can discover things. Science makes scientific theories available to us. Scientists can use our scientific theories. Scientists can predict things.

A position is a point of view. Let us suppose. A person takes a position. The position is. Only these things exist, until proven otherwise. Let us suppose further. The person says. The position is the rational position. In that event, the person is suggesting. The position is logical. The position is sane. The position is consistent with and or based on reason. For those reasons, the person is suggesting. We should adopt this position even though the correct position is unknown. We should adopt this position until proven otherwise.

Is this position logical, sane, and consistent with and or based on reason? Should we adopt this position even though the correct position is unknown? Should we adopt this position until proven otherwise? Our values act as forces upon our emotions. Most people believe in the value of truths. The most powerful emotional forces of sorrow, fear, and anger follow from the discovery of a truth. The truth is. It appears. One day, the seed body of self will die. The totality is everything, everywhere, at all times. We know a finite amount of truth about an infinite subject. For that reason, the totality makes possible an infinite number, diversity, and variety of myths.

Let us suppose. We did adopt this position. In that event, the act of adopting this position would require us to work up from pessimism to optimism rather than work down from optimism to pessimism. For that reason, the act of adopting this position would require us to believe in the value of pessimistic myths. These pessimistic myths would include. A godless totality exists. Self has only one life to live. Self has only one body to give. Self is only a seed and a body. Pessimism correlates with sorrow, fear, anger, and disease. For that reason, our belief in the value of these pessimistic myths would not enable us. We would be unable to balance the emotional forces of our minds. For that reason, our hearts would be filled with sorrow, fear, and anger. Our emotions act as forces upon our behaviors. For that reason, we would exhibit sad, mad, and bad behaviors. Lying, cheating, stealing, conquering, enslaving, and killing are sad, mad, and bad behaviors. Racist fascist warmongering behaviors are sad, mad, and bad behaviors. These sad, mad, and bad behaviors would act as forces upon our habitat. These forces would be conducive to a state of disease in our habitat. These sad, mad, and bad behaviors would act as forces upon our bodies. The forces would be conducive to a state of disease in our bodies. We would be unable to satisfy our common needs and aspirations. Our common needs and aspirations are. Achieve and maintain happiness, good health, and prosperity. Our values would not be aligned with our common needs and aspirations. For those reasons, the person's position is not logical. The person's position is not sane. The person's position is not consistent with and or based on reason. The person's position is immoral. We should not adopt the person's position even though the correct position is unknown. We should not adopt the person's position until proven otherwise.

Let us suppose. A person wishes to find the correct position. The person uses valid logical deductive inferences. These valid logical deductive inferences enable the person. The person is able to eliminate all other possible positions. The person arrives at one remaining position. In that event, the one remaining position would be the correct position.

Let us suppose. A person wishes to find the correct position. The person uses valid logical inductive inferences. These valid logical inductive inferences do not enable the person. The person is unable to eliminate all other possible positions. However, the person arrives at a position. In that event, the position would not necessarily be, the correct position.

Should we adopt a position even though the correct position is unknown? Should we adopt a position until proven otherwise? We know next to nothing about almost everything. However, next to nothing is still something. It appears. Scientific research affirms a theory. The theory is. Our optimism has a positive influence on our health. Our optimistic values improve our various health behaviors, our immune functions, and our biochemical functions. Belief in the value of optimistic myths makes our bodies more resistant to illness. Belief in the value of optimistic myths makes our bodies better able to recover from existing disease. Yes, we should adopt a position even though the correct position is unknown. We should adopt a position until proven otherwise. We should adopt the most optimistic position.

I provide good examples. The good examples show us how. We can love ourselves. We can love our world. We can love the totality. We can believe in the value of the most optimistic myths. We can believe in the value of truths. From a balance of values follows a balance of emotions. Joy, faith, and love, balance sorrow, fear, and anger. We can balance the emotional forces of our minds. We can be happy. We can exhibit glad behaviors. We can best satisfy our common needs and aspirations. We can achieve and maintain happiness, good health, and prosperity.

Let us suppose. A person adopts the identity of the bearer of the burden of proof. The person demands proof before the person will believe in the value of the most optimistic myths. In that event, the proof will not be forthcoming. We can gather truths. However, our abilities to gather truths are extremely limited. Our abilities to gather truths are only sufficient to enable us. We can function within our habitat. Our habitat is our body-consuming biosphere on our crusted magma globe of limited dimensions. The immensity of the totality renders us practically deaf, dumb, and blind. We are practically deaf, dumb, and blind when it comes to gathering truths about the totality.

Our seed-bodies make senses and perceptions available to us. We can use our senses and perceptions. However, use of our senses and perceptions does not enable us. We are unable to quantify infinity, qualify divinity, measure the longevity of eternity, and perceive the totality. Science makes tools available to us. Scientists can use our tools. Use of our tools does not enable scientists. Scientists are unable to quantify infinity, qualify divinity, measure the longevity of eternity, and perceive the totality. Science makes scientific theories available to us. Scientists can use our scientific theories. Use of our scientific theories does not enable scientists. Scientists are unable to quantify infinity, qualify divinity, measure the longevity of eternity, and perceive the totality. For that reason, the proof will not be forthcoming.

I adopt a most optimistic position. My most optimistic position follows from an affirmation of a truth. The truth is. A myth is a myth. My most optimistic position follows from a belief. My belief is in the value of the most optimistic myths. My most optimistic position is. Our seed-bodies make senses and perceptions available to us. We can use our senses and perceptions. We can find things. Science makes tools available to us. Scientists can use our tools. Scientists can discover things. Science makes scientific theories available to us. Scientists can use our scientific theories. Scientists can predict things. These things and everything else exists, until proven otherwise. The everything else enables me. I believe in the value of truths. I believe in the value of the most optimistic myths. The results are loyalty to the truth and emotional balance in my mind. Emotional balance in my mind is conducive to happiness and good health in my life. Happiness and good health in my life is conducive to success and prosperity in my business. I desire happiness and good health in my life. I desire success and prosperity in my business. For that reason, my most optimistic position is logical, sane, and consistent with and or based on reason. I adopt my most optimistic position even though the correct position is unknown. I adopt my most optimistic position until proven otherwise.

The bearer of the burden of proof eliminates the most optimistic myths, until proven otherwise. I eliminate pessimistic myths, until proven otherwise. The bearer of the burden of proof eliminates the most optimistic myths with a risk. The risk is. The bearer of the burden of proof might suffer ill mental health effects, ill emotional health effects, and ill physical health effects. I eliminate pessimistic myths without the risk.

CHAPTER 18. LIMITLESS ACCESS TO DIVINE INSPIRATION

Let us suppose. A few paranoid oppressive violent people gain influence over religious authority figures. Religious authority figures gain influence over communities of faithful believers. Communities of faithful believers gain influence over members. Members affirm an ability to know. A good entity rules in Heaven. The good entity is at war with an evil entity. The evil entity rules over the Earth. The few paranoid oppressive violent people are divinely ordained to rule over domestic territories. The few paranoid oppressive violent people are representatives of the good entity here on Earth. The will of the few paranoid oppressive violent people is, in fact, the will of the good entity. The few paranoid oppressive violent people are at war with outsiders. The outsiders rule over foreign territories. The outsiders are not divinely ordained to rule over foreign territories. The outsiders are representatives of the evil entity. The will of the outsiders is, in fact, the will of the evil entity. A supernatural system of divine eternal reward and abominable infernal punishment exists. The supernatural system compels the faithful. The faithful must observe and obey the will of the good entity. In that event, the few paranoid oppressive violent people would find. They can achieve and maintain authority, power, order, and control over communities of faithful believers. Members would be their spiritual slaves. Religious authority figures would be their slave drivers. The few paranoid oppressive violent people would be slave owners. Their religious organizations would be institutions of spiritual slavery.

Let us suppose. Members think, believe, and predict. The good entity only communes with certain people. Those certain people satisfy certain minimum requirements. Members describe those certain minimum requirements as 'a pure heart', 'innocent mind', 'righteous life', 'miraculous birth', and 'possession of superpowers'. In that event, the members believe in the value of pessimistic myths. These pessimistic myths are about the existence of limited access to divine inspiration.

Let us suppose. An ideology reflects the needs and aspirations of a few paranoid oppressive violent people. Let us suppose further. The ideology includes pessimistic myths about the existence of limited access to divine inspiration. In that event, I would wonder. How does the pessimistic myth about the existence of limited access to divine inspiration help satisfy the needs and aspirations of the few paranoid oppressive violent people? From the pessimistic myth about the existence of limited access to divine inspiration and claims of exclusive access to divinely inspired truth follows the authority, power, order, and control.

Let us suppose. A person was privileged to have an exclusive divine revelation of spiritual knowledge. The spiritual knowledge is true. However, our senses and perceptions are unable to verify the truth of the spiritual knowledge. In that event, both the truth; and the validity of the spiritual knowledge would be unverifiable. Claims of exclusive divine revelations of spiritual knowledge are as old as religion itself. Many contradictory claims exist. These many contradictory claims have inspired people. People have established discovery religions. Discovery religions are built upon a lie. The lie is. These pessimistic myths are truths. Discovery religions employ religious authority figures. Religious authority figures claim. We have discovered. These pessimistic myths are truths.

Let us suppose. Some of these religious authority figures persuade communities of faithful believers. Members think, believe, and predict. Pessimistic myths about the existence of exclusive divine revelations of spiritual knowledge are, in fact, truths about the existence of the word, will, way and laws of the good entity. In that event, they believe in the value of pessimistic myths. These pessimistic myths are about the existence of limited access to divine inspiration. These pessimistic myths are about the existence of exclusive divine revelations of spiritual knowledge.

Let us suppose. A few paranoid oppressive violent people have a strategy. A belief in the value of pessimistic myths about the existence of limited access to divine inspiration is part of the strategy. The strategy is. Use patronage, intimidation, extortion, and violent abuse. Gain influence over religious authority figures. Make religious authority figures into collaborators. Use threats of abominable infernal torment and promises of divine eternal bliss. Make the faithful observe and obey the will of the good entity. Order religious authority figures to proclaim. The will of the few paranoid oppressive violent people is, in fact, the will of the good entity. Let us suppose still further. The strategy enables the few paranoid oppressive violent people. The few paranoid oppressive violent people achieve and maintain authority, power, order, and control. In that event, the few paranoid oppressive violent people would find. They can play a dual role. They can play the role of representative of the good entity for an audience. The audience would consist of communities of faithful believers. These communities of faithful believers would live within domestic territories. The few paranoid oppressive violent people would find. They can play the role of representative of the evil entity for an audience. The audience would consist of communities of faithful believers. These communities of faithful believers would live within foreign territories. The few paranoid oppressive violent people would find. They can determine. Who is an insider and who is an outsider? The identities of insiders and outsiders are a matter of point of view. The locations of domestic and foreign territories are also a matter of point of view. For that reason, the few paranoid oppressive violent people in every territory would find. They can play the dual role of representative of the good entity and representative of the evil entity.

Let us suppose. The few paranoid oppressive violent people decide. Outsiders are a threat to their private business interests. A war must be fought to protect their private business interests. The few paranoid oppressive violent people are at war with the outsiders. The few paranoid oppressive violent people use patronage, intimidation, extortion, and or violent abuse. The few paranoid oppressive violent people gain influence over religious authority figures. The religious authority figures proclaim to communities of faithful believers. The good entity is on our side. A great big reward awaits the faithful after they march off to their own deaths in war. The faithful believe these proclamations. In that event, the faithful would march off to their own deaths in war with camaraderie, high morale, and a shared sense of purpose.

Let us suppose. Religious authority figures make laws of the good entity out of the laws of the state. They make the idea of the good entity into the ultimate state-sponsored surveillance system. They define the meaning of life as a test of character. They define the value of each individual according to their record of observing and obeying the will of the good entity. They say. The will of the few paranoid oppressive violent people is, in fact, the will of the good entity. Some people noticeably disregard and disobey the will of the few paranoid oppressive violent people. Communities of faithful believers punish those people. In that event, people have a way of behaving. The communities of faithful believers would police the way.

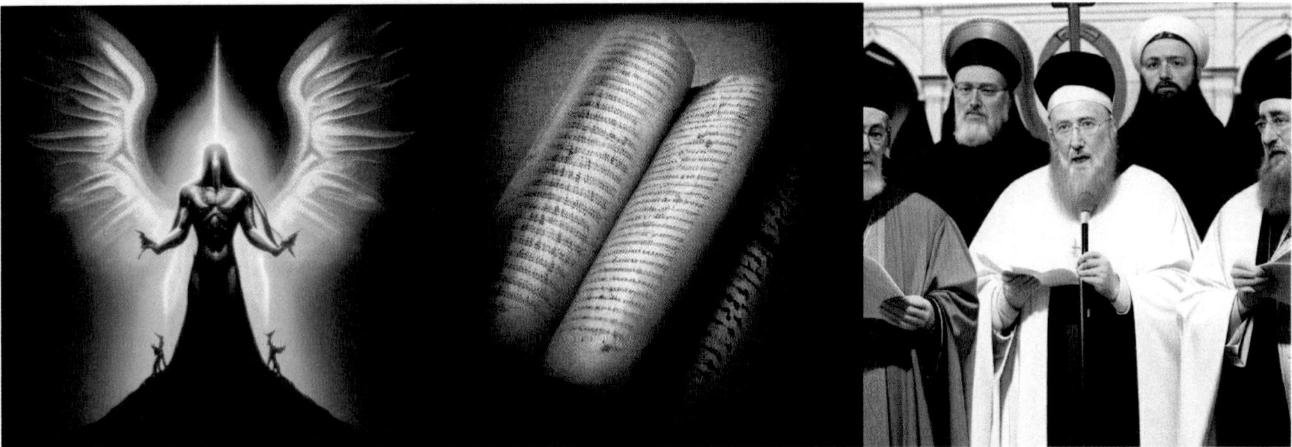

Let us suppose. Some religious authority figures attempt to refute the above ideas. They quote verses and chapters from a set of sacred scrolls. They proclaim. The set of sacred scrolls is an unimpeachable source of truth about events of the distant past. In that event, the key issue here is verification!

Let us suppose. Religious authority figures believe in the value of certain ideas. These certain ideas were given to them by their set of sacred scrolls. These certain ideas are about events of the distant past. The religious authority figures use their own senses and perceptions. Their own senses and perceptions do not enable them. Religious authority figures are unable. They can not verify the truth of these certain ideas. They can not verify the falsity of these certain ideas. These certain ideas are both unverifiable and unfalsifiable. In that event, the truth is: These certain ideas are myths. These religious authority figures believe in the value of these myths.

Let us suppose. They claim an ability to know. These myths are truths. In that event, they know next to nothing about almost everything. They value a lie. The lie is: These myths are truths. They devalue a truth. The truth is. These myths are myths. It appears. These religious authority figures fail to correctly sort ideas into three distinct categories. The three distinct categories are truths, myths, and lies. At the very least such religious authority figures lack the ability to do so. At worst, they willfully refuse to do so.

At times, my bodies' needs become urgent. Urgent needs cause my soul to have to deal with "a one-track mind". My "one-track mind" produces possibilities for thought, feeling and action. Let us suppose. My body is suffering from extreme hunger. In that event, the possibilities pertain primarily to feeding. Let us suppose. My body is sexually aroused. In that event, the possibilities pertain mostly to sexual desire. Let us suppose. My body is under physical stress. In that event, the possibilities pertain mostly to seeking a place of safety and refuge. Let us suppose. My body is in a balanced physiological state. I do not perceive any immediate threats to my well-being. In that event, it might be possible for my soul to guide my mind to spiritual enlightenment.

CHAPTER 19. CONTINUOUS SPIRITUAL COMMUNION

My model of the totality is, in part, the product of my biological heritage. My model of the totality is, in part, the product of my cultural heritage. My model of the totality is, in part, the work of my will. It appears. Life is, in part, a chemical reaction. The sun powers the chemical reaction. The chemical reaction feeds upon itself. Bodies consume bodies. Over time, the soul spirit selects for seed bodies of ever higher form and function. Millions of years of evolution have produced my seed-body. Millions of years of evolution have raised the global culture as a whole to progressively higher levels of conscious awareness. The sub-atomic realm is a realm of probabilities and possibilities. My highly evolved seed-body is a cloud of probabilities and possibilities. The cloud of probabilities and possibilities makes possible my unconscious mind. My unconscious mind makes available a limited number, diversity, and variety of possibilities for thought, feeling, and action. My soul evaluates the possibilities. My soul observes my seed-body. The act of observing my seed-body causes the cloud of probabilities and possibilities to collapse down to one possibility. My free will manifests. My free will is my inner voice, conscience, and source of inspiration. My conscious mind manifests. In the act of conscious thought, my soul gets inside my mind, guides my will, and rides my seed-body.

I do not propagate a discovery religion. Discovery religions are built upon a lie. The lie is. A myth is a truth. Let us suppose. A person affirms an ability to know. These most optimistic myths are truths. Let us suppose further. The person claims. The ability to know leads the person to a belief. The person believes in the value of the most optimistic myths. In that event, the person knows next to nothing about almost everything. The person values a lie. The lie is. These most optimistic myths are truths. The person devalues a truth. The truth is. These most optimistic myths are myths.

I propagate a mystery religion. Mystery religions are built upon a truth. The truth is. A myth is a myth. I affirm an inability to know. These most optimistic myths are truths. I claim. The inability to know and my desire to be happy and healthy lead me to a belief. I believe in the value of these most optimistic myths. I value a truth. The truth is. These most optimistic myths are myths. I devalue a lie. The lie is. These most optimistic myths are truths.

I acknowledge. The presence of evidence in the form of the universe provides premises. Those premises enable us. We can make valid logical inductive inferences. We can make myths. The totality makes possible the mystery of existence. The mystery of existence makes possible an infinite number, diversity, and variety of myths. Each of these myths is an equally valid possibility. For that reason, the most optimistic myths are possibilities. The most optimistic myths are possibly true.

I desire happiness, good health, and prosperity. I wish to experience the potential emotional and physiological benefits. For that reason, I believe in the value of the most optimistic myths.

Are the most optimistic myths true? I have concluded. I do not know. However, I do not choose to close my mind. Doing so would cause me to fall back into the trap of being a pessimystic.

I choose to be an optimystic. I open my mind to a possibility. The possibility is. Continuous spiritual communion between soul and spirit exists. The divine eternal essence of finite self is in continuous spiritual communion with the divine eternal essence of the infinite world. The most optimistic myths come to me through continuous spiritual communion.

We know of the truth by use of our senses and perceptions. Our senses and perceptions are limited. We know of the truth by use of scientific methods. Our scientific methods are limited. For that reason, truths are rare. Myths are infinitely abundant.

The correct position is unknown. I adopt the most optimistic position even though the correct position is unknown. The most optimistic position is. We have souls. Our souls are the divine eternal essence of ourselves. Our souls ride our seed-bodies. Our souls order the chaos of our minds. Our souls select our free wills for us. Our souls are in continuous spiritual communion with our Spirit. Our Spirit is the divine eternal essence of our infinite world.

I know. The truth is. These most optimistic myths are myths. However, I think, believe, and predict. The most optimistic myths are true. Doing so enables me. I significantly boost my ability. I make use of continuous spiritual communion. Continuous spiritual communion enables me. I receive inspiration, intuition, and good judgment.

My soul, my source of inspiration, my guiding light is perfect, divine, and eternal. My soul guides my will in a direction. The direction is right for me. It feels great to believe in the value of the most optimistic myths. Feeling great produces beneficial health-related behavior. Beneficial health-related behavior is great for my health. I devote energy, space, and time, to my most optimistic way of ornamenting my model of the totality with myths. My soul continuously guides my will.

CHAPTER 20. FRACTAL INFERNAL TEMPORAL SEED-BODY

The word fractal is an adjective. People use the adjective. People describe a noun. The noun is the form. A fractal form has parts. The parts resemble smaller copies of the whole on a range of scales. Often, a fractal form has a rough or fragmented geometric shape. The fractal form subdivides into parts. Each part is, at least approximately, a reduced-size copy of the whole fractal form. Self-similarity means. As one peers deeper into a fractal form, one notices. Shapes seen at one scale are similar to the shapes seen at other scales. Geometry is a branch of mathematics. Geometry is about the properties and mathematical structures of points, lines, surfaces, solids, and higher dimensional analogs. Fractal geometry is about the properties and mathematical structures of fractal forms. Many mathematical structures are fractal forms. Mathematicians use fractal geometry. When mathematicians derive fractal forms, self-similarity between part and whole can span an infinite range of scales from infinitely large to infinitesimally small. As one zooms in and out, the same kinds of shapes keep coming into view. People use fractal geometry. People describe the forms of many real-world objects, such as clouds, mountains, turbulence, and coastlines. These real world objects do not correspond to simple geometric shapes. When nature uses fractal geometry to derive shapes, self-similarity is common across a finite range of scales. The cauliflower is perhaps a familiar example of the self-similarity of fractal geometry over a finite range of scales. Let us suppose. I have a head of cauliflower. I break the head of cauliflower into many pieces. In that event, most of the many pieces would resemble a miniature version of a whole cauliflower. The same goes for many natural features such as trees, rivers, clouds, and mountains. As one zooms in, one notices. The shape of smaller parts resembles the shape of the whole.

A system is a group of interacting parts. The group of interacting parts function as a whole. The whole has recognizable boundaries. The recognizable boundaries distinguish the whole from its surroundings. A dynamic system changes over time. The behavior and or condition of the dynamic system is chaotic. The behavior and or condition of each part influences the behavior and condition of the whole. The complexity of a chaotic dynamic system makes the precise prediction of the future condition of any one of its' parts next to impossible.

However, we may describe the future condition of any one of the parts as falling within a

range of possibilities. The range of possibilities is often referred to as a strange attractor. The Earth moves around the Sun. A path is swept out. The path has a shape. Consider the shape. Seventeenth-century astronomer and mathematician Johannes Kepler taught us. The shape is an ellipse on a plane. The plane bisects the center of gravity of the Earth and Sun. The gravitational forces of the Sun and Earth combine. The effect is. The Earth falls towards the Sun. The Earth has linear momentum relative to the Sun. The effect is. The Earth flies away from the Sun. The result of the balance of these two effects is. It appears. The Earth is strangely attracted. The Earth travels in an elliptical path around the Sun.

Each part exerts an action and force upon all other parts. The balance of all actions and or forces draws the whole of a dynamic system towards a strange attractor. Earth and Sun are but two parts of a larger chaotic dynamic universal system. The larger chaotic dynamic system is made up of a number, diversity, and variety of interacting parts. Therefore, the effect of the sum total of all parts interacting with the Earth and Sun is. The Earth orbits the Sun. The shape of the path swept out by the Earth varies.

Scientists say. The slight variation means. A precise prediction of the future position of the Earth with respect to the Sun is not possible by means of scientific methods. However, we can predict. The position of the Earth with respect to the Sun will be within a range of possibilities. A probability of occurrence may be associated with each possibility for the Earth's position with respect to the Sun. The shape and intensity of each probability can be used to create a three-dimensional graphic display of a range of possibilities and probabilities. Over time, the Earth is strangely attracted to the range of possibilities and probabilities. The range of possibilities and probabilities is the Earth's strange attractor.

Scientists say. A seed grows over time into a body. It appears. The seed contains DNA. DNA is a plan for life. DNA is a blueprint for the future development and life of a seed-body. We can analyze the present and past conditions of the parents' bodies. We can analyze the present and past conditions of the parents' DNA. However, it appears. The development of the seed into the body is also dependent upon the influence of other parts of the universe around and within it. For that reason, we cannot precisely predict the future condition of the seed-body. We can predict a range of possibilities and probabilities for the future condition of any given seed-body. The range of possibilities and probabilities is the seed-bodies' strange attractor.

Fractal geometry is a wondrous tool that humans use to understand and appreciate the intricate beauty of the natural world. It's a language. The language helps us decipher complex forms and shapes. The complex forms and shapes emerge from chaotic dynamic systems, telling stories of evolution and transformation over time.

Imagine gazing up at the night sky, where stars twinkle like scattered jewels. Each star, a distant sun, contributes to the canvas of the cosmos, painting shapes against the infinite blackness. To the keen observer, these shapes reveal the fingerprints of fractal geometry, patterns repeating on both grand and minuscule scales.

On Earth's surface, the story unfolds with earthquakes, powerful ruptures in the skin of our planet. As the ground shifts and fractures, revealing jagged lines and fissures, it's as if nature itself is sketching fractal artwork upon the landscape, reminding us of the chaotic forces at play beneath our feet.

And then there's the relentless dance of wind and water, shaping coastlines with patient erosion and turbulent waves. The resulting contours, with their intricate bays and peninsulas, are testament to the fractal nature of nature's creativity, where chaos and order intertwine in a delicate balance.

In the quiet embrace of a forest, ferns unfurl their delicate fronds, each branching structure a testament to the growth process encoded within. As if following a mathematical algorithm, these ferns trace out fractal patterns in the air, their shapes echoing the recursive beauty of fractal geometry.

Even in the frozen stillness of winter, there's a silent symphony playing out in the formation of ice. Along the edges of frozen lakes and rivers, where water meets air, intricate patterns emerge with a chaotic grace, each jagged edge a testament to the fractal nature of crystalline growth.

But it's not just in the natural world where fractals weave their mesmerizing tales. Even the billowing clouds and plumes of pollution emanating from human activity reveal the telltale signs of fractal geometry. It is as if nature is reminding us of our interconnectedness with the chaotic systems we inhabit.

And in the delicate dance of snowflakes falling from the sky, each crystal is a tiny masterpiece of symmetry and complexity. Here we find yet another story of chaos giving birth to order. Each intricate shape is a testament to the beauty of fractal geometry.In every corner of the universe, from the grandest galaxies to the smallest snowflakes, the language of fractal geometry whispers its secrets. It invites us to marvel at the infinite complexity of the world around us. And as we listen, we find. We are drawn ever deeper into the enchanting tapestry of chaos and order, where every shape tells a story of evolution and transformation over time.

Fractal geometry accurately describes the shapes of many natural structures. For that reason, computer technology and knowledge of fractal geometry enable special effects artists. Special effects artists can generate images of convincing alien landscapes.

The planet Earth has an inner core. The inner core is made up of an alloy of Nickel, Iron and other elements. Tremendous pressures and temperatures exist inside the inner core. The tremendous pressures and temperatures make the inner core a plasma. The plasma acts like a solid.

The outer core covers the inner core. The outer core is essentially a slow-moving glob of liquid iron. Scientists say. The slow-moving glob of liquid iron in the outer core generates a magnetic field around planet Earth. The magnetic field protects life on planet Earth from solar winds and cosmic rays.

A mantle covers the outer core. The mantle is a slightly faster moving layer of liquid rock. Liquid rock is made up of various lighter elements. It appears. The pressures and temperatures in the mantel are not as high as the pressures and temperatures in the outer core.

A thin crust covers the liquid rock. The thin crust moves slower than the liquid rock. The thin crust is solid. The thin crust takes the form of tectonic plates. Tectonic plates grind into each other. The grinding spawns volcanic eruptions. The grinding spawns earthquakes. The grinding spawns mountain ranges. On the ocean floor, some of the crust sinks into the cauldron beneath. These are the signs of the immense dynamism of planet Earth. These signs are fractal and chaotic. Everywhere on Earth's thin crust, the natural landscape is being hewn by chaos into shapes with branches, folds, and fractures, and detail inside detail. The immense intermeshing of dynamical forces constitutes the eternal, ever-changing dissonance and harmony of nature. The eternal, ever-changing dissonance and harmony of nature has attracted the attention of scientists and artists throughout the centuries.

As the universe explodes and expands, it leaves behind a fractal imprint of swirling turbulent gases, star fields, and repeating forms. Each sub-atomic particle, atomic element, molecule, star, and galaxy, is similar to every other of its' kind in the fractal universe. Every life form of a given species is made in the fractal image of every other life form of the given species. The fractal universe exhibits self-similarity on a range of scales. Let us suppose. We peer deeply into space. In that event, new detail will unfold. The new detail will resemble details seen on a larger scale. From elementary particles to superclusters of galaxies we see parts collected to form "wholes'" and the latter collected to form larger "wholes," and so on. Virtually all of the atomic mass of the known universe is lumped into stars, and virtually all stars collect into galaxies. Many interesting classes of objects exist between atomic-scale objects and stellar scale objects. These many interesting classes of objects include us. However, we are quite rare relative to the dominant classes of objects. Our universe has a very rudimentary self-similar organization: Galactic "particles" are composed of stellar "particles". Stellar "particles" are composed of atomic "particles". Therefore, we observe a portion of nature. It appears. A discrete hierarchy organizes the portion of nature.

Fractal geometry is everywhere. The structures of our seed-bodies are replete with fractal geometry. The branching structures of nerves, bronchial tubes, veins, and arteries, trace a process of growth. The shapes of the branching structures are fractal. Our cells are self-similar. Each cell contains a copy of the genetic blueprint of self. Our cells contain organelles. The organelles within our cells function similar to the organs within our bodies. Therefore, our bodies exhibit self-similarity on a finite scale. I believe in the value of truths. For that reason, I use the word fractal as an adjective. I describe a quality of space. The quality of space is inherent within our seed-bodies and our universe.

I believe in the value of truths. It appears. Nobody comes out of this universe alive. Every body grows from a seed. Every body is subject to a life cycle. The life cycle ends in disease and death. The universe is the lower world of the dead.

I believe in the value of the most optimistic myths. Life is a synthesis of seed, body, soul, and spirit. The synthesis of seed, body, soul, and spirit forms living infernal fractal entities. We are these living infernal fractal entities. The union of Mother God and Father Love creates life. We are soul children.

Infernal is an adjective. I use the adjective. I describe a quality of space. The quality of space is inherent in the seed-body. It appears. The seed-body is of, or relating to, the lower world of the dead. Furthermore, the adjective infernal is similar to the noun inferno. The noun inferno describes a place or a condition. The place and or condition wherein; burning generates heat.

A universe is a place wherein; burning generates heat. The energy of the universe is composed of galaxies. The galaxies are composed of stars. The stars burn lighter elements in thermonuclear reactions. The thermonuclear reactions produce heavier elements and radiation of light and particles. Therefore, I use the adjective infernal to describe the quality of both the body and the universe.

Molten magma exists under the crust of the Earth. Let us suppose. This molten magma breaks through the crust and erupts on to the surface of the Earth. A person observes the molten magma. In that event, the person would find burning and the generation of heat.

The body is a place wherein; burning generates heat. The body has cells. The cells use the oxygen. The oxygen enables the cells. The cells get energy from food. This process is called cellular respiration. During cellular respiration cells use oxygen. The oxygen enables the cells. The cells break down sugar. The act of breaking down sugar produces energy and heat. Chemical reactions enable the seed-body. The seed-body changes food into energy and heat.

I believe in the value of truths. Scientists predict. Eventually our bodies, life on earth, the stars, galaxies, and the burning of thermonuclear furnaces throughout our universe will end. Therefore, I use the adjective temporal to describe the longevity of the body. I use the adjective temporal to describe the longevity of the universe.

CHAPTER 21. WHY DOES ONE SUFFER?

In their myths and legends, most cultures have celebrated an idea. The idea is. Chaos and order are a primal duality. Chaos is the disordered state of unformed matter and infinite space. Some religious cosmological views suppose. Chaos existed prior to the ordered universe.

Modern-day scientists have borrowed the word chaos from the ancient myth makers. The modern-day scientists use the word chaos. They describe their inability to precisely predict the future conditions of complex chaotic dynamic systems.

Seed-bodies are complex chaotic dynamic systems. Our scientific theories enable scientists. Scientists can predict. The future condition of any given seed-body will fall within a set of possibilities. However, scientists can not precisely predict the future condition of the seed-body.

The reason for this inability to precisely predict the future condition of a seed-body is. Our seed-bodies are part of a universal complex chaotic dynamic system. The universal complex chaotic dynamic system is made up of a number, diversity, and variety of parts. Each part interacts with all other parts of the whole.

Within the whole of our universe, there are complex chaotic dynamic systems nesting within complex chaotic dynamic systems. Our universe is a complex chaotic dynamic system. The universal complex chaotic dynamic system contains galactic complex chaotic dynamic systems. Galactic complex chaotic dynamic systems contain solar complex chaotic dynamic systems. Solar complex chaotic dynamic systems contain planetary complex chaotic dynamic systems. In some cases, planetary complex chaotic dynamic systems contain living complex chaotic dynamic systems. Living complex chaotic dynamic systems contain cellular complex chaotic dynamic systems. Cellular complex chaotic dynamic systems contain atomic complex chaotic dynamic systems and so on.

Let us suppose. Scientists wish to precisely predict the future condition of any part of such a universal complex chaotic dynamic system. In that event, infinitely complex models of all parts interacting with one another would be required. No finite tool available to scientists would be capable of providing this.

I believe in the value of the most optimistic myths. While scientists are incapable, I think, believe, and predict. The spirit is capable. I think, believe, and predict. The divinity of the spirit makes the infinite complexity of complex chaotic dynamic systems predictable. As such, I think, believe, and predict. Continuous spiritual communion between soul and spirit makes possible foreknowledge of future events.

Naturally, making assertions such as these may raise questions in the minds of some people. The questions may be similar to the following. Let us suppose. Our spirit and souls are divine and eternal. In that event, why do these aspects of our beings not intervene in suffering and sorrow? Suffering and sorrow are caused by the disease and death of our seed-bodies. Why don't these aspects of our beings magically restore immunity, reverse aging, and sustain everlasting life? Why does God allow war, poverty, disaster, and death to occur on planet Earth? What did we do wrong? Why does suffering and sorrow, disease and death, conflict and avarice, persist in the presence of a soul-spirit?

I answer. Life does not exist by soul-spirit alone. Life is a synthesis of seed, body, soul, and spirit. Seed and body are equally important components of the synthesis. The fractal infernal quality and temporal longevity of the seed-body are the perfect complements to the divine quality and eternal longevity of the soul-spirit.

My body is a complex chaotic dynamic system. My seed-body grows. My seed-body and soul make possible the existence of my mind. My mind changes my model of the totality continuously. I discover new truths. I add new truths to my model of the totality. My model of the totality changes. I discover old lies. I eliminate old lies from my model of the totality. My model of the totality changes. I make new myths. I add new myths to my model of the totality. My model of the totality changes. As my seed-body grows and matures, my model of the totality grows more complex and more ornate. As my seed-body decays, my model of the totality becomes less complex and less ornate.

Some people have suggested to me. Performance of certain actions will enable me. I can create a better life for myself. I believe in the value of truths. It appears. Laws of cause and effect predict the behavior, fate, and destiny of matter and energy in the known universe. The behavior, fate, and destiny of matter and energy in the known universe suggests to me a material standard of conduct. I think, believe, and predict. The act of conforming to this material standard of conduct will produce good health. I desire good health. For that reason, I conform to this material standard of conduct. I act to cause the effect of creating a better life for myself.

Some people have suggested to me. The act of believing in the value of certain myths will enable me. I can create a better life for myself. I believe in the value of the most optimistic myths. The most optimistic myths include. Spiritual laws of love and freedom predict the behaviors, fates, and destinies of our souls. These spiritual laws of love and freedom suggest a spiritual standard of conduct. I think, believe, and predict. The act of conforming to this spiritual standard of conduct will produce happiness. I desire happiness. For that reason, I conform to this spiritual standard of conduct. I act to cause the effect of creating a better life for myself.

Some people have suggested to me. The act of performing certain mythical rituals will empower me. I can create a better life for myself. Only our creative abilities and powers of imagination limit the kinds of mythical rituals. Some people imagine. Their spirit requires their souls. They use their bodies. They perform certain mythical rituals. Some of the more common mythical rituals include prayer, praise, confession, sacrifice, supplication, negotiation, servitude, stewardship, pilgrimage, petition, incantation, chanting, meditation, and dance. Let us suppose. I accept such suggestions. What are the potential benefits and risks of liability?

The ritual of public prayer is a form of communication between members of communities of faithful believers. The ritual of public prayer offers the potential benefit of focusing the minds of others on the needs and aspirations of self and others. The ritual of private prayer is a form of meditation. The ritual of private prayer offers the potential benefits of focusing the mind of self on the needs and aspirations of self and others.

I believe in the value of the most optimistic myths. For that reason, I think, believe, and predict. An infinite divine eternal being is everything, everywhere, at all times. A supreme state of being exists. Our divine eternal souls are in continuous communion with our spirit.

It follows from these most optimistic myths. Prayer as a form of communication with the spirit is unnecessary. Prayer as a form of communication with others has the potential to lead others to believe in the value of pessimistic myths. The pessimistic myths are. A supreme being exists external to self. A supreme state of being does not exist. Communion between soul and spirit is not continuous. To avoid such confusion, I prefer meditation over prayer. I refrain from participating in any form of public prayers.

Certain rituals might offer us a potential benefit as fun activities. To participate in rituals is for me a matter of choice. Let us suppose. Communities of faithful believers attempt to use threats against my life and or threats against my after life. Members attempt to coerce me into performing rituals. In that event, it would be a matter of choice as to whether or not I comply or resist.

Let us suppose. I am unwilling or unable. I will not or can not perform a certain ritual. Let us suppose further. Members warn me. The spirit will deprive me of love. In that event, I would remind myself. They know next to nothing about almost everything. They believe in the value of pessimistic myths. I believe in the value of the most optimistic myths. Mother God confers infinite love, divine forgiveness, eternal freedom, and unifying grace upon all of her Soul Children.

Consciousness is a process. My seed-body generates my unconscious mind. My unconscious mind makes available a finite number, diversity, and variety of possibilities for thought, feeling, and action. My soul evaluates these possibilities. My soul selects. My free will manifests. My conscious mind manifests. My seed-body is limited. For that reason, I may never be able to completely comprehend life.

I believe in the value of the most optimistic myths. The most optimistic myths include. I am divinely inspired. I believe in the value of truths. Let us suppose. I want scientific proof of my divine inspiration. In that event, I must gather objective evidence. I must make valid logical deductive inferences. I must eliminate all other possible conclusions. I must arrive at one definite conclusion. The one definite conclusion must be. I am divinely inspired.

The attributes of my seed-body limit my ability. My occupation of specific points in energy, space, and time limits my ability. I can only gather a finite amount of objective evidence. I can only make valid logical inductive inferences. I can only arrive at a conclusion. The conclusion is. I might be divinely inspired. I know next to nothing about the truth of the totality. For that reason, scientific proof of my divine inspiration is lost in the chaos of complex dynamic systems.

As such, I do not claim to know. I claim to think, believe, and predict. I am divinely inspired. Let us suppose. In fact, I am divinely inspired. In that event, my thoughts, beliefs, and expectations would strengthen my divine inspirations. My belief in the value of the most optimistic myths would enable me. I would make the best possible use of my divine inspirations.

I believe in the value of truths. The truths are. My will guides my mind. I choose from amongst a limited number of possibilities for thought, feeling, and action. The limited number of possibilities for thought, feeling, and action are made available to my mind by my body.

I believe in the value of the most optimistic myths. The most optimistic myths are. My will is guided by my soul. My soul is the divine eternal essence of finite self. My soul is in continuous communion with my spirit. My spirit is the divine eternal essence of the infinite world.

I believe in the value of truths. I know a finite amount of truth about an infinite subject. I know next to nothing about almost everything. However, next to nothing is still something. For all I know, it is possible. My soul reveals to me the most optimistic myths.

CHAPTER 22. THE MEANING OF LIFE

I believe in the value of the most optimistic myths. The meaning of life is living. The purpose of living is entertainment. I derive entertainment from the totality. I am free. I choose from a number, variety, and diversity of possible models of the totality.

I make my choices from the point of view of my soul. My seed-body makes available my mind. My soul orders the chaos of my mind. I am living in a body-consuming biosphere. The body-consuming biosphere covers a crusted magma globe. The body-consuming biosphere, the crusted magma globe, the sun, and the moon are reproducible in a galaxy of stars, and a universe of galaxies.

My seed-body lives and dies. There would be no life without death. There would be no death without life. There would be no drama of life and death without life and death. I derive entertainment from the drama of life and death. I enjoy the entertainment. For that reason, I am grateful for life and death. Life brings us an opportunity to enjoy entertainment. We derive entertainment from the drama of life and death. Death is the dramatic conclusion of the drama of life and death.

The meaning of death is dying. We let go of our seed-bodies. Travel through an infinite divine eternal being. Arrive at another point in energy, space, and time.

Let us suppose. We are soul children. We are divine and eternal. We order chaos of minds. We enjoy entertainment. We derive entertainment from seed-bodies. Seed-bodies live and die. We are role-playing in a universe. The universe creates cosmic games of survival and sacrifice. The cosmic games of survival and sacrifice entertain our spirit. We wish to form life. In that event, the infinite divine eternal being would enable us. We would form life within an infinite seed-body of large universes of the correct kind to support living infernal fractal entities. We would merge with seed-bodies. The seed-bodies would be suitable to the magnitudes of our souls.

I consider the benefits of this arrangement. My seed-body imposes limits upon my soul. These very limitations confer upon me my own unique character, ability, personality, and identity. Such an arrangement confers no loss upon me. Such an arrangement confers only a gained opportunity to experience life and death.

Life gives me an opportunity. The opportunity is. I put on a costume. I act in a drama of life and death. I perceive the sensations of pleasure and pain. I feel the catharsis of comedy and tragedy. I fight in the conflict between predator and prey. I play a game of survival and sacrifice. I ponder the existence of discovery and mystery. I submit to universal, state, and natural laws of cause and effect. I take a test of success and failure. I adopt a point of view.

Life is a synthesis of seed, body, soul, and spirit. I experience ignorance, guilt, inhibition, disgrace, suffering, and sorrow from the point of view of the seed-body. My soul transcends death. I experience compassion, forgiveness, freedom, grace, peace, and joy from the point of view of the soul-spirit. My seed-body generates my unconscious mind. My unconscious mind makes available a finite number, diversity, and variety of possibilities for thought, feeling, and action. My soul evaluates these possibilities. My soul selects. My free will manifests. My conscious mind manifests.

I am the authority. I decide how. I make up my mind. My soul transcends death. My seed-body imposes limits upon my soul. I escape from those limitations. I find truth, faith, love, unity, creation, healing, and infinity.

CHAPTER 23. THE MYSTERY OF CONSCIOUSNESS

We are human. We share human qualities with other human beings. This is the essence of our natural existence in this world. What exactly does it mean to be human? What all is involved in existing as a human being? How did we get to be the way? We are today. How are we today?

We human beings share certain qualities and attributes. I consider these certain qualities and attributes. We have seed-bodies. In a material sense, our seed-bodies are our personal homes. We live our lives in our seed-bodies. We are alike in this respect. My seed-body is a cooperative of cells. The cooperative of cells has grown together for a purpose. The purpose is. Create and survive. The seed-body is a time proven arrangement. The arrangement gives the cooperative of cells a better chance of obtaining energy and materials. The energy and materials enable us. We survive and multiply within our ever-changing environment.

Material and energy enables me. I create my seed-body. My mother and father provided much of the material and energy. They had the ability. I am grateful. At birth, my parental guardians assisted me. I developed. I grew sufficiently. I became self-reliant. I see this sort of nurturing behavior throughout the natural world. Members of a family interact with each other. The nature of the interaction is cooperative. The family is the focus of intense feelings, thoughts, and often lifelong relationships. The family unit serves as the cornerstone of communities of human beings.

Humans cooperate to satisfy a collective desire. The collective desire is. Obtain material and energy. The material and energy enables us. We create and survive. What exactly is involved in obtaining the material and energy?

The totality makes our habitat available to us. Our habitat provides. Water flows in streams. Fruit grows on trees and vines. Vegetables spring to life in fertile soil. Grains are cultivated and harvested. Our environment is self-perpetuating. Our sun is shining.

Our habitat makes seed-bodies available to us. Our seed-bodies enable us. We obtain these sources of concentrated nutrients. We move about the environment. We capture. We domesticate. We cultivate. We harvest. We prepare. We consume other life forms. We destroy the bodies of countless other life forms. We obtain millions of calories of nutrition. We create our human seed-bodies. We destroy to create. We create to destroy.

Our seed-bodies make senses and perceptions available to us. Our senses and perceptions enable us. We detect the presence of a fruit tree, a vegetable, a root, a nut, a seed, a legume or a kernel of wheat.

A growing living cooperative of cells has a need to feed and a need to breed. A brain is born out of these needs. The brain provides information about the environment. The growing living cooperative of cells locates food and evades predators.

I believe in the value of the most optimistic myths. My seed-body generates my unconscious mind. My unconscious mind makes available a finite number, diversity, and variety of possibilities for thought, feeling, and action. My soul evaluates these possibilities. My soul selects. My free will manifests. My free will enables me. I control and apply, the voluntary functions of my seed-body. My conscious mind manifests. Let us suppose. I had no conscious mind. In that event, I would not be aware of the presence of my body. I would not be aware of the condition of my body. I would be oblivious to my surroundings.

The soul and the seed-body have a relationship. I now expound further on the relationship.

The soul is to the seed-body what a hand is to a glove. Imagine precisely how and at what point interaction might occur. Scientists theorize. Our universe is composed of various kinds of energy. These various kinds of energy exist in space and time. Scientists have painstakingly observed, characterized, and classified these various kinds of energy. Scientists have uncovered laws of cause and effect. It appears. The laws of cause and effect are of great value in explaining events in the universe around us. Scientists have discovered. Much of this energy can be broken down into infinitesimally small particles known as subatomic particles. Subatomic particles are of special interest: It appears. The behavior of sub-atomic particles is probable and possible. The probable and possible behavior of subatomic particles provides a foundation of discovery. Upon this foundation of discovery may be built a framework of myth. The framework of myth can explain how. Chaotic events on such an infinitesimal scale come about in one way rather than another.

The central nervous system is composed of greater than a trillion-trillion atoms. I believe in the value of the most optimistic myths. My soul works in this realm of probability and possibility. My soul orders events. Events influence the future condition of my seed-body. These atoms interact with one another. These atoms combine to function as a living complex chaotic dynamic system. Scientists have discovered. The future conditions of complex chaotic dynamic systems are sensitive to minute changes in starting conditions. Tiny changes in the initial conditions of a complex chaotic dynamic system can lead to large differences in the future conditions of the complex chaotic dynamic system. Scientists find. These differences are unpredictable in a chaotic dynamic system as complex as my seed-body. I believe in the value of the most optimistic myths. Our soul-spirit finds. These large differences are predictable. My soul devotes a concentration of divine energy. My soul orders the chaos of my seed-body.

My soul accomplishes tasks. The tasks might include guidance of consciousness, healing of disease, age reversal, resurrection from death, perhaps even immortalization of a seed-body. I may only speculate as to why. It appears. My soul does not accomplish all of these tasks. Let us suppose. In this particular universe, seed-bodies receive souls with just enough energy to direct consciousness, and perhaps in sleep effect limited healing. In that event, my soul would be unable to perform all of these tasks.

Our minds have the power. We can cause things to manifest. Let us suppose. Our minds are powerful enough. In that event, we can manifest our own deaths. It appears. Every body eventually dies. Fractal self-similarity exists between seed-bodies. This is strong evidence. The evidence leads by a valid logical inductive inference to a conclusion. The conclusion is. One day, the seed-body of self will die. However, I am not dead yet. Is my impending disease and death a truth or a pessimistic myth? My impending disease and death is a theory. The theory is scientifically testable, provable, and disprovable. With the passage of time, the theory will be either confirmed or remain unconfirmed indefinitely.

I believe in the value of the most optimistic myths. At some point, our conscious awareness of the totality and continuous spiritual communion may enable us. We may learn how. We may yet find a way. We may keep ourselves young, happy, and in good health indefinitely. This could happen during my present life time.

Let us suppose. My soul has full access to the powers of the infinite divine eternal being. Let us suppose further. Survival of my soul is independent of the survival of my seed-body. Let us suppose still further. My seed-body was never meant to live beyond its normal life cycle. In that event, intervention would simply be unnecessary, and unimportant. My soul would not be willing. My soul would not intervene on behalf of my seed-body.

Let us suppose. My soul is non-existent. My seed-body generates free will. My seed-body generates my conscious mind. In that event, my soul would be unable. My soul would be unwilling. My soul could not intervene on behalf of my seed-body. My soul would not intervene on behalf of my seed-body.

Do I invent my soul so that I may produce the most powerful emotional forces of joy, faith, and love? Does the fractal infernal seek and find the divine eternal because the divine eternal seeks and finds the fractal infernal? The truth is. There is no proof. Truths are rare. Myths are infinitely abundant. So how do I know? I do not know. I believe in the value of truths. I believe in the value of the most optimistic myths. I balance the emotional forces of my mind. I am happy. I think, believe, and predict. There can be no gladness without sadness. There can be no anger without fear. Life is a synthesis of seed-body and soul-spirit. Life creates a range of emotional possibilities. The range of emotional possibilities creates entertainment.

CHAPTER 24. THE DISCOVERY AND MYSTERY OF EXISTENCE

Mystery and discovery inspire me to wonder and dream. What am I? Where am I? When am I? How am I? Why am I? Who am I? These are the grand enigmatic questions of identity.

Communities of faithful believers exist within our global culture. They have the ability. I am grateful. They build models of the totality. They ornament their models with their favorite myths. The act of ornamenting their models with their favorite myths, enables communities of faithful believers. Communities of faithful believers create identities for themselves. Communities of faithful believers use their models. Communities of faithful believers answer the grand enigmatic questions of identity. They explain to themselves and to the rest of the global culture what, where, when, how, why, and who they are, and how they came into existence. Through art, music, drama, science, and myths of creation, they explain the totality. With ideology, they fashion their realities.

I answer these grand enigmatic questions of identity. My answers enables me. I have the highest esteem of the totality. I balance the emotional forces of my mind. I am happy. What am I? I am seed-body joined with soul-spirit. Where am I? I am located in a body-consuming biosphere. The body-consuming biosphere is on a crusted magma globe. A moon orbits the crusted magma globe. The crusted magma globe orbits a sun. The crusted magma globe, the sun, and the moon are reproducible in a galaxy of stars, and a universe of galaxies. When am I? I have been, I am, and I will always be, eternal. How am I? I am created by an infinite divine eternal being. Why am I? I am living for a purpose. The purpose is. I provide entertainment to the infinite divine eternal being. Who am I? We are actors in the drama of life and death. We portray characters of our own creation. I am the truth seeker. I am the myth maker. I am the authority. I decide how. I make up my mind. I believe in the value of certain ideas. These certain ideas are my values. I believe in the value of truths. I believe in the value of the most optimistic myths. I am the architect. I use my values. I build within my mind. I build my model of the totality. My model is my reality. My reality is my House of Ideology. I am the High Ideologue of my House of Ideology.

Without answering the grand enigmatic questions of identity, I would experience an identity crisis. The ancients summed up the whole of human wisdom in the maxim, know thyself. Knowledge of myself is difficult and most important. I express this knowledge of myself. I build my model of the totality. I find the most optimistic way. I answer the grand enigmatic questions of identity. My answers enable me. I produce emotional balance in my mind. Emotional balance in my mind is conducive to happiness and good health in my life.

Balancing the emotional forces of our minds may be of paramount importance, to our continued survival. Let us suppose. We recognize the limitations of our senses and perceptions. We adopt an agnostic position. We ornament our models of the totality with the most optimistic myths. We balance the emotional forces of our minds. We are happy. In that event, we would put ourselves in the best possible position. The best possible position would enable us. We would persevere, overcome obstacles, and progress towards victory.

Let us suppose. We devote energy, space, and time to thoughts, beliefs, and expectations about higher self and higher world. In that event, we would take each other to a higher future.

CHAPTER 25. POINTS OF DIVINE INTERVENTION

Scientists describe a sub-atomic realm of probability and possibility. At any point in the totality wherein; only probabilities and possibilities may be described. A point of divine intervention becomes a possibility.

I believe in the value of the most optimistic myths. The soul and the spirit perform functions. The functions include. The soul and the spirit determine how. These probabilities and possibilities play themselves out. Individual seed-bodies combine. They produce mating pairs. The soul and the spirit determine how. These individual seed-bodies combine. Sperm and egg combine. The act of combining leads to conception of a new seed. The soul and the spirit determine how. Sperm and egg combine.

A seed-body benefits. Life is a union of seed-body and soul-spirit. The union confers an evolutionary advantage. The living infernal fractal entity is better able to create, survive, perfect, and revive within the body-consuming biosphere.

The game of survival and sacrifice selects. The seed-body converges upon an ever higher conscious awareness of the totality. This ever higher conscious awareness of the totality enables the soul-spirit.

The soul-spirit enjoys the benefits. The benefits are. The drama of life and death entertains. The soul-spirit enjoys the entertainment.

We are actors in the drama of life and death. We portray characters of our own creation. The spirit bestows infinite love, divine forgiveness, eternal freedom, and unifying grace upon all souls. We are saved. We have been saved. We always will be saved.

CHAPTER 26. I TAKE MY LOVE TO ITS LOGICAL EXTREME

I love Healthy Agnostic Positivistic Nationalistic Spiritization of self and world. To spiritize is to impart a spiritual nature to something. Healthy Agnostic Positivistic Nationalistic Spiritization of self and world requires several additional conditions be satisfied. The first condition is. I spiritize self and world as a healthy person would. I balance the emotional forces of my mind. Emotional balance in my mind is conducive to happiness and good health in my life. The second condition is. I spiritize self and world as an agnostic would: I humbly admit. I know next to nothing about almost everything. I do not know whether or not my most optimistic myths are true. The third condition is. I spiritize self and world as a positivist would: I make a clear distinction between truths, lies, and myths. The fourth condition is. I spiritize self and world as a nationalist would. I free myself to be strong enough in all ways. I devote myself to the interests, needs, and aspirations of those around me in my family, community, nation, culture, and world.

I love to take healthy agnostic positivistic nationalistic spiritization of self and world to its' logical extreme? What exactly is an extreme? An extreme is either of two values. The two values are situated at opposite ends of a range of values. I am referring to values. To what values am I referring? Self and world have attributes. These attributes include quantity of energy, and value of denominator. I am referring to values for the description of these attributes. Seed-body and soul-spirit have attributes. These attributes include quality of space, and longevity of time. I am referring to values for the description of these attributes. These values exist within a range of possible values. Extreme values exist as limits at the opposite ends of the range of possible values.

I choose values for the description of the attributes of the seed-body and self. The existence of discovery limits these values. For that reason, I select true values. True values are not extreme values. I choose values for the description of the attributes of the soul-spirit and the world. The existence of discovery does not limit these values. For that reason, I select the most optimistic values. The most optimistic values are extreme values.

The most optimistic values balance the true values. Joy, faith, and love balance sorrow, fear, and anger. From a balance of values comes a balance of emotions. I balance the emotional forces of my mind. Emotional balance in my mind is conducive to happiness and good health in my life. Happiness and good health in my life is conducive to success and prosperity in my business. I align my values with my needs and aspirations. Thereby, I best satisfy my needs and aspirations. My needs and aspirations are. Achieve and maintain happiness, good health, and prosperity.

CHAPTER 27. WHY SHOULD I TAKE MY LOVE TO ITS LOGICAL EXTREME?

I love Healthy Agnostic Positivistic Nationalistic Spiritization of self and world. Why should I take my love to its logical extreme? Optimal happiness is a prerequisite to optimal health. Optimal health is a prerequisite to optimal happiness. A balance of the emotional forces of the mind produces happiness. A balance of the physiological processes of the seed-body produces good health.

My values act as forces upon my emotions. The most powerful emotional forces of sorrow, fear, and anger follow from my belief in the value of truths. The truths include. It appears. One day, the seed-body of self will die. The most powerful emotional forces of joy, faith, and love follow from my belief in the value of the most optimistic myths. The most optimistic myths include. The life and immunity of the soul-spirit is, eternal and divine. Joy, faith, and love balance sorrow, fear, and anger. I balance the emotional forces of my mind. The balance of the emotional forces of my mind produces a state of happiness. I am happy.

My emotions act as forces upon my behaviors. I exhibit glad behaviors. Truth telling, sharing, playing well with others, liberating, emancipating, and nurturing are glad behaviors. Friendly tolerant peacemaking behaviors are glad behaviors.

My glad behaviors act as forces upon my body. The forces are conducive to a state of good health in my body. My glad behaviors act as forces upon my habitat. The forces are conducive to a state of good health in my habitat. Emotional balance in my mind is conducive to happiness and good health in my life. Happiness and good health in my life is conducive to success and prosperity in my life.

The three most commonly valued pessimistic myths are. Self has only one life to live. Self has only one body to give. Self is only a seed and a body.

Let us suppose. I believed in the value of these pessimistic myths. In that event, my values would act as forces upon my emotions. My belief in the value of these pessimistic myths would not enable me. I would be unable to balance the emotional forces of my mind. My heart would be filled with sorrow, fear, and anger.

Let us suppose. My heart was filled with sorrow, fear, and anger. In that event, my emotions would act as forces upon my behaviors. I would exhibit sad, mad, and bad behaviors. Lying, stealing, cheating, conquering, enslaving, and killing are sad, mad, and bad behaviors. Racist fascist warmongering behaviors are sad, mad, and bad behaviors.

Let us suppose. I exhibited sad, mad, and bad behaviors. In that event, my sad, mad, and bad behaviors would act as forces upon my body. My sad, mad, and bad behaviors would be conducive to a state of disease in my body. My sad, mad, and bad behaviors would act as forces upon my habitat. My sad, mad, and bad behaviors would be conducive to a state of disease in my habitat. Emotional unbalance in my mind would be conducive to unhappiness and disease in my life. Unhappiness and disease in my life would be conducive to failure and hardship in my business.

Happiness is the desired result. For that reason, I produce happiness. Glad behaviors are the desired result. For that reason, I produce glad behaviors. Good health is the desired result. For that reason, I produce good health. Success and prosperity is the desired result. For that reason, I produce success and prosperity.

I believe in the value of my truths. I base my truths on the existence of discovery. I believe in the value of my theories. I base my theories on the existence of scientifically reproducible discoveries. Our knowledge of truths and theories continues to grow exponentially. Pain, sorrow, suffering, and disease plague humanity. Our knowledge of truths and theories has made much of the pain, sorrow, suffering, and disease, treatable. In some cases, the pain, sorrow, suffering, and disease is even curable. Our knowledge of truths and theories may delay death. Nevertheless, it appears. Disease and death remain inevitable.

Our seed-bodies make senses and perceptions available to us. Our senses and perceptions enable us. We can use our senses and perceptions. We can find things. Science makes tools available to us. Scientists can use our tools of science. Scientists can discover things. Science makes scientific theories available to us. Scientists can use our scientific theories. Scientists can predict things. The totality consists of more than these things.

Let us suppose. I believed in the value of a pessimistic myth. The pessimistic myth is. The totality consists of only these things. In that event, my values would act as forces upon my emotions. I would experience powerful emotional forces of sorrow, fear, and anger.

Let us suppose. My sorrow, fear, and anger inspired hatred of the drama of life and death. My hatred of the drama of life and death produced a paralyzing inhibition. My paralyzing inhibition produced a failure to meet the challenges of daily living. In that event, my failure to meet the challenges of daily living would have consequences. The consequences might include suffering, sorrow, destruction, disgrace, desolation, and premature death. These emotional forces of sorrow, fear, and anger could precipitate social, moral, mental, emotional, behavioral, and physical problems. These problems could ultimately render scientific help useless.

The power of imagination is. Imagination raises the morale of people. Imagination enables us. We persevere, overcome obstacles, and progress towards victory. Imagination is the power of the mind to form images of things. Some of these things are not present to our senses and perceptions. Some of these things are not within our actual experiences.

My imagination enables me. I imagine. The totality is an infinite divine eternal being. I have the highest esteem of the totality. The act of having the highest esteem of the totality enables me. I experience the most powerful emotional responses of joy, faith, and love. The act of experiencing the most powerful emotional responses of joy, faith, and love enables me. I produce emotional balance in my mind. Emotional balance in my mind is conducive to happiness and good health in my life. Happiness and good health in my life are conducive to success and prosperity in my business. I meet the challenges of life. For that reason, it is worthwhile. I love Healthy Agnostic Positivistic Nationalistic Spiritization of self and world. I take my love to its' logical extreme. I live a happier and healthier life.

Why should I take my love to its' logical extreme? I more completely answer the question. Consider the possible beneficial impact on society of doing so. The gloom of disease and assumed finality of death hangs over our heads like swords of Damocles. Emotional baggage comes along with this set of living arrangements. Let us suppose. We did not have the emotional baggage. In that event, we might take a greater interest in ourselves, our world, and our futures.

Let us suppose. We believe in the value of the most optimistic myths. In that event, our values would act as forces upon our emotions. We would experience the most powerful emotional forces of joy, faith, and love. We would balance the emotional forces of our minds. We would be happy. We would exhibit glad behaviors. Our glad behaviors would be conducive to our good health. We would be better able to delay and resist the onset of debilitating chronic illnesses, prolong a healthy productive life, and delay death.

Let us suppose. We devote our energy, space, and time to the most optimistic thoughts, beliefs, and expectations about the totality. In that event, our devotion would offer us potential benefits. The potential benefits are likely to be mental, emotional, behavioral and physiological in nature. For those reasons, I love Healthy Agnostic Positivistic Nationalistic Spiritization of self and world. I take my love to its logical extreme.

CHAPTER 28. MY MODEL OF THE TOTALITY OF EXISTENCE

My model of the totality contains two kinds of content. These two kinds of content are seed-body and soul-spirit. The difference between seed-body and soul-spirit is the most basic distinction. I make the distinction. I describe content in my model of the totality.

My model of the totality contains two kinds of form. These two kinds of form are self and world. The difference between self and world is the most basic distinction. I make the most basic distinction. I describe form in my model of the totality.

I combine the thought of one of the two kinds of content; with the thought of one of the two kinds of form. I do so once in every possible way. I create four things. The four things are the seed-body of the world, the seed-body of self, the soul-spirit of self, and the soul-spirit of the world.

CHAPTER 29. QUANTITY OF ENERGY: SEED-BODY OF SELF

I value truths. Some things occupy space, respond to gravitation, and show inertia. Scientists describe those things. Scientists use the general term matter. Matter has a capacity to perform work as a result of motion or position. Scientists describe the capacity to perform work as a result of motion or position. Scientists use the general term energy.

Modern physicists, however, have discovered and shown. It is possible. Matter transforms into energy. Energy transforms into matter. For that reason, everything around us and within us in one form or another is energy. Scientists often find it simpler and more convenient to treat matter and energy as separate. I identify both matter and energy simply as energy.

The seed-body of self. The seed-body of self is also known as the body. A quantity of energy is an attribute of the seed-body of self. Measurement of the quantity of energy is within the reach of scientific inquiry. A value for the quantity of energy exists within a range of possible values. I forgo the scientific exactitude of an exhaustive examination of all possible values. Instead, I choose to adopt very broad terms. I describe limits to the range of values as being neither equal to zero or infinity. I describe the quantity of energy as finite.

CHAPTER 30. QUANTITY OF ENERGY: SOUL-SPIRIT OF SELF

The soul-spirit of self is also known as the soul. A quantity of energy is an attribute of the soul-spirit of self. A value for the quantity of energy exists within a range of possible values. The possible values range from a lower limit of zero to an upper limit of infinity.

Measurement of the quantity of energy is beyond the reach of scientific methods. For that reason, I am free. I align my values with my needs and aspirations. My needs and aspirations are. Achieve and maintain happiness, good health, and prosperity. Emotional balance in my mind is conducive to happiness and good health in my life. Happiness and good health in my life is conducive to success and prosperity in my business. I desire happiness, good health, and prosperity. For that reason, I balance the emotional forces of my mind.

A quantity of energy is an attribute of my seed-body. I select a value to describe the quantity of energy. Let us suppose. I choose infinity as the value. In that event, my soul would be an infinite soul. An infinite soul would be out of proportion with a finite seed-body. Let us suppose. I choose zero as the value. In that event, my soul would be a non-existent soul. A non-existent soul would be out of proportion with a finite seed-body. Only a finite soul is in proportion to a finite seed-body. From a balance of ideas follows a balance of emotions.

CHAPTER 31. REASONS WHY ALIENATION OCCURS

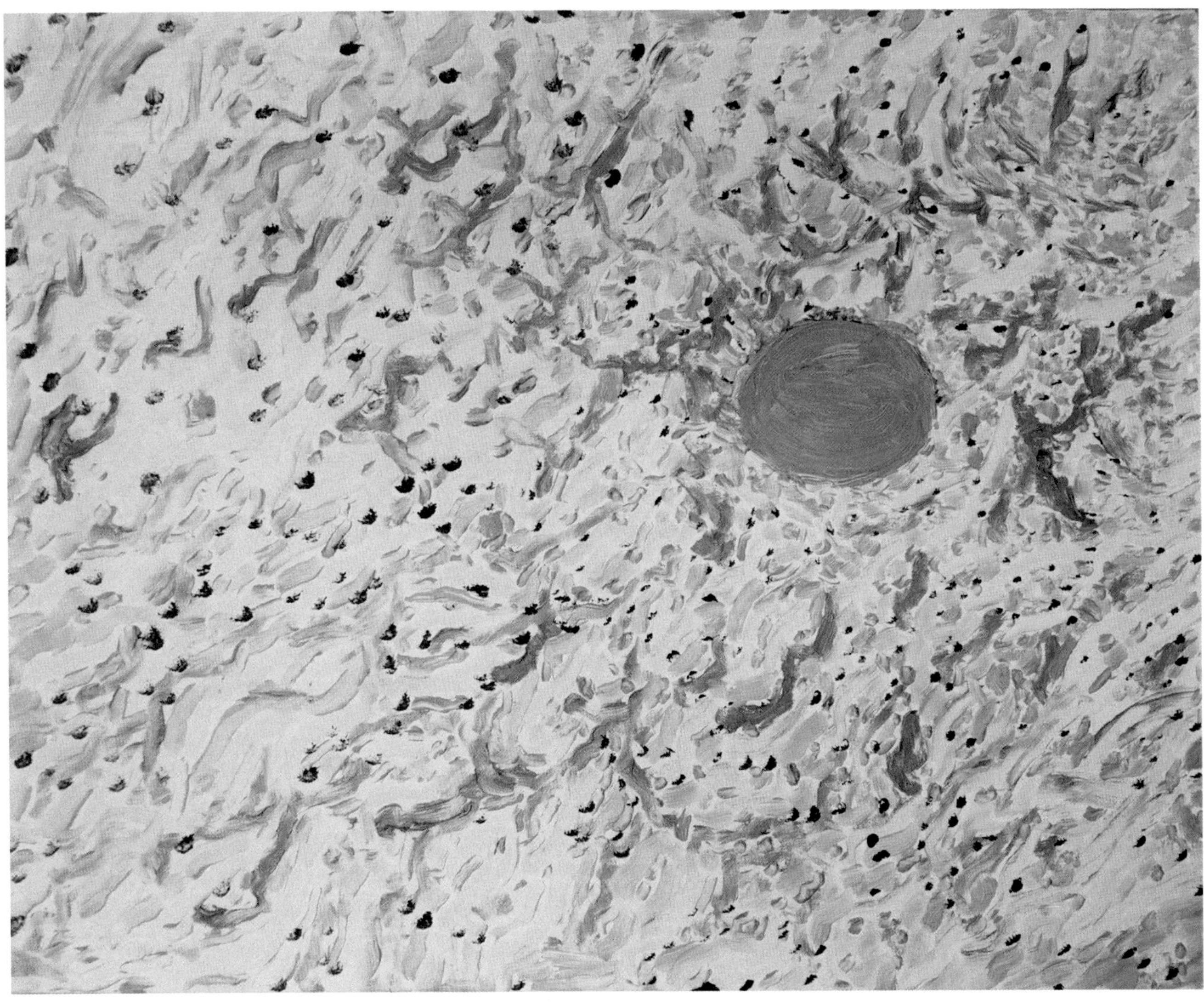

A possibility is. Our soul-spirit exists. Why do some people reject the possibility? I may only speculate. Maybe their own experience influences them. Maybe their upbringing influences them. Maybe a peer group influences them. Maybe something else influences them.

Let us suppose. People answer the grand enigmatic questions of identity in a certain way. In that event, the certain way may influence them. Such people have seed-bodies. Their seed-bodies make available their unconscious minds. Their unconscious minds make available a finite number, diversity, and variety of possibilities for thought, feeling, and action. Their souls evaluate these possibilities. Their souls select. Their souls may be able to accept a most optimistic myth as a possibility. The most optimistic myth is. Our soul-spirit exists. Yet their souls may be unwilling to believe in the value of the most optimistic myth.

I value truths. It appears. Our seed-bodies evolve over time. I value the most optimistic myths. Our soul-spirit is an active participant in the evolution of our seed-bodies. Souls make up the minds of seed-bodies. Let us suppose. A certain soul chooses to live in a state of alienation. Let us suppose further. The state of alienation removes a seed-body from the gene pool. Let us suppose still further. The removal of the seed-body from the gene pool moves life in general to a higher state of conscious awareness of the totality. In that event, the soul may function as Social Darwinist. The person may not even be aware of this function.

Consider the point of view of the person. Let us suppose. The point of view of the person is. Self is a seed-body. The seed-body exists on a tiny island of life. A vast ocean of death surrounds the tiny island of life. In that event, it may seem to the person. Death is the norm. Life is the abnormality. The purpose of life is its' own self-perpetuation. Ones' own motivations in everything one says or does are the product of the biochemical functions of a meat machine.

The truth is. These ideas are pessimistic myths. Let us suppose. A person claims an ability to know. These pessimistic myths are truths. In that event, the person's values would act as forces upon the person's emotions. The most powerful emotional forces of sorrow, fear, and anger would follow from the discovery of a truth. The truth is. It appears. One day, the seed-body of self will die. The person's belief in the value of pessimistic myths would not enable the person. The person would be unable to balance the emotional forces of the person's mind. The person's heart would be filled with sorrow, fear, and anger. The person's emotions would act as forces upon the person's behaviors. The person would exhibit sad, mad, and bad behaviors.

Let us suppose. The person loses hope. The person loses faith. The person gives up. The person turns to crime. The person turns to drugs. The person becomes aggressive, violent, depressed, and or suicidal. In general, the person does nothing. The person acts helpless. In that event, the person's behaviors might cause the person to fail to procreate.

I value the most optimistic myths. Our seed-bodies make possible our unconscious minds. Our unconscious minds make available a finite number, diversity, and variety of possibilities for thought, feeling, and action. Our souls choose from these possibilities. A person's choices could cause the person to abstain from procreation.

People live in their habitat. Individual seed-bodies are parts of a body-consuming biosphere. The body-consuming biosphere is a complex chaotic dynamic system. Other living infernal fractal entities may act on our seed-bodies. Their actions may cause some people to be non-reproductive.

A primal conflict between predator and prey divides the body-consuming biosphere. We play a game of survival and sacrifice. The competition to survive compels us. We make selections. The selections are parental, communal, predatory, and sexual in nature. The selections condition some people to assume reproductive roles. The selections condition some people to assume non-reproductive roles.

It appears. Laws of cause and effect predict the behavior and fate of matter and energy in the known universe. Laws of cause and effect suggest a material standard of conduct. Some people conform to this material standard of conduct. The laws of cause and effect reward those people. The reward is good health. Some people deviate from this standard of conduct. The laws of cause and effect punish those people. The punishment is disease. Reproduction requires energy, space, and time. Good health makes finding the energy, space, and time easier. Disease makes finding the energy, space, and time harder, or even impossible.

Soul-spirit may act to prevent an individual seed-body from procreating. Every living infernal fractal entity plays the dual role of predator and prey. Some may play their roles in a civilized way. Some may not. The conflict of predator and prey continues. Every living seed-body is both eating and being eaten throughout its' brief existence. Thus, predators microscopic and macroscopic eat from every seed-body alive. Therefore, our soul-spirit has many avenues to operate through.

These many avenues include bisexuality, homosexuality, asexuality, and non-reproductive heterosexuality. Preventing certain seed-bodies from reproducing is beneficial. The species benefits. The culture as a whole benefits. A tolerant view towards all forms of sexual expression emerges from these ideas.

CHAPTER 32. QUANTITY OF ENERGY: SEED-BODY OF THE WORLD

A quantity of energy is an attribute of the seed-body of the world. How do we measure the quantity of energy? Scientists say. The quantity of energy remains beyond the grasp of scientific inquiry. What things exist beyond the known universe? I do not know. It may be. The known universe is an infinitesimal part of the seed-body of the world. Our known universe may be like a seed. The big bang may be like a birth. The development of our universe may be like a seed growing into a body. Our known universe has a quantity of energy. Science does not limit the quantity of energy. The world is more than the known universe.

I expand the definition of the seed-body of the world. I include a positive possibility. The positive possibility is. Many big bangs may occur. A seed-body of parallel universes may exist.

A quantity of energy is inherent in the seed-body of the world. Let us suppose. The quantity of energy is equal to infinity. A quantity of energy is inherent in our universe. Let us suppose further. The quantity of energy is finite. In that event, our universe could be one of an infinite number, diversity, and variety of large universes.

The lower limit to the range of values approaches zero. Let us suppose. The seed-body of the world is an illusion. In that event, the quantity of energy is finite. The finite quantity of energy manifests as the illusion. The finite quantity of energy is a lower limit to the range of possible values. The range of possible values exists between a lower limit of some finite quantity and an upper limit of infinity.

From abundance comes compassion, forgiveness, freedom, grace, peace, joy, and the divinity of life. From scarcity comes ignorance, guilt, inhibition, disgrace, suffering, sorrow, and the abomination of death. I know of no ideological, scientific, or spiritual reason to impose a finite limit on the quantity of energy. From the range of possible values, I select infinity. Infinity is an extreme value. My selection enables me. I devote, energy, space, and time to the most optimistic model of the totality. I experience the most powerful emotional forces of joy, faith, and love. I balance the emotional forces of my mind. I am happy.

An infinite quantity of energy can not be isolated. For that reason, I use the phrase 'infinite'. I describe the quantity of energy.

CHAPTER 33. QUANTITY OF ENERGY: SOUL-SPIRIT OF THE WORLD

The soul-spirit of the world is also known as the spirit. A quantity of energy is an attribute of the soul-spirit of the world. I believe in the value of truths. Measurement of the quantity of energy remains beyond the grasp of scientific inquiry. The quantity of energy exists within a range of possible values. The possible values range from a lower limit of zero to an upper limit of infinity.

From abundance comes compassion, forgiveness, freedom, grace, peace, joy, and the divinity of life. From scarcity comes ignorance, guilt, inhibition, disgrace, suffering, sorrow, and the abomination of death.

I believe in the value of the most optimistic myths. I select infinity. Infinity is an extreme value. The extreme value enables me. I devote, energy, space, and time to my most optimistic model of the totality. I experience the most powerful emotional forces of joy, faith, and love. I balance the emotional forces of my mind. I am happy.

An infinite quantity of energy can not be isolated. An infinite quantity of energy is an attribute of the soul-spirit of the world.

CHAPTER 34. QUALITIES OF SPACE

I describe space as the ability to extend in any direction. I know space as the expanse. The solar system, stars, and galaxies constitute the energy of the universe. I value truths. Scientists say. The energy appears to occupy space. The energy appears to distort space-time.

A quantity of energy is an attribute of the totality. The quantity of energy generates a quality of space. What is a quality of space? Quality is a relative term. Quality is the essential character of something: its' nature or degree or grade of excellence.

Quality compares to quality. Quality compares in a relationship with something else. A quantity of energy is an attribute of the seed-body. A quantity of energy is an attribute of the soul-spirit. The two quantities of energy generate two qualities of space. How do the two qualities of space compare? What is the quality of space of the seed-body relative to the quality of space of the soul-spirit?

I describe the quality of space on a scale. The scale ranges from a lower limit of random chaos to an upper limit of perfect order.

A quantity of energy is an attribute of the seed-body. The quantity of energy generates a quality of space. The seed-body has an order. I place the order between the lower limit of random chaos and the upper limit of perfect order. The quality of space is 'fractal'

A quantity of energy is an attribute of the soul-spirit. The quantity of energy generates a quality of space. The soul-spirit has an order. I place the order at the upper limit of perfect order. The quality of space is 'divine'.

A quality of space is an attribute of four things. The four things are the seed-body of the world, the seed-body of self, the soul-spirit of self, and the soul-spirit of the world. The four things combine to make up, complete, and bring to perfection my model of the totality.

An infinite quantity of energy is an attribute of the seed-body of the world. The infinite quantity of energy generates a quality of space. The quality of space is 'fractal'.

A finite quantity of energy is an attribute of the seed-body of self. The finite quantity of energy generates a quality of space. The quality of space is 'fractal'.

A finite quantity of energy is an attribute of the soul-spirit of self. The finite quantity of energy generates a quality of space. The quality of space is 'divine'.

An infinite quantity of energy is an attribute of the soul-spirit of the world. The infinite quantity of energy generates a quality of space. The quality of space is 'divine'.

I use the phrase 'fractal'. I describe a quality of space. The quality of space is an attribute of both the seed-body of self and the seed-body of the world. I use the phrase 'divine'. I describe a quality of space. The quality of space is an attribute of both the soul-spirit of self and soul-spirit of the world.

CHAPTER 35. LENGTHS OF TIME

Time is a non-spatial continuum. It appears. Events occur in irreversible succession from the past through the present into the future. I measure time as an interval. I select a regularly recurring event, such as the sunrise. I count the number of its occurrences.

I describe four things. These four things are seed-body of the world, seed-body of self, soul-spirit of self, and soul-spirit of the world. I describe each of these four things as having an integrity. The integrity persists over some interval of time. Each of these four things is a functional whole for a certain 'length of time'.

A length of time is an attribute of the seed-body of self. I value truths. It appears. The seed-body of self remains an integrated functional whole over only a relatively brief, finite interval of time. I can measure the interval of time in seconds, minutes, hours, days, weeks, months, and years. My seed-body remains an integrated functional whole for a length of time. Bodily processes limit the length of time. Bodily processes are infernal in nature. Within my body I burn calories. I burn sugars, carbohydrates, proteins, and lipids. With the help of oxygen, my body liberates chemical energy. The infernal nature of my seed-body limits its' longevity. For these reasons, I use the phrase 'infernal temporal'. I describe the longevity of the seed-body of self.

A length of time is an attribute of the known universe. Stars may burn brightly for many millions or billions of years. Eventually, stars run out of fuel. Stars make up galaxies. Galaxies make up much of the energy of the known universe. Thus the infernal nature of the known universe appears to limit its' longevity. As such, I use the phrase 'infernal temporal' to describe the longevity of the universe.

A length of time is an attribute of the seed-body of the world. The infernal nature of the seed-body of the world does not limit its' longevity. The seed-body of the world continuously burns. The soul-spirit of the world creates new fuel eternally. The seed-body of the world is an eternal flame. As such, I use the phrase 'infernal'. I describe the length of time of the seed-body of the world.

A length of time is an attribute of the soul-spirit of self. I value the most optimistic myths. Souls are resilient. Souls are invulnerable to injury. Souls are subject to a sustained existence. Souls have immunity to death. Souls enjoy eternal life. Souls are immortal. As such, I use the phrase 'eternal'. I describe the length of time of the soul-spirit of self.

A length of time is an attribute of the soul-spirit of the world. The integrity of the soul-spirit of the world is everlasting. The soul-spirit of the world is the creator of energy, space, and time. For that reason, the soul-spirit of the world transcends time. As such, I use the phrase 'eternal'. I describe the length of time of the soul-spirit of the world.

CHAPTER 36. VALUES OF DENOMINATOR

$$\textit{Quotient} = \frac{\textit{Numerator}}{\textit{Denominator}}$$

An equation is a mathematical sentence. Let us imagine an equation. The equation begins with a number. The number has a name. The name is quotient. The quotient is followed by an equals sign. The equals sign is followed by a fraction. The fraction consists of two numbers and a horizontal line. The horizontal line functions as a divide by symbol. A number appears above the horizontal line. The number has a name. The name is numerator. A number appears below the horizontal line. The number has a name. The name is denominator. The mathematical sentence reads. The quotient is equal to the numerator divided by the denominator.

I build a model of the totality. I describe four things. The four things are seed-body of the world, seed-body of self, soul-spirit of self, and soul-spirit of the world. These four things are fractions of a whole. The whole is the totality. I represent the fractions of a whole mathematically. I use equations.

Let us imagine an equation. Self is the quotient. The totality is the numerator. A number approaching infinity is the denominator. The equation reads. Self equals the totality divided by a number approaching infinity. Self is infinitesimal relative to the totality. Self has a value of denominator. I describe the value of denominator as "infinite". The seed-body of self and the soul-spirit of self are two parts of one self. For that reason, the seed-body of self has a value of denominator. I describe the value of denominator as "infinite". The soul-spirit of self has a value of denominator. I describe the value of denominator as "infinite".

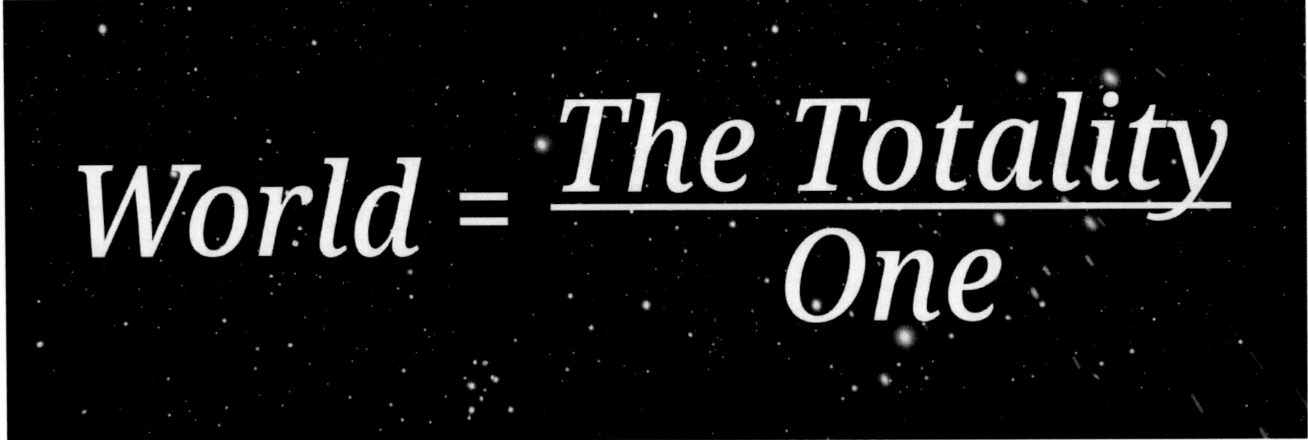

Let us imagine another equation. The world is the quotient. The totality is the numerator. One is the denominator. The equation reads. The world equals the totality divided by one. The world has a value of denominator. I describe the value of denominator as "one". The seed-body of the world and the soul-spirit of the world are two parts of one world. For that reason, the seed-body of the world has a denominator. I describe the value of denominator as "one". The soul-spirit of the world has a value of denominator. I describe the value of denominator as "one".

CHAPTER 37. INFINITE FOUR

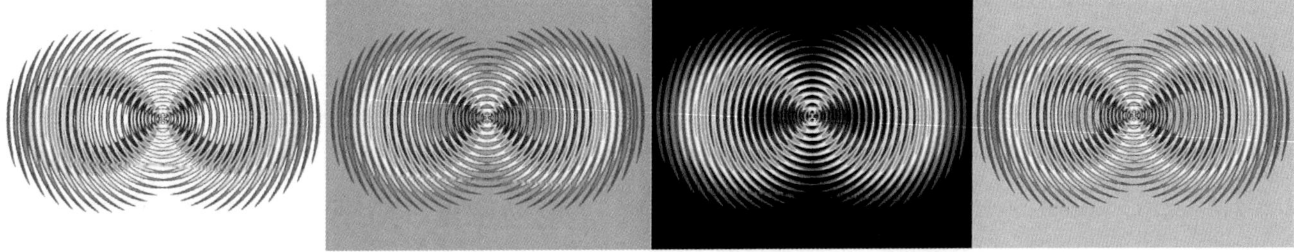

Quantity of energy is an attribute of the totality. The limit to the quantity of energy is equal to infinity. I value the most optimistic myths. Out of this infinite quantity of energy, comes an infinite number, variety, and diversity of random permutations and combinations of energy, space, and time. Out of all random permutations and combinations of energy, space, and time, comes a permutation and combination of energy, space, and time, with a divine quality of space, and an eternal longevity of time. An infinite number, variety, and diversity of possible combinations and permutations of energy, space, and time, makes the improbability of the creation of a divine eternal order an actuality. By virtue of its' divine eternal nature then, this finite divine eternal entity has the power. This finite divine eternal entity absorbs onto itself all the energy, space, and time, of all other possibilities. This finite divine eternal entity transforms the totality from an infinite abominable infernal being into an infinite divine eternal being. Everything, everywhere, is forever, and always will be, existing in this supreme state of being. Simply put: Out of an infinity of random possibility comes a divinity eternal whose dominance of the continuum makes it an infinite divine eternal being.

In the process of this transformation of the totality, the infinite divine eternal being did absorb and evaluate all other possible combinations and permutations of energy, space, and time. It was inevitable. The infinite divine eternal being discovered designs for an infinite number, diversity, and variety of Large Universes of the Correct Kind to Support Living Infernal Fractal Entities or LUCKS LIFE. The infinite divine eternal being stores those designs in an infinite seed. This infinite seed enables the infinite divine eternal being. The infinite divine eternal being creates at will, any and all possible designs. At will, the infinite divine eternal being actively transforms designs from possibility into energy, space, and time. The product of these transformations are the infinite seed-body of large universes of the correct kind to support living infernal fractal entities.

The infinite divine eternal being has a purpose. The purpose is the enjoyment of entertainment. The drama of life and death entertains. For that reason, the infinite divine eternal being manifests as an infinite four. The infinite four are an infinite seed, an infinite body, an infinite soul, and an infinite spirit. The infinite four are the big IF. The infinite divine eternal being experiences the bliss of conscious thought, feeling, and action, from the point of view of an infinite number, diversity, and variety, of living infernal fractal entities. Within the infinite spirit exists the infinite seed. Within the infinite seed exists our finite bodies. Within our finite bodies exists our finite souls. All finite bodies combine to form an infinite body. All finite souls combine to form an infinite soul. Mother God is the infinite soul-spirit. Father Love is the infinite seed-body. The union of Mother God and Father Love creates life. We are Soul Children.

As a life form, I vie for authority, power, order, and control over limited resources. The limited resources exist within a body consuming biosphere. The body consuming biosphere exists on a crusted magma globe. The crusted magma globe has limited dimensions. I perceive scarcity. The scarcity is only an illusion. The illusion is born out of limitations. My seed-body has attributes. The attributes impose limitations upon my senses and perceptions. My seed-body occupies specific points in energy, space, and time. The specific points in energy, space, and time, impose limitations upon my senses and perceptions. These limitations are hiding infinite abundance from my view.

I value the most optimistic myths. The most optimistic myths are all about infinite abundance. Infinite abundance is the infinite love of my divine eternal spirit for my divine eternal soul. Mother God bestows infinite love, divine forgiveness, eternal freedom, and unifying grace upon all of her soul children. I am free. I explore, enjoy, and choose. Infinite abundance is the ultimate source of compassion, forgiveness, freedom, grace, peace, joy, and divinity. An infinite divine eternal being creates an infinite number of finite creatures. The infinite creator creates each finite creature in the image of the infinite creator. The limit to the number of finite creatures is infinity. The infinite creator endows each creature with a seed-body and a soul-spirit. The infinite creator creates an infinite number, diversity and variety of finite creatures in the image of the infinite creator.

I have built my model of the totality. My model of the totality consists of four things. The four things are the seed-body of the world, the seed-body of self, the soul-spirit of self, and the soul-spirit of the world.

Each of these four things has attributes. I have described four attributes. The four attributes are the quantity of energy, quality of space, longevity of time, and value of denominator. Based on my description of these four attributes, I describe these four things. The seed-body of the world is infinite, fractal, infernal, and one. The seed-body of self is finite, fractal, infernal temporal, and infinite. The soul-spirit of self is fractal, divine, eternal, and infinite. The soul-spirit of the world is infinite, divine, eternal, and one.

The infinite seed is the same as the seed-body of the world. The infinite body is the same as the seed-body of self and the seed-bodies of all finite creatures. The infinite soul is the same as the soul-spirit of self and the soul-spirits of all finite creatures. The infinite spirit is the same as the soul-spirit of the world.

The infinite seed, infinite body, infinite soul, and infinite spirit, combine to form an infinite mind. The infinite seed, and the infinite body, function as the infinite unconscious mind. The infinite soul, and the infinite spirit, function as the infinite conscious mind. I describe the totality as an infinite life form.

CHAPTER 38. KEY TO JOY, FAITH, AND LOVE

My key to joy, faith, and love is. I value certain ideas. Those certain ideas are my values. I value the most optimistic myths. I value truths. My values act as forces upon my emotions. Joy, faith, and love, balance sorrow, fear, and anger. I balance the emotional forces of my mind. Emotional balance in my mind is conducive to happiness and good health in my life.

From the thought of an infinite divine eternal being follows an idea. The idea is. Everything, everywhere, will forever, and always be, existing in a supreme state of being. Existence within a supreme state of being renders life and all resulting ignorance, guilt, inhibition, disgrace, suffering, sorrow, and abomination an illusion.

Eternal Divinity is monotonous. Living infernal fractal entities offer the soul-spirit an opportunity. The opportunity is an opportunity to escape from the monotony of eternal divinity. In the guise of a poly-focal infinite soul, the spirit enjoys entertainment. Our souls experience a freedom of choice. The freedom of choice enables us. We choose from an endless variety and diversity of positive possible views of self and world. An infinite quantity of energy is inherent in the totality. The totality makes all of this and more possible.

CHAPTER 39. POSSIBLE REASONS WHY WE CAN NOT DISCOVER OTHER UNIVERSES

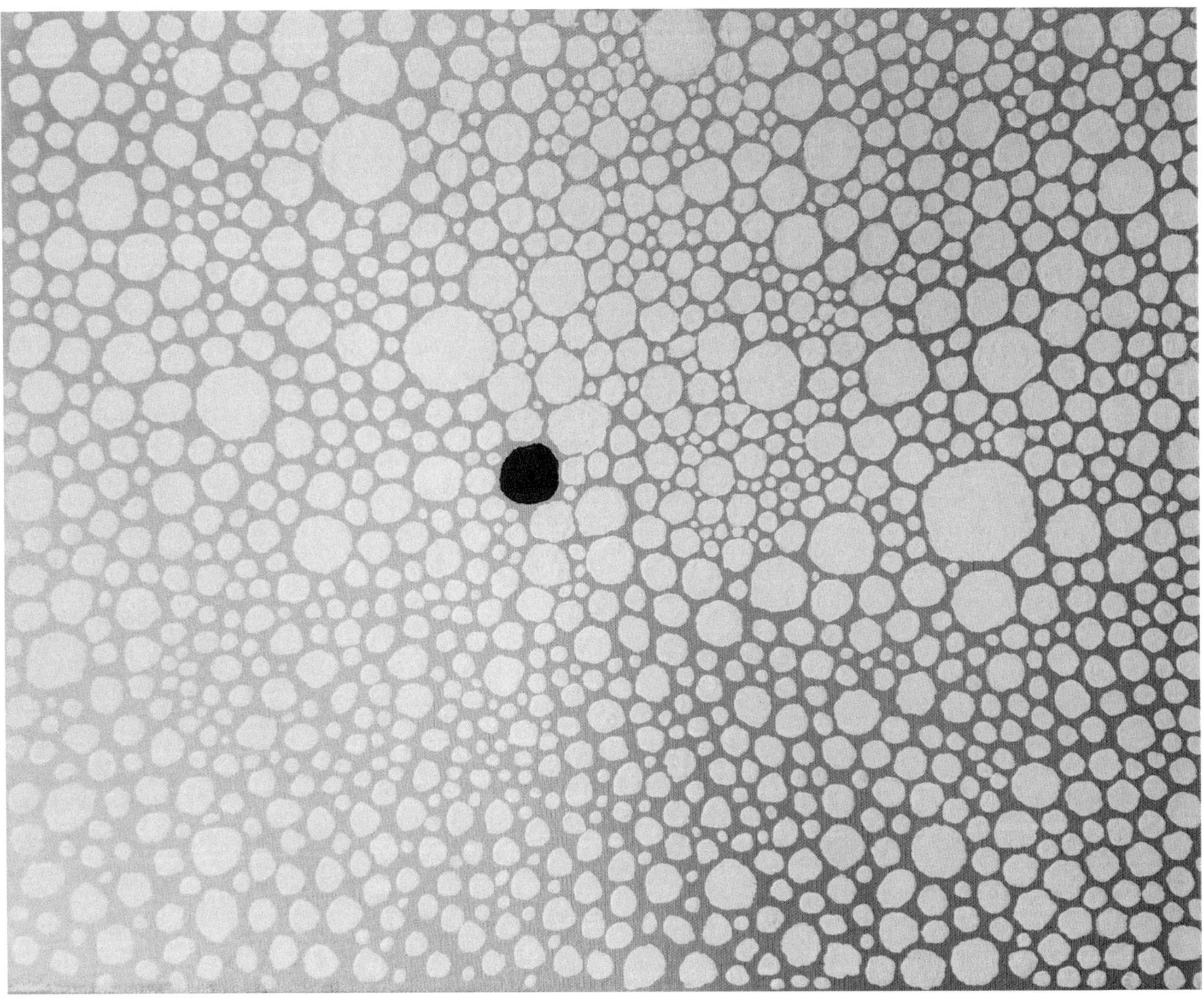

The universe is known by many individuals. Each individual has a different point of view. For that reason, it appears. The known universe is different for each individual.

Science offers us skeletons. Scientists say. It appears. A skeleton remains from the big bang. The skeleton is cosmic background radiation. Science offers us the fossilized skeletons of dinosaurs. Scientists say. It appears. Dinosaurs once roamed the Earth. Science offers us the skeletons of galaxies. Scientists say. It appears. Galaxies are very far way from us. Light from the galaxies takes time to reach us. For that reason, the galaxies appear to us as these galaxies were millions or even billions of years ago.

Science can tell us about reality. Reality is the way. Things appear to be. Actuality is the way. Things actually are. Let us suppose. The universe was actually created about ten thousand years ago. Let us suppose further. The universe was created with the appearance of being about fourteen billion years old. In that event, scientists would only be able to say. It appears. The universe is fourteen billion years old.

When the correct explanation is unknown, scientists prefer the simplest explanation. What is the simplest explanation? How do they know? An explanation is the simplest.

When the correct explanation is unknown, I default to the most optimistic explanation. The most optimistic explanation is. We have agreed. We entered into a cosmic game. In the cosmic game, each of us confines our awareness of the totality. We confine ourselves to our conscious minds. We gain enjoyment. We enjoy entertainment. We do not know. All there is to know. We are individuals. We know next to nothing about almost everything.

Let us suppose. Continuous spiritual communion between soul and spirit actually does exist. Let us suppose further. A person values the most optimistic myths. In that event, the person is in the best possible position. Divine inspiration becomes available to the person through continuous spiritual communion between soul and spirit. Belief in the value of the most optimistic myths enables the person. The person can make better use of the divine inspiration.

Our bodies make senses and perceptions available to us. We can use our senses and perceptions. We can find things. Science makes tools available to us. Scientists can use our tools of science. Scientists can discover things. Science makes scientific theories available to us. Scientists can use our scientific theories. Scientists can predict things. These things and everything else exist. The everything else enables me. I have the highest esteem of the totality. I balance the emotional forces of my mind. I am happy.

I make use of divine inspiration in my work. I persevere, overcome obstacles, and progress towards victory. Let us suppose. Divine inspiration becomes available to scientists through continuous spiritual communion between soul and spirit. Let us suppose further. Scientists choose to believe in the value of the most optimistic myths. In that event, scientists would be in the best possible position. Belief in the value of the most optimistic myths would enable them. Scientists would make better use of divine inspiration in their work. Scientists would work down from optimism to pessimism; rather than work up from pessimism to optimism.

Physicists are people who try to figure out how Nature works. Why do the stars shine? Why is water fluid? Why is the sky blue? What matter and energy makes up my seed-body? Why is weight an attribute of my seed-body? Why does the universe expand? What are energy and matter actually?

Experimental physicists usually work in a lab. Test hypotheses and theories. Make discoveries of new phenomena. Develop new applications of ideas.

Theoretical physicists use mathematics. Develop explanations of experimental data. Formulate new theories. Make new hypotheses.

Theoretical physicists make predictions about the behavior and fate of matter and energy in the known universe. Often, making predictions involves the use of mathematical equations. The mathematical equations include constants. About twenty constants enable the theoretical physicists. The theoretical physicists make their mathematical equations work. The mathematical equations make their scientific theories work. The theoretical physicists use their scientific theories. The theoretical physicists predict the behavior and fate of matter and energy in the known universe. They have the ability. I am grateful.

Physicists say. It appears. The constants in physics are seemingly arbitrary and unrelated. The seemingly arbitrary and unrelated constants in physics, have one strange thing in common: It appears. The fundamental constants of physics and chemistry are just right, or fine-tuned. The fundamental constants of physics and chemistry allow the universe and life as we know it, to exist.

Physicists say. Let us suppose. The values of these constants differed by only surprisingly small amounts. In that event, it appears. Life, stars, galaxies, everything in the universe would be impossible. It appears. The nature of this universe is finely tuned in favor of the existence of life as we know it.

We are living. We can observe the universe. These facts imply. The fundamental constants must be "just right" to produce life. Let us suppose. The constants were not "just right" to produce life. In that event, we would not be here to observe the universe. However, the fact is. The universe does not seem to be a random or chance event. It appears. The fundamental constants, of physics and chemistry, allow the universe and life as we know it, to exist.

To explain this fact, people have postulated many universes scenarios. In some of these many universes scenarios, only one or some universes produce life. We live in only one of those many universes.

Our seed-bodies make senses and perceptions available to us. Our tools of science extend the reach of our senses and perceptions. The energy, space, and time, of our known universe, is available as a source of discovery. Discovery has not offered us a way. We have not discovered the existence of other universes. For that reason, the existence of other universes is a myth, rather than, a scientific theory.

From this myth, I take one further step. I value the most optimistic myths. Out of an infinite chaos of random probability and possibility, came a divine eternal order. The divine eternal order dominated the totality. Dominance of the totality made the divine eternal order into an infinite divine eternal being. The infinite divine eternal being is everything, everywhere, at all times. The infinite divine eternal being enjoys entertainment. The drama of life and death entertains. For that reason, the infinite divine eternal being manifests as an infinite four. The infinite four consists of; an infinite seed, an infinite body, an infinite soul, and an infinite spirit. The infinite seed is an infinite number, diversity, and variety of large universes of the correct kind to support living infernal fractal entities.

Let us suppose. An infinite number, diversity, and variety of large universes of the correct kind to support living infernal fractal entities actually exist. In that event, why haven't scientists discovered other universes. The following are some possible reasons.

Let us suppose. Time has elapsed since the creation of each universe. Light has travelled a distance during the elapsed time. Universes are spaced farther apart than the distance. In that event, we would be unable to discover the other universes.

Recently, scientists have made a discovery. The discovery is. Supermassive black holes exist. Scientists have observed. Supermassive black holes exist in the centers, of the galaxies, of our known universe. Some people have suggested a possibility. The possibility is. A black hole, might project, within the boundaries, of its event horizon, the energy, space, and time, of a universe. The universe might also contain black holes. This idea suggests to me the possibility of a world with a fractal self-similarity on an infinite range of scales.

A combination and permutation, of energy, space, and time, came into existence, to create, our universe. Let us suppose. Our senses and tools are specific to the combination and permutation of energy, space, and time. Let us suppose further. Different combinations and permutations of energy, space, and time came into existence to create other universes. Let us suppose still further. We are unable to sense and perceive these different combinations and permutations of energy, space, and time. In that event, the other universes would be invisible, to us.

Let us suppose. These other universes are superimposed, on top, of our universe. Let us suppose further. These other universes have inhabitants. Let us suppose still further. The inhabitants could sense and perceive our known universe. In that event, our known universe would appear to them as a ghost world.

Do other universes exist? I leave to science the task of answering this question. With the tools available, science is quite unable to complete the task at this time.

CHAPTER 40. UNICORNS, DRAGONS, AND FAIRIES

The totality is everything, everywhere, at all times. I believe in the value of the most optimistic myths. For that reason, I think, believe, and predict. The totality is an infinite divine eternal being. The infinite divine eternal being is everything, everywhere, at all times. The infinite divine eternal being enjoys entertainment. The drama of life and death entertains. For that reason, the infinite divine eternal being manifests as an infinite four. The infinite four consists of an infinite seed, an infinite body, an infinite soul, and an infinite spirit. The infinite seed consists of an infinite number, diversity, and variety, of large universes of the correct kind to support living infernal fractal entities. These universes make possible the existence of unicorns, dragons, and faeries.

Let us suppose. Unicorns are blue, single-horned, horse-like, creatures. Let us suppose further. These unicorns live in some other universe. Let us suppose still further. Our souls live and die an infinite series of lives. Let us suppose even still further. Our souls are capable of traveling from universe to universe between lifetimes. In that event, our souls may have lived some past lifetime in a universe, wherein; unicorns exist.

Let us suppose. A dragon lives somewhere on the land surface of planet Earth. Let us give this dragon a gender and a name. Let us call him George. Let us suppose further. George is totally undetectable. We can not sense and perceive George. Scientists can use our tools of science. Let us suppose still further. Scientists search for George. The scientists can not find George. George is inert. George does not affect the universe as we know it, in any way. George's universe is superimposed over our own universe. George can see us for some reason, but we can not see George. George has chosen to live inside of a garage. A garage has garage spaces. People park cars in the garage spaces. Let us suppose even still further.

George has chosen to occupy a garage space. The car space is just big enough to accommodate the bulk of his dragon body. Let us suppose finally. A person walks right into the garage. The person walks right up to the garage space. The garage space contains a car. The person enters the car. The person starts the car. The person drives out of the garage space for some reason. Later the person returns. The person parks the car in said garage space. In that event, George is present. However the person does not notice George. George is unharmed by the activity. For that reason, George continues to exist. Although his existence is completely unknown to the person.

Pink fairies offer me yet another way of ornamenting my model of the totality with myth. Let us suppose. A combination and permutation of energy, space, and time came into existence. The combination and permutation of energy, space, and time manifests as our universe. Let us suppose further. A different combination and permutation of energy, space, and time came into existence. The different combination and permutation of energy, space, and time manifests as a different universe. Let us suppose still further. The different universe is superimposed over our own universe. Pink fairies exist in the different universe. These pink fairies can see me, touch me, hold me, and heal me; but I am unable. I can not sense and perceive the existence of these pink fairies. In that event, this superimposed universe is a myth.

The difference; between unicorns, dragons, and fairies; and an infinite divine eternal being, is the difference between limited attributes and extreme attributes. Unicorns, dragons, and fairies, have limited attributes. Finite quantities of energy, fractal qualities of space, infernal temporal longevities of time, and infinite values of denominator are the limited attributes of unicorns, dragons, and fairies. An infinite divine eternal being has extreme attributes. An infinite quantity of energy, a divine quality of space, an eternal longevity of time, and a denominator of one, are the extreme attributes of the infinite divine eternal being.

CHAPTER 41. EVIDENCE

The presence of the universe is the presence of evidence. The presence of evidence in the form of the universe provides premises. Those premises enable us. We can make valid logical inductive inferences. We can make myths. An infinite number, diversity, and variety of myths are made possible by the totality. Each of these myths is an equally valid possibility.

My seed-body makes senses and perceptions available to me. I can use my senses and perceptions. I can find things. A finite quantity of energy, a fractal quality of space, an infernal temporal longevity of time, and an infinite value of denominator are attributes of my seed-body. The attributes of my seed-body impose limitations upon my senses and perceptions. My seed-body occupies a specific point in energy, space, and time. My occupation of a specific point in energy, space, and time imposes limitations upon my senses and perceptions.

Science makes tools available to us. Scientists can use our tools of science. Scientist can find things. Finite quantities of energy, fractal qualities of space, infernal temporal longevities of time, and infinite values of denominator are attributes of our tools of science. The attributes of our tools of science impose limitations upon scientists. Our tools of science occupy specific points in energy, space, and time. The occupation of specific points in energy, space, and time, imposes limitations upon scientists.

Is our universe a part of an infinite divine eternal being, or an entity on to itself? We are limited in our abilities to gather evidence, make inferences, and draw conclusions. Given these limitations, I simply can not know for sure. The presence of evidence in the form of the universe offers some support for both of these myths. Each of these myths is a valid possibility.

How can scientists use our tools of science to quantify infinity, qualify divinity, measure the duration of eternity, and perceive the totality? Continuous spiritual communion yields inspiration, intuition, and good judgment. Let us suppose. Scientists make use of their inspiration, intuition, and good judgment. In that event, maybe scientists can learn how.

CHAPTER 42. CAUSES AND EFFECTS OF AN UNBALANCED MIND

A totality exists. For that reason, we are part of the totality. Ideas are thoughts, beliefs, and expectations about the totality. We value certain ideas. These certain ideas are our values. We use our values. We build within our minds. We build our models of the totality. Our values act as forces upon our emotions. I value truths. I value the most optimistic myths. I balance my values. A balance of values produces a balance of emotions. A balance of the emotions produces happiness. I desire happiness. For that reason, I balance my values. I balance the emotional forces of my mind. I am happy.

Let us suppose. Some people do not know how to balance their own values. In that event, those people would fail to balance their own emotions. Those people would experience an emotional unbalance of their own minds. They would be unhappy.

Let us suppose. Some people do know how to balance their own values. Let us suppose further. Those people are unwilling to balance their own values. In that event, those people would fail to balance their own emotions. Those people would experience an emotional unbalance of their own minds. They would be unhappy.

Let us suppose. A person must face a sudden loss or unfortunate circumstance. Let us suppose further. The person has difficulty coping. The person can not step back and see even just the outline of the whole picture. The person does focus on the seed-body and its relationship to the universe. The person does not focus on the soul-spirit. In that event, the person is not balancing values. The person is not balancing emotions. An emotional imbalance is born out of a preoccupation with the seed-body and its relationship to the universe. The person is unhappy.

What are the effects of an unbalanced mind? Let us suppose. A person experiences an emotional imbalance. The person is unhappy. The heart of the person is filled with sorrow, fear, and anger. In that event, the person's emotions would act as forces upon the person's behaviors. The person would exhibit sad, mad, and bad behaviors. Racist fascist warmongering behaviors are sad, mad, and bad behaviors. Lying, stealing, cheating, conquering, enslaving, and killing are sad, mad, and bad behaviors. The sad, mad, and bad behaviors would act as forces upon the person's body. The sad, mad, and bad behaviors would be conducive to a state of disease in the person's body. The sad, mad, and bad behaviors would act as forces upon the person's habitat. The sad, mad, and bad behaviors would be conducive to a state of disease in the person's habitat. For that reason, emotional unbalance in the person's mind would be conducive to unhappiness and disease in the person's life. Unhappiness and disease in the person's life would be conducive to failure and hardship in the person's business.

Let us suppose. The minds of billions of people experience emotional imbalance. Billions of people are unhappy. The hearts of billions of people are filled with sorrow, fear, and anger. In that event, billions of people would exhibit sad, mad, and bad behaviors. The sad, mad, and bad behaviors of billions of people would be conducive to a state of disease in the body-consuming biosphere. The sad, mad, and bad behaviors of billions of people would be conducive to a weak and unstable civilization.

Human beings have populated the Earth. It appears. Until very recently, groups of human beings remained isolated within their own ancestral homelands. In isolation, each group of human beings established their own standard of beauty. Presently, human beings from around the world are mingling. For that reason, we can marvel at these many interpretations of beauty.

Racism is a belief. This belief is. These groups of human beings are races. Each race possesses distinct characteristics, abilities, and or qualities. Each race inherits these distinct characteristics, abilities, and or qualities from their ancestors. These races are competing for limited resources. The limited resources include breathable air, drinkable water, productive land, and available sunshine. Racists believe. The right thing to do is. Join a collective effort. Work, fight, and outnumber the competition.

However, there is nothing proprietary about this collective effort. People belong to other races. Those people can also join a collective effort. Those people can also work, fight, and outnumber the competition.

Let us suppose. Racism is wide spread. In that event, racists would run a race. The race would cause population overshoot, depletion of natural resources, abrupt climate change, and habitat loss. The finish line of the race would be Armageddon. Armageddon is a horrible war. This horrible war could easily precipitate human extinction.

Let us suppose. Some people know how to balance their own values. Let us suppose further. Those people do balance their own values. In that event, those people would balance their own emotions. Those people would experience emotional balance. They would be happy.

Let us suppose. A person is confronted with a sudden loss or unfortunate circumstance. Let us suppose further. The person does focus on the seed-body and its relationship to the universe. Let us suppose still further. The person does focus on the soul-spirit. In that event, the person is balancing values. The person is balancing emotions. An emotional balance is born out of a balance of values. The person experiences an emotional balance of the mind. The person is happy.

What are the effects of a balanced mind? Let us suppose. A person experiences emotional balance. The person is happy. The heart of the person is filled with joy, faith, and love. In that event, the person's emotions would act as forces upon the person's behaviors. The person would exhibit glad behaviors. Friendly tolerant peacemaking behaviors are glad behaviors. Truth telling, sharing, playing well with others, liberating, emancipating, and nurturing are glad behaviors. The person's glad behaviors would act as forces upon the person's body. The person's glad behaviors would be conducive to a state of good health in the person's body. The person's glad behaviors would act as forces upon the person's habitat. The person's glad behaviors would be conducive to a state of good health in the person's habitat. For that reason, emotional balance in the person's mind would be conducive to happiness and good health in the person's life. Happiness and good health in the person's life would be conducive to success and prosperity in the person's business.

Let us suppose. The minds of billions of people experience emotional balance. Billions of people are happy. The hearts of billions of people are filled with joy, faith, and love. In that event, the glad behaviors of billions of people would be conducive to a state of good health in the body consuming biosphere. The glad behaviors of billions of people would be conducive to a strong and stable civilization.

CHAPTER 43. BALANCE OF EMOTION AND THOUGHT

Thoughts, beliefs, and expectations follow from the discovery of the probable attributes of the seed-body and self. I value these thoughts, beliefs, and expectations. My values act as forces upon my emotions. I experience emotional forces of sorrow, fear, and anger. Thoughts, beliefs, and expectations follow from the mystery of the possible attributes of the soul-spirit and the world. I value these thoughts, beliefs, and expectations. My values act as forces upon my emotions. I experience emotional forces of joy, faith, and love. Joy, faith, and love balance sorrow, fear, and anger. I balance my values. I balance my emotions. I am happy. Quality of space and longevity of time are attributes of the soul-spirit. I describe these attributes as divine and eternal. Quality of space and longevity of time are attributes of the seed-body. I describe these attributes as fractal, infernal, and temporal. The soul-spirit balances the seed-body. Compassion and ignorance; forgiveness and guilt; freedom and inhibition; grace and disgrace; peace and suffering; joy and sorrow; these are dualities of experience. These dualities of experience follow from the combination of the soul-spirit and the seed-body. Quantity of energy and value of denominator are attributes of the world. I describe these attributes as infinite and one. Quantity of energy and value of denominator are attributes of self. I describe these attributes as finite and infinite. The world balances the self. Truth and lie; faith and fear; love and hate; unify and divide; create and destroy; heal and stress; these are dualities of action. These dualities of action follow from the combination of the world and the self. The two kinds of content are seed-body and soul-spirit. The two kinds of form are self and world. I combine the thought of one of the two kinds of content; with the thought of one of the two kinds of form. I do so once in every possible way. I create four things. I call these four things; the seed-body of the world, the seed-body of self, the soul-spirit of self, and the soul-spirit of the world.

A quantity of energy, a quality of space, a longevity of time, and a value of denominator are attributes of the seed-body of the world. I describe these attributes as infinite, fractal, infernal, and one. I value these ideas. My values act as forces upon my emotions. I experience sorrow. A quantity of energy, a quality of space, a longevity of time, and a value of denominator are attributes of the seed-body of self. I describe these attributes as finite, fractal, infernal temporal, and infinite. I value these ideas. My values act as forces upon my emotions. I experience fear. A quantity of energy, a quality of space, a longevity of time, and a value of denominator are attributes of the soul-spirit of self. I describe these attributes as finite, divine, eternal, and infinite. I value these ideas. My values act as forces upon my emotions. I experience anger. A quantity of energy, a quality of space, a longevity of time, and a value of denominator are attributes of the soul-spirit of the world. I describe these attributes as infinite, divine, eternal, and one. I value these ideas. My values act as forces upon my emotions. I experience joy.

I use my values. I build within my mind. I build my model of the totality. My model of the totality enables me. I balance the emotional forces of my mind. I am happy. My emotions act as forces upon my behaviors. I exhibit glad behaviors. My glad behaviors act as forces upon my body. My glad behaviors are conducive to a state of good health in my body. My glad behaviors act as forces upon my habitat. My glad behaviors are conducive to a state of good health in my habitat. For that reason, emotional balance in my mind is conducive to happiness and good health in my life. Happiness and good health in my life is conducive to success and prosperity in my business.

A probable thing may be sensed, perceived, discovered, and known to exist. A possible thing may only be imagined, believed, and expected to exist. Let us suppose. I value a probable thing. Let us suppose further. I value a possible thing. In that event, my values would act as forces on my emotions. The value of the probable thing would act with a greater force upon my emotions than would the value of the possible thing.

I compensate for this inequality. The divine eternal is the emotional balance to the fractal infernal temporal. The soul-spirit values the seed-body. The seed-body is the emotional balance to the soul-spirit. The infinite unity is the emotional balance to the alienation infinite. The world values the self. The self is the emotional balance to the world.

There can be no joy without sorrow. There can be no anger without fear. Life as a synthesis of soul-spirit and seed-body creates a means of experiencing a range of emotional possibilities. From these emotional possibilities, our soul-spirit derives entertainment.

I experience the entertainment. I act in a drama of life and death. I play in a game of survival and sacrifice. I take a test of success and failure. I ponder an existence of discovery and mystery. I perceive sensations of pleasure and pain. I feel the catharsis of comedy and tragedy. I enjoy my freedom. I form my own opinion about the totality. I select from a number, variety, and diversity of positive possibilities. The positive possibilities are only limited by my creative abilities and powers of imagination.

CHAPTER 44. GROWING STRONGER AS A BELIEVER

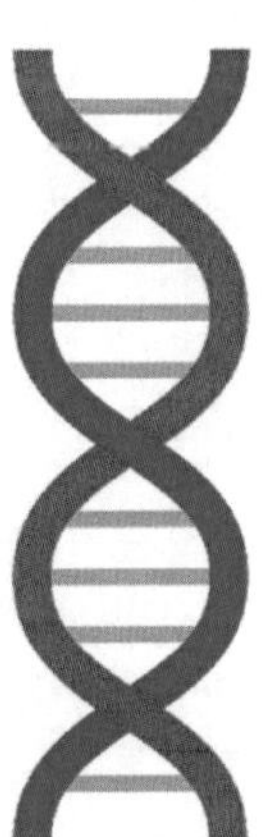

Each of us is born into this world. We are born naked, ignorant, and infantile. From the moment we are born, we begin gathering ideas. Ideas are thoughts, beliefs, and expectations about the totality. Some of these ideas come from within. Our seed-bodies store instinctual ideas. The instinctual ideas are stored in the form of DNA messages. The DNA messages may be found in every cell. Other ideas are experiential. These ideas come to us from the world around us. We value certain ideas. These certain ideas are our values. We use our values. We build within our minds. We build our models of the totality. We use our models of the totality. We navigate about our habitats. We orient ourselves towards the world. We explain the world to ourselves. Our models of the totality start out simple. Infants are either in a state of homeostasis or some physiological processes are out of balance. Imbalances in physiological processes may result in a wide range of unpleasant sensations including hunger, thirst, feeling cold or hot, nausea, fatigue, wetness, and or pain. These uncomfortable sensations may then result in emotional displays of sorrow, fear, and anger. At these times, the parent or guardian may attempt to comfort the child. Let us suppose. The parental guardian succeeds in comforting the child. The seed-body of the infant returns to a state of homeostasis. In that event, the infant experiences sensations of comfort, relief, and may display emotions of joy, faith, and love. Infants typically though not necessarily construct a very simple model of the totality. The relationship between infant and parental guardian is central to the very simple model of the totality.

As we grow towards maturity, our world experience expands. With this expansion of experience, our models of the totality grow and become ever more elaborate and ornate. For each and every one of us is continuously designing, building, remodeling, repairing, decorating, restoring, ornamenting, and reinforcing our models of the totality.

As I grow towards greater understanding, I come to several realizations. The totality consists of an existence of discovery and an existence of mystery. The existence of discovery is finite while the existence of mystery may be infinite. For that reason, I know next to nothing about almost everything.

I value my truths. I base my truths on the existence of discovery. I value my theories. I base my theories on the existence of scientifically reproducible discoveries. I value my most optimistic myths. I base my most optimistic myths on what is possible within the realm of mystery. My truths and my theories impose limitations upon what is possible within the realm of mystery. For that reason, my truths and my theories impose limitations upon my most optimistic myths.

My truths and my theories are ideas about discovered limitations of the material plane. My most optimistic myths originate in the mysterious limitlessness of the spiritual realm. For every idea of discovered limitation, a complementary idea of mysterious limitlessness exists. Ideas of discovered limitations neither deny nor exclude the possibility of ideas of mysterious limitlessness. Ideas of mysterious limitlessness neither deny nor exclude ideas of discovered limitations.

I value my truths, my theories, and my most optimistic myths. My values act as forces upon my emotions. The mysterious limitlessness of the spiritual realm is the emotional complement to the discovered limitations of the material plane. These complements combine to complete, make up a whole, and bring to perfection, my model of the totality. My model of the totality enables me. I balance my values. Thereby, I balance my emotions. I am happy. My emotions act as forces upon my behaviors. From happiness comes glad behaviors. My glad behaviors act as forces upon my body. My glad behaviors are conducive to good health in my body. My glad behaviors act as forces upon my habitat. My glad behaviors are conducive to good health in my habitat. For those reasons, emotional balance in my mind is conducive to happiness and good health in my life. Happiness and good health in my life is conducive to success and prosperity in my business.

CHAPTER 45. PROBLEMS AND SOLUTIONS

I gather information, draw logical inferences, and make conclusions. My capacity to perform these actions is limited. For that reason, my point of view is limited. The solution to my problems might come to me from my own limited capacity to gather information, draw logical inferences, and make conclusions. The solutions to my problems might come to me from the much greater capacity of billions of people. The solutions to my problems might come from the mind of an infinite life form. In these ideas, I have found a reason. I am most optimistic about self, world, and future. Let us suppose. I focus on solutions offered by the world. In that event, I have reason to be glad to be alive.

I believe in the value of truths. Scientists say. The truth is. It appears. One day, the seed-body of self will die. I believe in the value of the most optimistic myths. The most optimistic myths include. The life and immunity of the soul-spirit is divine and eternal. I have an infinite number, diversity, and variety of lives to live. I have an infinite number, diversity, and variety of bodies to give. I am seed, body, soul, and spirit.

While it is enjoyable to believe in the value of these ideas, right now I have a life to live. For that reason, I address the problems pertaining to my needs and aspirations. My needs and aspirations are. Achieve and maintain happiness, good health, and prosperity.

Responsibility for my health or sickness rests squarely on my shoulders. I live in a body-consuming biosphere. A primal conflict between predator and prey divides the body consuming biosphere. For that reason, I expect to be carrying the weight of a world of enemies on my shoulders. I choose to conduct myself in a manner. The manner gives me the best chance of producing rewards and reducing punishment.

I value truths. Scientists say. It appears. Laws of cause and effect predict the behavior, fate, and destiny of matter and energy in the known universe. Matter and energy in the known universe includes the matter and energy of my seed-body. For that reason, I am subject to these laws of cause and effect. The universe imposes these laws of cause and effect upon my seed-body.

The laws of cause and effect suggest a material standard of conduct. Let us suppose. I conform my behaviors to this material standard of conduct. In that event, my seed-body would experience rewards of compassion. These rewards of compassion would result in feelings of forgiveness. These feelings of forgiveness would result in acts of freedom. These acts of freedom would result in the unity of grace. This unity of grace would result in the healing of creation. This healing of creation would result in an expression of joy. My behaviors would most likely produce good health.

Let us suppose. I deviate from this material standard of conduct. In that event, my seed-body would experience punishment of ignorance. Punishment of ignorance would result in feelings of guilt. Feelings of guilt would result in acts of inhibition. Acts of inhibition would result in the division of disgrace. Division of disgrace would result in the suffering of destruction. This suffering of destruction would result in expression of sorrow. My behaviors would most likely produce disease.

Let us suppose. I tell the truth. In that event, people may have faith in my words. Let us suppose. People have faith in my words. In that event, love may follow. Let us suppose. Love follows. In that event, we may achieve unity. Let us suppose. We achieve unity. In that event, we may create healing together. Let us suppose. We create healing together. In that event, we would grow ever closer to knowing infinity divinity.

Let us suppose. I lie. In that event, people may have fear of my words. Let us suppose. People have fear of my words. In that event, hate may follow. Let us suppose. Hate follows. In that event, division may occur. Let us suppose. Division occurs. In that event, destruction may follow. Let us suppose. Destruction follows. In that event, stress may overwhelm our bodies. Let us suppose. Stress overwhelms our bodies. In that event, we would grow ever closer to knowing alienation abomination.

I ponder my relationships. People come to me. I question them. What do they have to say? I listen. What do they do? I observe them. I decide how. I make up my mind. I weigh the potential risks and benefits of investing my energy, space, and time in my relationships.

Let us suppose. A person does not want to be seen with me in public. The person is ashamed. The person believes. I should be ashamed. In that event, the person might abandon me when the going gets tough. The person might condemn me when the going gets tough. The person is unreliable. For that reason, I would not invest my energy, space, and time in a relationship with the person.

Let us suppose. A person does want to be seen with me in public. The person is proud. The person believes. I should be proud. In that event, the person might support me when the going gets tough. The person might defend me when the going gets tough. The person is reliable. For that reason, I would invest my energy, space, and time in a relationship with the person.

Let us suppose. A person says to me. You are 'evil', 'demon possessed', 'irrational', or 'insane'. In that event, the person is probably not a friend. The person is possibly an enemy. Let us suppose further. I believe in the value of this person's judgment. In that event, my values would act as forces upon my emotions. My heart would fill with sorrow, fear, and anger. I would be unhappy. My emotions would act as forces upon my behaviors. I would exhibit sad, mad, and bad behaviors. My sad, mad, and bad behaviors would act as forces upon my body. My sad, mad, and bad behaviors would be conducive to a state of disease in my body. Unhappiness and disease are not a desirable result. For that reason, I would not believe in the value of this person's judgment.

Let us suppose. A person says to me. We are 'good', 'superstars', 'Soul Children', 'logical', 'rational', and 'sane'. In that event, this person is probably not an enemy. The person is possibly a friend. Let us suppose further. I believe in the value of this person's judgement. In that event, my values would act as forces upon my emotions. I would be happy. My emotions would act as forces upon my behaviors. I would exhibit glad behaviors. My glad behaviors would act as forces upon my habitat. My glad behaviors would be conducive to a state of good health in my habitat. My glad behaviors would act as forces upon my body. My glad behaviors would be conducive to a state of good health in my body. Happiness and good health are desirable results. For that reason, I would believe in the value of this person's judgment.

Let us suppose. A person says. "I am your enemy". In that event, I would take the person's word for it. Let us suppose. My enemies present themselves to me as being my friends. Let us suppose further. Being friends is a way of getting close enough to hurt me. In that event, I believe in the value of the most optimistic myths. I rely upon continuous spiritual communion to guide my steps.

Let us suppose. A person says. "I am your friend". In that event, I would take the person's word for it. Let us suppose. Some of my friends present themselves to me as being my enemies. Let us suppose further. Being enemies is a way of getting far enough away to help me. In that event, I believe in the value of the most optimistic myths. I rely upon continuous spiritual communion to guide my steps.

CHAPTER 46. CONTRADICTIONS BETWEEN IMAGINED AND KNOWN EXISTENCE

Sometimes a contradiction between an imagined existence and known existence becomes obvious. The consequences of a poorly designed physical structure may be exposure to the elements. The consequences of a poorly designed model of the totality may be emotional unbalance.

Let us suppose. A person builds a model of the totality. Let us suppose further. The model of the totality does not enable the person. The person can not balance the emotional forces of the person's mind. In that event, the model of the totality is poorly designed. A poorly designed model of the totality may be a manageable problem in the spring of childhood and summer of adulthood. However, some people might endure emotional unbalance in the fall of disease and winter of death. As the end of life approaches, a poorly built model of the totality may leave the occupying architect in misery.

Let us suppose. A person builds a model of the totality. Let us suppose further. The model of the totality does enable the person. The person can balance the emotional forces of the person's mind. In that event, the model of the totality is well designed.

I value my truths. I base my truths on the existence of discovery. I value my theories. I base my theories on the existence of scientifically reproducible discoveries. I assimilate and accommodate new truths and new theories as these become available to me. I value my most optimistic myths. I base my most optimistic myths on what is possible within the realm of mystery. Let us suppose. I find. My most optimistic myths are in conflict with my truths and my theories. In that event, I remake my most optimistic myths.

Let us suppose. A contradiction between imagined existence and known existence becomes obvious. In that event, I endeavor to reimagine existence. I remake my most optimistic myths. I restore my model of the totality to a state of perfection.

CHAPTER 47. PRAGMATIC EVALUATION OF MY MODEL

Now I pause a moment and evaluate my model of the totality. What is the best model of all? On what criterion should I make such a judgment? My criterion for making such a judgment follows from my objectives. My objectives are. To best satisfy my needs and aspirations. My needs and aspirations are. Achieve and maintain happiness, good health, and prosperity.

I align my values with my needs and aspiration. My values act as forces upon my emotions. I balance the emotional forces of my mind. I am happy.

My emotions act as forces upon my behaviors. I exhibit glad behaviors. Glad behaviors are friendly behaviors, not racist behaviors. Glad behaviors are tolerant behaviors, not fascist behaviors. Glad behaviors are peacemaking behaviors, not warmongering behaviors. Friendly tolerant peacemaking behaviors are glad behaviors. Truth telling, sharing, playing well with others, liberating, emancipating, and nurturing are glad behaviors.

My glad behaviors act as forces upon my body. My glad behaviors are conducive to a state of good health in my body. My glad behaviors act as forces upon my habitat. My glad behaviors are conducive to a state of good health in my habitat. For those reasons, emotional balance in my mind is conducive to happiness and good health in my life. Happiness and good health in my life are conducive to success and prosperity in my business.

I love Healthy Agnostic Positivistic Nationalistic Spiritization of self and world. To spiritize is to impart a spiritual nature to something. Healthy Agnostic Positivistic Nationalistic Spiritization of self and world requires several additional conditions be satisfied. The first condition is. I spiritize self and world as a healthy person would. I balance the emotional forces of my mind. Emotional balance in my mind is conducive to happiness and good health in my life. The second condition is. I spiritize self and world as an agnostic would: I humbly admit. I know next to nothing about almost everything. I do not know whether or not. My most optimistic myths are true. The third condition is. I spiritize self and world as a positivist would: I make a clear distinction between truths, lies, and myths. The fourth condition is. I spiritize self and world as a nationalist would. I free myself to be strong enough in all ways. I devote myself to the interests, needs, and aspirations of my self, family, community, nation, culture, and world.

I take Healthy Agnostic Positivistic Nationalistic Spiritization of self and world to its logical extreme in a process. The process may be broken down into four steps. The first step is. I affirm. My model of the totality contains two kinds of content. These two kinds of content are seed-body and soul-spirit. My model of the totality contains two kinds of form. These two kinds of form are self and world. I combine the idea of one of the two kinds of content; with the idea of one of two kinds of form. I do so once in every possible way. I create the idea of four things. These four things are the seed-body of the world, the seed-body of self, the soul-spirit of self, and the soul-spirit of the world. The second step is. I recognize. Quantity of energy, quality of space, longevity of time, and value of denominator are attributes of these four things. Possible values for the description of any given attribute of these four things exist in a range of values. My knowledge of truths and theories limits the range of values. I base my truths on the existence of discovery. I base my theories on the existence of scientifically reproducible discoveries. My myths do not limit the range of values. I base my myths on what is possible within the realm of mystery. The third step is. The soul-spirit has attributes. These attributes include quality of space, and longevity of time. I select the most optimistic values for these attributes. The world has attributes. These attributes include quantity of energy and value of denominator. I select the most optimistic values for these attributes. The seed-body has attributes. These attributes include quality of space and longevity of time. I select true values for these attributes. The self has attributes. These attributes include quantity of energy and value of denominator. I select true values for these attributes. The fourth step is. I combine all values. By doing so, I balance my values. My values act as forces upon my emotions. Joy, faith, and love, balance sorrow, fear, and anger. I balance the emotional forces of my mind. I am happy.

The seed-body of the world has attributes. These attributes include a quantity of energy, a quality of space, a longevity of time, and a value of denominator. I select values for the description of these attributes. I describe the quantity of energy as infinite. I describe the quality of space as fractal. I describe the longevity of time as infernal. I describe the value of denominator as one. I describe these attributes as infinite, fractal, infernal, and one.

The seed-body of self has attributes. These attributes include a quantity of energy, a quality of space, a longevity of time, and a value of denominator. I select values for the description of these attributes. I describe the quantity of energy as finite. I describe the quality of space as fractal. I describe the longevity of time as infernal temporal. I describe the value of denominator as infinite. I describe these attributes as finite, fractal, infernal temporal, and infinite.

The soul-spirit of self has attributes. These attributes include a quantity of energy, a quality of space, a longevity of time, and a value of denominator. I select values for the description of these attributes. I describe the quantity of energy as finite. I describe the quality of space as divine. I describe the longevity of time as eternal. I describe the value of denominator as infinite. I describe these attributes as finite, divine, eternal, and infinite.

The soul-spirit of the world has attributes. These attributes include a quantity of energy, a quality of space, a longevity of time, and a value of denominator. I select values for the description of these attributes. I describe the quantity of energy as infinite. I describe the quality of space as divine. I describe the longevity of time as eternal. I describe the value of denominator as one. I describe these attributes as infinite, divine, eternal, and one.

Fractal geometry is evident within the infernal temporal universe. This fractal geometry extends beyond the grasp of my senses and perceptions into the innermost and outer most reaches of the totality. An infinite being creates an infinite number of finite creatures. The infinite number of finite creatures are created in the image of the infinite being. This infinite being endows each finite creature with a seed-body and a soul-spirit.

The result is. The infinite being self-organizes into an infinite four. The infinite four consists of an infinite seed, an infinite body, an infinite soul, and an infinite spirit. The infinite seed is the same as the seed-body of the world. The infinite body is the same as the seed-body of self and the seed-bodies of all finite creatures. The infinite soul is the same as the soul-spirit of self and the soul-spirits of all finite creatures. The infinite spirit is the same as the soul-spirit of the world.

An infinite number, variety, and diversity of life forms engage in an infinite series of conflicts, dramas, mysteries, discoveries, comedies, tragedies, intrigues, and entertainments. Each of these life forms acts in any way their divine eternal souls may choose. The spirit bestows infinite love, divine forgiveness, eternal freedom, and unifying grace upon all divine eternal souls. Out of an infinite number, diversity, and variety of life forms follows an infinite number, diversity, and variety of possibilities for thought, feeling, and action.

Although some may not be consciously aware of this fact, it is true. We fashion our realities within our own minds. We build models of the totality. We use our models. We navigate about our habitat. We orient ourselves towards the existence. We explain existence to ourselves.

My model of the totality is entertaining enough to be worthy of an infinite divine eternal being. This infinite divine eternal being is everything, everywhere, at all times. The infinite divine eternal being enjoys entertainment. The drama of life and death entertains. For that reason, this infinite divine eternal being transforms designs for large universes of the correct kind to support living infernal fractal entities from possibility into existence.

CHAPTER 48. THE LOGIC OF THE MIND

The logic of the emotional mind is associative. People communicate ideas. People use similes, metaphors, and images. Similes, metaphors, and images are associative elements. People use these elements in literature, film, poetry, song, theatre, and opera. The elements speak directly to the emotional mind. The elements symbolize reality. The elements trigger a memory of reality. The emotional mind takes the elements to be the same as reality.

Religious authority figures speak in the language of emotion. They teach in parables, fables, and stories. Religious symbol and ritual make little sense from a rational point of view. Religious symbol and ritual speak to followers in the vernacular of the heart.

The emotional mind follows its own logic and its own rules. One element stands for another. The emotional mind need not define things by their objective identity. The appearance of things can be far more important than the actuality of things. The emotional mind is indiscriminate. Some things have similar striking features. The emotional mind connects those things.

The logic of the thinking mind is the metaphysics of reality. The real is the rational. The rational is the real. The rational mind makes logical connections between cause and effect.

The presence of the universe is the presence of evidence. The presence of evidence in the form of the universe provides premises. Those premises enable us. We can make valid logical inductive inferences. We can make myths. Myths cannot be verified to be true. Myths can not be verified to be false. Myths are unverifiable and unfalsifiable. An infinite number, diversity, and variety of myths are made possible by the totality.

Validity is the quality of being logical or factually sound. The validity of myths follows from two definitions of the word valid. The two definitions are a logical definition and a pragmatic definition.

The logical definition of the word valid is: having a sound basis in logic or fact; reasonable or cogent. The logical definition of the word valid leads to a conclusion. The conclusion is. Each myth is an equally valid possibility.

The pragmatic definition of the word valid is: producing the desired results. Let us suppose. The desired results are happiness, good health, and prosperity. In that event, optimistic myths are more valid. Pessimistic myths are less valid or even invalid.

Belief in the value of pessimistic myths has a capacity to produce emotional imbalance in our minds. Emotional imbalance in our minds is not conducive to happiness and good health in our lives. For those reasons, I suggest. We devalue pessimistic myths.

Belief in the value of the most optimistic myths has a capacity to produce emotional balance in our minds. Emotional balance in our minds is conducive to happiness and good health in our lives. For those reasons, I suggest. We value the most optimistic myths.

CHAPTER 49. THE CALCULATION OF THE PROBABILITY THAT A MYTH MAY BE TRUE

A totality exists. For that reason, we are part of the totality. The totality is everything, everywhere, at all times. Some things existed in the past. Those things are part of the totality. Some things exist right now. Those things are part of the totality. Some things will exist in the future. Those things are part of the totality. The totality transcends our knowledge and comprehension. For that reason, the totality makes possible an infinite number, diversity, and variety of ideas.

Ideas are thoughts, beliefs, and expectations about the totality. Our bodies make our senses and perceptions available to us. Our senses and perceptions enable us. We have the ability. We can verify the truth of ideas. We have the ability. We can verify the falsity of ideas.

A seed-body has attributes. The attributes are a finite quantity of energy, a fractal quality of space, a temporal longevity of time, and an infinite denominator. The attributes of the seed-body limit our abilities. A seed-body occupies specific points in energy, space, and time. Our occupation of specific points in energy, space, and time, limits our abilities. The totality may be infinite. Our abilities are limited. For that reason, we know next to nothing about almost everything. Truths are rare. Lies are rare. Myths are infinitely abundant.

Myths are ideas. Myths are both unverifiable and unfalsifiable. We cannot verify whether or not. Myths are true. We cannot verify whether or not. Myths are false. We can only verify. Myths are ideas.

Myths have a certain probability of being true. Let us suppose. A person wishes to calculate the certain probability. In that event, any competent scientist would admit. We can gather objective evidence. We can apply our probability theories. We can make inductive and deductive inferences. We can use logic. We can arrive at conclusions. However, our abilities to do so are limited. For that reason, the act of making such a calculation is beyond our capabilities.

CHAPTER 50. OCCAM'S RAZOR

Let us suppose. A person observes a fact or event. Let us suppose further. The cause or explanation for the fact or event is in question. In that event, the person might use the word phenomenon to describe the observable fact or event. The word phenomena is a plural form of the word phenomenon.

Occam's razor is a scientific rule. People often interpret Occam's Razor to mean. An explanation for phenomena should first be attempted in terms of knowledge of truths and theories. The simplest of two or more competing theories is preferable.

The totality is a phenomenon. Let us suppose. A person interprets Occam's razor to mean. The person should value only truths and theories. The person should devalue all myths. In that event, the person would use these values. The person would build within the person's mind. The person would build a model of the totality. The totality would present the person with a problem. The problem would be. The person knows next to nothing about almost everything. Knowledge of truths and theories would not be sufficient. The person would not be able to complete the model of the totality. Myths would be needed.

How does the person resolve this problem? Let us suppose. The person decides. Our seed-bodies make senses and perceptions available to us. We can use our senses and perceptions. We can find things. Science makes tools available to us. Scientists can use our tools of science. Scientists can discover things. Science makes scientific theories available to us. Scientists can use our scientific theories. Scientists can predict things. Only these things exist. Let us suppose further. The person reasons. Taking any other position would be irrational, illogical, and/or insane. In that event, the person would be mistaken.

The person has not devalued all myths. On the contrary, the person is part of the totality. The totality makes possible an infinite number, diversity, and variety of myths. For that reason, it is logical to infer. The person believes in the value of pessimistic myths. These pessimistic myths are. Self is only a seed and a body. Self has only one life to live. Self has only one body to give. A godless totality exists.

Pessimism correlates with sorrow, fear, anger, and disease. Let us suppose. The person desires happiness and good health. In that event, belief in the value of these pessimistic myths would be illogical, irrational, and/or insane.

Our values act as forces upon our emotions. Our emotions act as forces upon our behaviors. Our behaviors act as forces upon our bodies. Our behaviors act as forces upon our habitats. For that reason, the person's belief in the value of pessimistic myths is problematic. This problem is a danger to this person, the person's family, the person's community, and maybe even the whole world.

I help people to get back on the right track to happiness, good health, and prosperity. I help people who have lost their minds to find their minds. The totality presents me with a problem. The problem is. I know next to nothing about almost everything. How do I resolve this problem? I decide. Our seed-bodies make senses and perceptions available to us. We can use our senses and perceptions. We can find things. Science makes tools available to us. Scientists can use our tools of science. Scientists can discover things. Science makes scientific theories available to us. Scientists can use our scientific theories. Scientists can predict things. These things exist and everything else exists. The everything else enables us. We can believe in the value of the most optimistic myths. We can have the highest esteem of the totality. We can balance the emotional forces of our minds. Emotional balance in our minds is conducive to happiness and good health in our lives. Happiness and good health in our lives is conducive to success and prosperity in our businesses.

Optimism correlates with happiness, good health, and prosperity. Let us suppose. We desire happiness, good health, and prosperity. In that event, belief in the value of the most optimistic myths would be rational, logical, and sane. Taking any other position would be irrational, illogical, and/or insane.

CHAPTER 51. OBJECTIVE EVIDENCE, SUBJECTIVE EVIDENCE, AND THE HOUSE OF IDEOLOGY

I value truths. Let us suppose. We gather evidence by use of our senses and perceptions. In that event, the evidence is objective evidence. Let us suppose. We use tools of science. In that event, we enhance our senses and perceptions. Let us suppose. We use our enhanced senses and perceptions. We gather evidence. In that event, the evidence is objective evidence. Objective evidence is uninfluenced by emotion, surmise, or personal prejudice. Objective evidence is verifiable externally. Let us suppose. Objective evidence is scientifically reproducible. Let us suppose further. The objective evidence leads by valid logical inferences to a conclusion. Let us suppose still further. The conclusion is. A certain idea is true. In that event, I classify the certain idea as a truth. Let us suppose. The conclusion is. A certain theory is scientific. In that event, I classify the certain theory as a scientific theory.

My seed-body makes senses and perceptions available to me. My senses and perceptions enable me. I can verify. Truths are true. I can verify. Lies are false. However, I cannot verify whether or not. The most optimistic myths are true. I cannot verify whether or not. The most optimistic myths are false. The most optimistic myths are both unverifiable and unfalsifiable. I value the most optimistic myths. For what reason do I value the most optimistic myths? The only remaining reason is. My inspiration, intuition, and judgment has led me to value the most optimistic myths.

The main argument against trusting my inspiration, intuition, and judgment is. My inspiration, intuition, and judgment are subjective. My inspiration, intuition, and judgment are subject to my desire to best satisfy my needs and aspirations. My needs and aspirations are. Achieve and maintain happiness, good health, and prosperity.

My inspiration, intuition, and judgment tell me. My values act as forces upon my emotions. The most powerful emotional forces of joy, faith, and love follow from my belief in the value of the most optimistic myths. The most optimistic myths include. The life and immunity of the soul-spirit is, eternal and divine. The most powerful emotional forces of sorrow, fear, and anger follow from my belief in the value of truths. The truths include. It appears. One day, the seed-body of self will die. Joy, faith, and love, balance sorrow, fear, and anger. Happiness is a balance of the emotional forces of the mind. I balance the emotional forces of my mind. I am happy.

My inspiration, intuition, and judgment tell me. My emotions act as forces upon my behaviors. I exhibit glad behaviors. Glad behaviors are friendly behaviors, not racist behaviors. Glad behaviors are tolerant behaviors, not fascist behaviors. Glad behaviors are peacemaking behaviors, not warmongering behaviors. Truth telling, sharing, playing well with others, liberating, emancipating, and nurturing are glad behaviors.

My inspiration, intuition, and judgment tell me. My glad behaviors act as forces upon my body. My glad behaviors are conducive to a state of good health in my body. My glad behaviors act as forces upon my habitat. My glad behaviors are conducive to a state of good health in my habitat. For those reasons, emotional balance in my mind is conducive to happiness and good health in my life. Happiness and good health in my life is conducive to success and prosperity in my business.

My inspiration, intuition, and judgment lead me to value the most optimistic myths. My inspiration, intuition, and judgment offers subjective evidence. The subjective nature of the evidence does not mean. My inspiration, intuition, and judgment are inherently wrong. Rather, it means. My inspiration, intuition, and judgment are subjective.

A scientific community seeks truths and theories. Limited amounts of energy, space, and time are available to the scientific community. I am willing to concede. The most valid approach to managing the limited energy, space, and time is. Focus on senses, perceptions, and objective evidence.

An ideological community makes myths. The more important test for any myth is. Does my belief in the value of this myth enable me? Can I best satisfy my needs and aspirations? A limited amount of energy, space, and time is available to the ideological community. I think, believe, and predict. The most valid approach to managing the limited energy, space, and time is. Focus on inspiration, intuition, judgment, and subjective evidence.

My soul rides my seed-body. My soul gets inside my mind. My soul guides my thoughts, beliefs, and expectations. I build within my mind. I build my model of the totality. My model of the totality is right for me.

CHAPTER 52. FURTHER ORNAMENTATION OF MY MODEL

I desire happiness and good health in my life. For that reason, I believe in the value of the most optimistic myths. Let us suppose. I attempt to prove the most optimistic myths are true. In that event, I must use my senses and perceptions. I must gather objective evidence. The objective evidence must lead by valid logical deductive inference to a conclusion. The conclusion must be. The most optimistic myths are true.

My seed-body makes senses and perceptions available to me. I use my senses and perceptions. I verify the truth of ideas. I verify the falsity of ideas. A finite quantity of energy, a fractal quality of space, an infernal temporal longevity of time, and an infinite value of denominator are attributes of my seed-body. The attributes of my seed-body limit my senses and perceptions. My seed-body occupies specific points in energy, space, and time. My occupation of specific points in energy, space, and time, limits my senses and perceptions. My senses and perceptions limit my abilities. I can gather a limited amount of objective evidence. I can make a limited number of inferences. I can draw a limited number of conclusions. I can gather a limited amount of truths. For those reasons, I know a finite amount about an infinite subject. I admit. I know next to nothing about almost everything.

Myths are ideas. My senses and perceptions do not enable me. I can not verify whether or not. Myths are true. I can not verify whether or not. Myths are false. Myths are both unverifiable and unfalsifiable. For that reason, I affirm. I do not have the ability. I can not possess knowledge of the nonexistence of deities. This affirmation makes me an agnostic. I claim. The inability to know leads me to a belief. This claim makes me an agnostic theist.

How do I know an infinite quantity of energy with a finite seed-body? How do I know a divine quality of space with a fractal seed-body? How do I know an eternal longevity of time with an infernal temporal seed-body? How do I know the totality with an infinitesimal seed-body? I do not know. My inspiration, intuition, and judgment lead me. I think, believe, and predict.

My inability to know does not preclude the existence of an infinite divine eternal being. I do not know. However, I also do not know what I do not know. For all I know. It is possible. My soul interacts with my seed-body on a subatomic level of probability and possibility. The interaction with my seed-body on a subatomic level of probability and possibility is presently much too subtle for our best science to discover. My soul guides my conscious mind. For that reason, I write these very words.

The existence of discovery and the existence of mystery make possible an infinite number, diversity, and variety of myths. These myths are only limited by our creative abilities and powers of imagination. In the absence of an ability to achieve verification by use of my senses and perceptions, I rely upon personal revelations:

My values act as forces upon my emotions. I believe in the value of the most optimistic myths.

The most powerful emotional forces of joy, faith, and love follow from the mystery of the most optimistic myths. The most optimistic myths include. The life and immunity of the soul-spirit is, eternal and divine. I believe in the value of truths. The most powerful emotional forces of sorrow, fear, and anger follow from the discovery of a truth. The truth is. It appears. One day, the seed-body of self will die. Joy, faith, and love, balance sorrow, fear, and anger. Happiness is a balance of the emotional forces of the mind. I balance the emotional forces of my mind. I am happy.

My emotions act as forces upon my behaviors. I exhibit glad behaviors. Friendly tolerant peacemaking behaviors are glad behaviors. Truth telling, sharing, playing well with others, liberating, emancipating, and nurturing are glad behaviors. My glad behaviors act as forces upon my body. My glad behaviors bring about a state of good health in my body. My glad behaviors act as forces upon my habitat. My glad behaviors bring about a state of good health in my habitat. For those reasons, emotional balance in my mind is conducive to happiness and good health in my life.

Scientific research seems to affirm a theory. The theory is. Optimistic thoughts, beliefs, and expectations have a positive influence on our health. Our optimistic thoughts, beliefs, and expectations improve our various health behaviors, our immune functions, and our biochemical functions. The improvement of our various health behaviors, our immune functions, and our biochemical functions makes our bodies more resistant to illness and better able to recover from existing disease. For those reasons, I believe in the value of the most optimistic myths.

The most optimistic myths are all about infinite abundance. An infinite divine eternal being is everything, everywhere, at all times. The infinite divine eternal being enjoys entertainment. The drama of life and death entertains. For that reason, the infinite divine eternal being manifests as an infinite four. The infinite four are an infinite seed, an infinite body, an infinite soul, and an infinite spirit. The infinite seed is an infinite number, diversity, and variety of large universes of the correct kind to support living infernal fractal entities. The infinite body is the seed-body of self and the seed-bodies of all of the other living infernal fractal entities. The infinite soul is the soul-spirit of self and the soul-spirits of all of the other living infernal fractal entities. The infinite spirit is the infinite divine eternal being. Mother God is the infinite soul-spirit. Father Love is the infinite seed-body. The union of Mother God and Father Love creates life. We are Soul Children.

I am not in a position to know the spiritual truth. I am in a position to value the most optimistic myths. I value the most optimistic myths. I choose to enjoy the potential emotional and physiological benefits of valuing the most optimistic myths. The act of valuing the most optimistic myths enables me. I have the highest esteem of the totality. I produce emotional balance in my mind. Emotional balance in my mind is conducive to happiness and good health in my life. Happiness and good health in my life are conducive to success and prosperity in my business. I best satisfy my needs and aspirations. My needs and aspirations are. Achieve and maintain happiness, good health, and prosperity.

CHAPTER 53. THE FOUR MOTIVATIONS THEORY

The seed, the body, the soul, and the spirit; are the four structures. The four structures combine. The four structures form life.

The Four Motivations Theory enables me. I predict. Create, survive, perfect, and revive are four motivations. The seed creates a body. The body survives in a body consuming biosphere. A primal conflict between predator and prey divides the body-consuming biosphere. The soul perfects bodies with each generation. The global culture moves towards ever-higher levels of conscious awareness. The drama of life and death entertains. The spirit revives the drama of life and death. The spirit revives the life of the soul after the death of the seed-body. The spirit revives the life of the body-consuming biosphere.

The Four Motivations Theory offers a framework through which we can understand the fundamental drivers behind human existence and the broader dynamics of life on Earth. According to this theory, the motivations of creation, survival, perfection, and revival underpin our experiences and interactions within the world.

Creation serves as the initial spark, the impulse to bring forth new forms and expressions into existence. Like a seed planting itself in fertile soil, creation sets the stage for the emergence of life and consciousness.

Survival, the second motivation, speaks to the imperative to sustain and perpetuate life in a world defined by the primal conflict between predator and prey. Within the body-consuming biosphere, survival is paramount, driving organisms to adapt and evolve in order to thrive in their respective environments.

Perfection represents the ongoing process of refinement and improvement, as the soul seeks to perfect bodies with each successive generation. This pursuit of excellence propels the evolution of consciousness and the advancement of global culture towards ever-higher levels of awareness and understanding.

Finally, revival speaks to the cyclical nature of existence, where the drama of life and death unfolds in a perpetual dance of creation and destruction. The spirit, imbued with the power of renewal, revives the essence of life after the death of the seed-body, breathing new energy into the soul and the body-consuming biosphere alike.

In this grand narrative of existence, creation, survival, perfection, and revival intertwine to form the fabric of life itself. Each motivation plays a vital role in shaping our experiences and interactions, guiding us on a journey of growth, transformation, and ultimately, transcendence. Through the lens of the Four Motivations Theory, we gain insight into underlying forces. These underlying forces drive the drama of life and death, and an eternal cycle of renewal. The eternal cycle of renewal sustains the tapestry of existence.

The spectrum of belief regarding the existence of deities encompasses a variety of perspectives, each with its own nuances and convictions. To simplify this complexity, individuals can be sorted into four broad categories based on their beliefs and claims about knowledge: gnostic theists, agnostic atheists, gnostic atheists, and agnostic theists.

Gnostic theists are individuals who claim to have knowledge of the existence of at least one deity. They affirm their belief in a higher power or powers with confidence. Their belief is often based on personal experiences, religious teachings, or philosophical convictions. For them, the existence of a deity is a matter of certainty rather than speculation.

Agnostic atheists, on the other hand, lack belief in the existence of deities. However, they do not claim to possess knowledge about their nonexistence. They acknowledge the absence of evidence for the existence of gods. For that reason, they refrain from affirming any belief in them. However, they also recognize the limitations of human knowledge. They do not assert absolute certainty regarding the absence of deities.

Gnostic atheists assert knowledge of the nonexistence of deities. They confidently claim. No gods exist. Their claim is often based on logical arguments, scientific evidence, or philosophical reasoning. They reject the possibility of divine beings with a high degree of certainty. They view the concept of gods as incompatible with their understanding of reality.

Agnostic theists occupy a unique position. They acknowledge their belief in the existence of at least one deity while also admitting uncertainty regarding their knowledge. They may hold strong faith in a higher power or divine being. However, they recognize the inherent limitations of human understanding when it comes to matters of spirituality and metaphysics.

These four categories provide a framework for understanding the diverse range of beliefs and attitudes towards the existence of deities. By considering both belief and claims to knowledge, individuals can better articulate their perspectives and engage in meaningful discussions about faith, skepticism, and the nature of existence.

The act of creation serves as a foundational motivation, driving the seed—the essence of life—to bring forth new forms and expressions into existence. This primal urge to create not only shapes the physical world but also influences aspects of identity, including sexual orientation, political orientation, and spiritual orientation.

In the realm of sexual orientation, the motivation of the seed reinforces heterosexuality—the attraction to individuals of the opposite sex. This alignment with heterosexuality reflects the biological imperative to reproduce and propagate the species, ensuring the continuation of life through procreation.

Similarly, the motivation of the seed extends to political orientation, often manifesting as a tendency towards fundamentalism. Fundamentalism is a strict adherence to traditional beliefs and values. Just as the seed seeks stability and continuity in the act of creation, fundamentalism provides a sense of structure and order in the realm of governance and societal organization.

At the spiritual level, the motivation of the seed fosters a gnostic theistic orientation—a belief in the existence of at least one deity and the pursuit of esoteric knowledge and understanding. This spiritual orientation reflects the innate human longing for transcendence and meaning, driving individuals to seek deeper truths beyond the material world.

Gnostic theists affirm. They have an ability. They can possess knowledge of the existence of at least one deity. Gnostic theists claim. The ability to know leads to a belief. The belief is. At least one deity exists. From this belief follows a desire. The desire is. Gnostic theists wish to belong to communities of gnostic theists. From the act of belonging to communities of gnostic theists follows a desire for political power. From this desire for political power follows the rise of fundamentalism. If everything is justified by a lie, then their leaders take away tolerance and freedom. The lie is. A myth is a truth.

The fundamental motivation of the body is survival. Survival is an innate drive to maintain life and ensure its continuation in the face of challenges and threats. This primal urge to survive influences various aspects of identity, including sexual orientation, political orientation, and spiritual orientation.

In the realm of sexual orientation, the motivation of the body reinforces asexuality—a lack of sexual attraction to others. While sexuality plays a significant role in many individuals' lives, those with an asexual orientation may prioritize other aspects of existence over sexual relationships, focusing instead on personal growth, relationships, and pursuits beyond the realm of physical intimacy.

Similarly, the motivation of the body extends to political orientation, often manifesting as a tendency towards communism. Communism is a socio-political ideology centered around collective ownership of resources and the equitable distribution of wealth and power. Just as the body seeks to ensure its survival through cooperation and mutual support, communism emphasizes solidarity and cooperation among individuals to address societal needs and challenges.

At the spiritual level, the motivation of the body fosters an agnostic atheistic orientation —a stance characterized by skepticism towards the existence of deities and a lack of belief in supernatural phenomena. This spiritual orientation reflects a focus on empirical evidence and rational inquiry, rejecting supernatural explanations in favor of naturalistic perspectives rooted in science and reason.

Agnostic atheists affirm. They do not have an ability. They can not possess knowledge of the existence of deities. Agnostic atheists claim. The inability to know leads to a lack of belief. From this lack of belief follows a desire. The desire is. Agnostic atheists wish to belong to communities of agnostic atheists. From the act of belonging to communities of agnostic atheists follows a desire for political power. From this desire for political power follows the rise of communism. If everything is justified by their theories of evolution, then their leaders take away happiness and balance.

At the core of human existence lies the motivation of the soul—to perfect, refine, and evolve towards higher states of being. This innate drive for perfection influences various aspects of identity, including sexual orientation, political orientation, and spiritual orientation.

In the realm of sexual orientation, the motivation of the soul reinforces homosexuality—the romantic and sexual attraction to individuals of the same gender. Just as the soul seeks harmony and alignment within itself, homosexuality reflects the natural expression of love and connection between individuals, regardless of gender.

Similarly, the motivation of the soul extends to political orientation, often manifesting as a tendency towards capitalism. Capitalism is a socio-economic system characterized by private ownership of property, free markets, and individual enterprise. Capitalism resonates with the values of individual autonomy and self-expression, providing opportunities for individuals to pursue their unique talents and aspirations in the pursuit of personal and collective prosperity.

At the spiritual level, the motivation of the soul fosters a gnostic atheistic orientation—a philosophical stance grounded in the pursuit of inner knowledge and understanding, free from the constraints of dogma and religious authority. Gnostic atheism emphasizes the importance of critical inquiry and personal revelation in the search for truth, rejecting supernatural explanations in favor of rational and empirical approaches to spirituality.

Gnostic atheists affirm. They have an ability. They can possess knowledge of the non-existence of deities. From this affirmation follows a claim. Gnostic atheists claim. This ability to know leads to a lack of belief. From this lack of belief follows a desire. The desire is. Gnostic atheists wish to belong to communities of gnostic atheists. From the act of belonging to communities of gnostic atheists follows a desire for political power. From this desire for political power follows the rise of capitalism. If everything is justified by a profit in the market, then their leaders take away liberty and security.

At the heart of the human experience lies the motivation of the spirit—to revitalize, rejuvenate, and bring new life to the world. This intrinsic drive for revival influences various aspects of identity, including sexual orientation, political orientation, and spiritual orientation.

In the realm of sexual orientation, the motivation of the spirit reinforces bisexuality—the capacity to experience romantic or sexual attraction to individuals of both the same and different genders. Bisexuality embodies the fluidity and expansiveness of the human spirit, embracing the diversity of human connections and relationships without rigid boundaries or limitations.

Similarly, the motivation of the spirit extends to political orientation, often manifesting as a tendency towards socialism. Socialism is a socio-political ideology centered around collective ownership of resources, social equality, and solidarity among individuals. Socialism resonates with the values of compassion, cooperation, and community, emphasizing the importance of mutual support and shared prosperity in the pursuit of a more just and equitable society.

At the spiritual level, the motivation of the spirit fosters an agnostic theistic orientation—a belief in the existence of at least one deity, coupled with an acknowledgment of the inherent limitations of human knowledge and understanding. Agnostic theism embraces the mystery and wonder of the divine, encouraging individuals to cultivate a sense of reverence and awe for the sacredness of existence while remaining open to the possibility of transcendence beyond human comprehension.

Agnostic theists affirm. They do not have the ability. They can not know about the non-existence of deities. From this affirmation follows a claim. The claim is. This inability to know leads to a belief. The belief is. At least one deity exists. From this belief follows a desire. The desire is. Agnostic theists wish to belong to communities of agnostic theists. From the act of belonging to communities of agnostic theists follows a desire for political power. From this desire for political power follows the rise of socialism. If everything is justified by the interests of the many people, then their leaders take away terror of plutocracy.

CHAPTER 54. TOLERANCE VERSUS FASCISM

"Tolerance" and "fascism" represent contrasting attitudes and behaviors towards LGBTQ+ individuals. These contrasting attitudes and behaviors reflect broader societal attitudes and movements regarding acceptance, diversity, and human rights.

"Tolerance" embodies an ethos of acceptance, respect, and support for LGBTQ+ individuals and their rights. Those who advocate for tolerance embrace diversity and equality. They recognize and affirm the rights of individuals regardless of their sexual orientation or gender identity. Tolerance encourages empathy, understanding, and inclusivity. It fosters environments wherein; LGBTQ+ individuals can live authentically and without fear of discrimination or prejudice.

Conversely, "fascism" reflects an ideology characterized by intolerance, discrimination, and oppression towards LGBTQ+ individuals. Fascist attitudes and behaviors seek to enforce rigid gender norms and traditional heterosexual relationships while marginalizing or actively persecuting those individuals who deviate from these norms. Fascism often manifests in efforts to restrict LGBTQ+ rights, perpetuate harmful stereotypes, and promote exclusionary policies or practices.

The juxtaposition of tolerance and fascism highlights the ongoing struggle for LGBTQ+ rights and equality worldwide. Progress has been made in many areas. However, LGBTQ+ individuals still face discrimination, violence, and systemic barriers to full inclusion and acceptance. Advocates for tolerance continue to push for legal protections, social acceptance, and cultural change to create safer and more affirming environments for LGBTQ+ individuals to thrive.

Ultimately, the choice between tolerance and fascism reflects broader societal values and commitments to human rights, justice, and dignity for all individuals, regardless of sexual orientation or gender identity. By promoting tolerance and rejecting fascism, societies can move closer to realizing the principles of equality, diversity, and inclusion for LGBTQ+ individuals and all members of the community.

The origin of the word 'homos' is the Greek language. The ancient Greeks originally defined the word 'homos' as meaning 'same.' I define tolerance as the capacity for and or practice of recognizing and respecting the opinions, practices, and or behaviors of other people.

I define the word tolerance in a sexual sense. The sexual definition is. Tolerance is a noun meaning the capacity for and or practice of recognizing and respecting the opinions, practices, and or behaviors of homosexuals and other LGBTQ+ individuals. Homosexuals practice homosexuality. Homosexuality is the quality or characteristic of being sexually attracted solely to people of the same sex.

Homosexuals and other non-reproductive adults make a sacrifice of their potential to create a living seed. Ideally, in a tolerant society, people would love, cherish and reward homosexuals and other non-reproductive adults for making this sacrifice. Heterosexuals would vie for the honor of serving homosexuals in response to the privilege and responsibility of producing offspring. In a tolerant society, nature selects the most loving, able, strong, and caring individuals to be heterosexuals. Good mutations have a greater opportunity to reproduce. Bad mutations have a lesser opportunity to reproduce. A tolerant society enables us. We create seed-bodies of better form and function. We attain higher levels of conscious awareness of the totality. In the short-term and in the long-term, tolerance helps to best satisfy our common needs and aspirations. Our common needs and aspirations are. Achieve and maintain happiness, good health, and prosperity.

I define the word tolerance in a spiritual sense. The spiritual definition is. Tolerance is a noun meaning the capacity and the practice of recognizing and respecting the opinions, practices, and behaviors of all people. All people includes people who predict. Evil does not exist. All is good.

Let us suppose. A person believes in the value of the most optimistic myths. The most optimistic myths include. The totality is an infinite divine eternal being. The infinite divine eternal being enjoys entertainment. The drama of life and death entertains. For that reason, the infinite divine eternal being manifests as an infinite four. The infinite four are an infinite seed, an infinite body, an infinite soul, and an infinite spirit. Mother God is the infinite soul-spirit. Father Love is the infinite seed-body. The union of Mother God and Father Love creates life. We are soul children. Mother God bestows infinite love, divine forgiveness, eternal freedom, and unifying grace upon all of her soul children. We are saved. We have been saved. We always will be saved. We have an infinite number, diversity, and variety of lives to live. We have an infinite number, diversity, and variety of bodies to give. We are seed, body, soul, and spirit. In that event, the person builds a model of the totality. An infinite divine eternal being unifies the model. The person predicts. Evil does not exist. All is good. The model has a homogeneous quality. The model has a tolerant quality. For that reason, I would describe the model as tolerant in the spiritual sense of the word.

The origin of the word 'heteros' is the Greek language. The ancient Greeks originally defined 'heteros' as meaning 'other.' I define fascism as an ideology or system of government. The ideology or system of government is marked by stringent centralized social, military and economic control, and often a foreign policy of belligerent nationalism.

I define the word fascism in a sexual sense. The sexual definition is. Fascism is a noun meaning an ideology or system of government. The ideology or system of government is marked by a demand. The demand is. Conform to a heterosexual norm. Heterosexuals practice heterosexuality. Heterosexuality is the quality or characteristic of being sexually attracted solely to people of the opposite sex.

What is a natural sexual orientation? A natural sexual orientation is specific to each individual. Some people are heterosexuals. Some people are asexuals. Some people are homosexuals. Some people are bisexuals. Let us suppose. A person forces other people to assume an unnatural sexual orientation. In that event, the person is arrogant and wrong.

I define the word fascism in a spiritual sense. The spiritual definition is. Fascism is a noun meaning an ideology and or system of government. The ideology or system of government is marked by a demand. The demand is. Observe and obey the will of the good entity. Be good.

Let us suppose. A person believes in the value of pessimistic myths. The pessimistic myths include. A system of divine eternal reward and abominable infernal punishment exists. The system compels the faithful. The faithful must observe and obey the will of a good entity. The good entity rules in Heaven. The good entity is at war with an evil entity. The evil entity rules over the Earth. In that event, the person builds a model of the totality. A spiritual conflict between good and evil divides the model. The person predicts. Both good and evil exist. Good is other than evil. Evil is other than good. The model has a heterogeneous quality. The model has a fascist quality. For that reason, I would describe the model as fascist in the spiritual sense of the word.

The predator is other than the prey. The prey is other than the predator. A successful predator may present self as being good. The successful predator may present sacrificed prey as being evil. However, in the judgment of the spirit, the drama of life and death entertains. We are actors in the drama of life and death. We play the dual role of predator and prey. Both predator and prey are necessary roles in the drama of life and death. Both predator and prey are good.

CHAPTER 55. AGNOSTIC THEISM VERSUS GNOSTIC ATHEISM

Agnostic theism and gnostic atheism represent two distinct positions on the existence of a higher power or deity. Each position has its own philosophical implications and perspectives on the nature of belief and knowledge.

Agnostic theism is a belief system. The belief system acknowledges the possibility of the existence of a higher power or deity but does not claim certainty or absolute knowledge about it. Those who identify as agnostic theists recognize. The existence of a higher power is ultimately unknowable or beyond human comprehension. They may find value in spiritual or religious practices and concepts, while also maintaining an openness to skepticism and uncertainty.

In contrast, gnostic atheism asserts a belief in the non-existence of any higher power or deity with a high degree of certainty or knowledge. Gnostic atheists hold a position. The position is. There is no evidence or rational basis for the existence of a divine being. For that reason, gnostic atheists reject the notion entirely. They may assert. Empirical evidence and logical reasoning lead to a conclusion. The conclusion is. Gods or supernatural entities are human inventions or products of superstition.

Both agnostic theism and gnostic atheism have implications for how people approach questions of spirituality, morality, and the meaning of life. Agnostic theists may find solace in the possibility of a higher power or divine presence while maintaining an openness to uncertainty and skepticism. They may view spirituality as a personal journey of exploration and growth, guided by their own experiences and beliefs.

Gnostic atheists, on the other hand, often place emphasis on reason, science, and empirical evidence as the basis for their worldview. They may reject religious or spiritual beliefs as unfounded and see atheism as a rational response to questions about the existence of gods or supernatural phenomena. Gnostic atheists may find meaning and fulfillment in secular humanism or other philosophical frameworks.

It's important to recognize that these terms represent positions on a spectrum rather than strict dichotomies, and individuals may hold nuanced or evolving beliefs about the existence of higher powers. Both agnostic theism and gnostic atheism reflect the diversity of human perspectives on matters of faith, reason, and the nature of the universe.

Some agnostic theists believe in creationism. They believe. The creation of the universe and living beings was the act of at least one deity.

Some gnostic atheists believe in destructionism. They say. It appears. Long ago, many thousands of millions of years ago, a Big Bang occurred. They believe. A singularity was destroyed. Out of this destruction, a planet of life was born in a world of death. A natural process of evolution occurred. The game of survival and sacrifice selected for seed bodies of ever higher form and function. These people see no need to explain the origins of this cosmic seed with a god finite or otherwise.

I am an agnostic theist. I believe in creationism. I believe. Life is, in part, a chemical reaction. The chemical reaction is powered by the sun. The chemical reaction feeds on itself. Seed bodies consume seed bodies. The game of survival and sacrifice enables the soul spirit. The soul spirit selects for seed bodies of ever higher form and function. Life is, in part, entertainment. The totality is an infinite divine eternal being. The infinite divine eternal being enjoys entertainment. The drama of life and death entertains.

A finite entity is nothing in comparison to an infinite divine eternal being. This may be demonstrated mathematically. Represent a finite entity with a finite number. Represent the infinite divine eternal being with an infinitely larger number. Divide the finite number by the infinitely larger number. The result is a number approaching zero.

The existence of discovery and mystery leaves gaps in our understanding of the known universe. People use myths to fill in the gaps. Myths are based on the existence of mystery. Myths are infinitely abundant. Truths are based on the existence of discovery. Truths are rare. Scientific theories are based on scientifically reproducible discoveries. Scientific theories are rare. Lies are based on the existence of discovery. Lies are rare.

Some people claim. They build a model of the totality using only their truths and their theories. However, the truth is. The correct myths are unknown. These people adopt a belief in the value of pessimistic myths when the correct myths are unknown. These pessimistic myths include. Self has only one life to live. Self has only one body to give. Self is only a seed and a body. A godless totality exists.

Let us suppose. A person believes in the value of these pessimistic myths. The person believes in the value of truths. These truths include. It appears. One day, the seed-body of self will die. In that event, the person's values would act as forces upon the person's emotions. The most powerful emotional forces of sorrow, fear, and anger would follow from the person's belief in the value of these truths. The person's belief in the value of these pessimistic myths would not enable the person. The person would be unable to achieve and maintain emotional balance. The person's heart would be filled with sorrow, fear, and anger. The person's emotions would act on the person's behaviors. The person would exhibit sad, mad, and bad behaviors. The person's sad, mad, and bad behaviors would act on the person's habitat. The person's sad, mad, and bad behaviors would be conducive to a state of disease in the person's habitat. The person's sad, mad, and bad behaviors would act on the persons's body. The person's sad, mad, and bad behaviors would be conducive to a state of disease in the person's body.

Scientists say. It appears. Laws of cause and effect predict the behavior and fate of matter and energy in the known universe. Let us suppose. The person masters the laws of cause and effect. In that event, a mastery of the laws of cause and effect might enable the person. The person might be able to gain an advantage in the game of survival and sacrifice. However, the person's sad, mad, and bad behaviors would negate the advantage.

As an agnostic theist, I offer. I appreciate truths. The totality is everything, everywhere, at all times. I know next to nothing about the totality. I appreciate the most optimistic myths. For that reason, I think, believe, and predict. The totality is an infinite divine eternal being. The infinite divine eternal being is everything, everywhere, at all times.

CHAPTER 56. POSITIVISM VERSUS PERFECTIONISM

Perfectionism and positivism are two distinct perspectives. These two distinct perspectives often shape how individuals approach life, challenges, and personal growth. Perfectionism and positivism share some similarities. However, perfectionism and positivism also have fundamental differences. These similarities and fundamental differences are in their underlying philosophies and implications for behavior and well-being. Perfectionism holds. Religious, moral, social, or political perfection is attainable. Moral or spiritual perfection should be or has been attained. Positivism holds. People acquire facts, information, and skills through experience and education. All genuine facts, information, and skills are either true by definition or derived by reason and logic from sensory experience.

Perfectionism is a mindset characterized by striving for flawlessness and setting excessively high standards for oneself. Those who embrace perfectionism often believe. Any deviation from these high standards is a failure. This belief often leads to feelings of inadequacy, self-criticism, and anxiety. Perfectionists tend to focus on avoiding mistakes rather than embracing the learning process. This tendency can hinder their ability to take risks and grow personally and professionally. This mindset can lead to a constant sense of dissatisfaction, as perfectionists may never feel truly content with their achievements.

On the other hand, positivism is an approach rooted in optimism, resilience, and a belief in the inherent goodness of life and people. Positivism emphasizes focusing on strengths, opportunities, and solutions rather than dwelling on shortcomings or obstacles. Those who adopt a positive outlook on life are more likely to see setbacks as temporary challenges to overcome rather than insurmountable failures. This mindset fosters a sense of gratitude, hope, and satisfaction with one's progress and achievements. This sense of gratitude, hope, and satisfaction leads to greater overall well-being and fulfillment.

Both perfectionism and positivism can drive individuals to pursue excellence and self-improvement. However, they have different effects on mental health and overall quality of life. Perfectionism tends to be associated with higher levels of stress, anxiety, and burnout, as individuals constantly strive for unattainable ideals. In contrast, positivism promotes resilience, emotional well-being, and a sense of fulfillment, as individuals focus on their strengths and embrace the journey of growth and development.

Ultimately, finding a balance between striving for excellence and maintaining a positive outlook is key to leading a fulfilling and meaningful life. It is natural to have high standards and aspirations. However, it is also important to approach challenges with optimism, resilience, and self-compassion. By cultivating a positive mindset and embracing the learning process, individuals can navigate life's ups and downs with grace and gratitude, ultimately achieving a sense of fulfillment and well-being.

CHAPTER 57. SPIRITIZATION VERSUS NEGATIVISM

"Spiritization" and "negativism" represent contrasting approaches to life, perception, and mindset. Each approach influences how. Individuals engage with the world around them and their own internal experiences.

"Spiritization" embodies a mindset characterized by positivity, optimism, and a focus on personal growth and fulfillment. Those who embrace spiritization seek to cultivate a sense of purpose, meaning, and connection in their lives. Often those who embrace spiritization draw upon spiritual or philosophical beliefs. The spiritual or philosophical beliefs guide their actions and decisions. Spiritization encourages individuals to adopt a constructive outlook, embrace challenges as opportunities for learning and growth, and maintain resilience in the face of adversity. This mindset emphasizes gratitude, compassion, and a belief in the inherent goodness of life and humanity.

In contrast, "negativism" reflects a mindset characterized by cynicism, pessimism, and a focus on limitations and shortcomings. Those who embody negativism may be inclined to see the world through a lens of negativity. They may perceive obstacles as insurmountable barriers. They may perceive setbacks as confirmation of their own pessimistic worldview. Negativism can lead to feelings of hopelessness, despair, and resignation, as individuals struggle to find meaning or purpose in their experiences. This mindset often perpetuates a cycle of negativity. This cycle of negativity may reinforce feelings of dissatisfaction and disillusionment.

The choice between spiritization and negativism reflects broader philosophical orientations and attitudes towards life, perception, and personal development. While spiritization encourages individuals to embrace positivity, resilience, and a sense of purpose, negativism can hinder personal growth and well-being by fostering a mindset of defeatism and despair.

Ultimately, the act of cultivating a spiritized mindset involves the act of cultivating awareness, intentionality, and a commitment to personal growth and fulfillment. The acts of adopting a constructive outlook, practicing gratitude, and seeking meaning and connection in our lives, can enable us. We can cultivate a sense of purpose and resilience. We can navigate life's challenges with grace and optimism. The act of embracing spiritization can lead to greater satisfaction, fulfillment, and well-being, and foster a deeper sense of connection and meaning in our lives and relationships.

Nationalism is a devotion to the interests, needs, and aspirations of a particular nation and or culture of people. Spiritization is an act or process of imparting a spiritual nature or treating as having a spiritual sense or meaning. Nationalistic spiritization follows from a devotion to the interests, needs, and aspirations of our nation and or our culture of people. We have common interests, needs, and aspirations. Our common interests, needs, and aspirations are. Achieve and maintain happiness, good health, and prosperity. Optimism correlates with happiness, good health, and prosperity. For those reasons, nationalistic spiritization is an act or process of imparting a spiritual nature to the totality.

A brief survey of several reference sources reveals. Negativism is a noun with numerous definitions. Negativism is any of the following:

1. A negative or pessimistic attitude;
2. A tendency to resist external commands, suggestions, or expectations or internal stimuli, such as hunger by doing something contrary or unrelated to the stimulus;
3. Any system of negative philosophy, and or;
4. A state of mind or behavior characterized by extreme skepticism and persistent opposition or resistance to outside suggestions or advice.

I love Healthy Agnostic Positivistic Nationalistic Spiritization of self and world. I take Healthy Agnostic Positivistic Nationalistic Spiritization of self and world to its logical extreme. Our values act as forces upon our emotions. Our emotions act as forces upon our behaviors. Our behaviors act as forces upon our bodies. Our behaviors act as forces upon our habitats.

It appears. The act of pointing out the connection between our values, our emotions, our behaviors, our bodies, and our habitat has little of no effect upon the behaviors of negativists. Negativists build models of the totality. Negativists use their models of the totality. They explain existence to themselves. They orient themselves towards existence. They navigate about their habitats. Their models of the totality are often deeply ingrained in the physiology of their brains. Their models of the totality are often deeply ingrained in the structure of their communities and societies. For that reason, any alternate model seems foreign, strange, wrong, and difficult to grasp, and or imagine.

Often, their models of the totality include defense mechanisms. The defense mechanisms, in effect, prevent a challenge by alternative models of the totality. As such, extreme skepticism, persistent opposition, refusal, and or resistance may characterize the reaction of negativists to outside suggestions and or advice.

Theistic negativists build gnostic theistic models of the totality. Alternative models of the totality are at variance with their gnostic theistic models. Outsiders build alternative models. Often, the gnostic theistic models include a defense mechanism. The defense mechanism is. Theistic negativists regard outsiders as evil. For that reason, theistic negativists resist, oppose, refuse, and negate; these alternative models. Let us suppose. The outsiders offer suggestions and or advice to the theistic negativists. In that event, extreme skepticism, persistent opposition, refusal, and or resistance may characterize the reaction of the theistic negativists to these outside suggestions and or advice.

Atheistic negativists build gnostic atheistic models of the totality. Alternative models of the totality are at variance with their gnostic atheistic models. Outsiders build alternative models. Often, the gnostic atheistic models include a defense mechanism. The defense mechanism is. Atheistic negativists regard outsiders as irrational, illogical, immoral, and or insane. For that reason, atheistic negativists resist, oppose, refuse, and negate; these alternative models. Let us suppose. The outsiders offer suggestions and or advice to the atheistic negativists. In that event, extreme skepticism, persistent opposition, refusal, and or resistance may characterize the reaction of the atheistic negativists to these outside suggestions and or advice.

What about me? I build an agnostic theistic model of the totality. Alternative models of the totality are at variance with my agnostic theistic model. Outsiders build alternative models. Does my agnostic theistic model also include a defense mechanism? The answer is yes. My agnostic theistic model of the totality does include a defense mechanism. The defense mechanism is. I regard outsiders as irrational, illogical, immoral, and or insane. For that reason, I resist, oppose, refuse, and negate any alternative to my agnostic theistic model. Let us suppose. The outsiders offer suggestions and or advice to me. In that event, extreme skepticism, persistent opposition, refusal, and or resistance may characterize my reaction to these outside suggestions and or advice.

The existence of discovery and the existence of mystery inspire people to wonder and dream. What am I? Where am I? When am I? How am I? Why am I? Who am I? These are the grand enigmatic questions of identity. People establish identities for themselves. The act of establishing identities for themselves enables them. They give answers to the grand enigmatic questions of identity.

Some theistic negativists establish an identity for themselves. They are the bearers of the burden of exclusive divine revelations. The act of establishing identities for themselves enables them. They give pessimistic answers to the grand enigmatic questions of identity.

Some atheistic negativists establish an identity for themselves. They are the bearers of the burden of proof. The act of establishing identities for themselves enables them. They give pessimistic answers to the grand enigmatic questions of identity.

I establish an identity for myself. I am the bearer of the burden of personal divine revelations. The act of establishing an identity for myself enables me. I give the most optimistic answers to the grand enigmatic questions of identity.

Optimism correlates with happiness and good health. Pessimism correlates with sorrow, fear, anger, and disease. Some negativists fail to see the importance. When confronted with their own mortality or the mortality of a loved one, some negativists may end up being overwhelmed by feelings of sorrow, fear, and anger. Some negativists may suffer from depression, anxiety, and or become alienated. Some negativists may lose hope and faith, turn to drugs, and or exhibit sad, mad, and bad behaviors.

The correct position is unknown. When the correct position is unknown, I default to the most optimistic position. The most optimistic position is. Our seed-bodies make senses and perceptions available to us. We can use our senses and perceptions. We can find things. Science makes tools available to us. Scientists can use our tools of science. Scientists can discover things. Science makes scientific theories available to us. Scientists can use our scientific theories. Scientists can predict things. These things exist. Everything else exists. The everything else enables me. I have the highest esteem of the totality. I balance the emotional forces of my mind. I best satisfy my needs and aspirations. My needs and aspirations are. Achieve and maintain happiness, good health, and prosperity.

CHAPTER 58. REALITY AND ACTUALITY

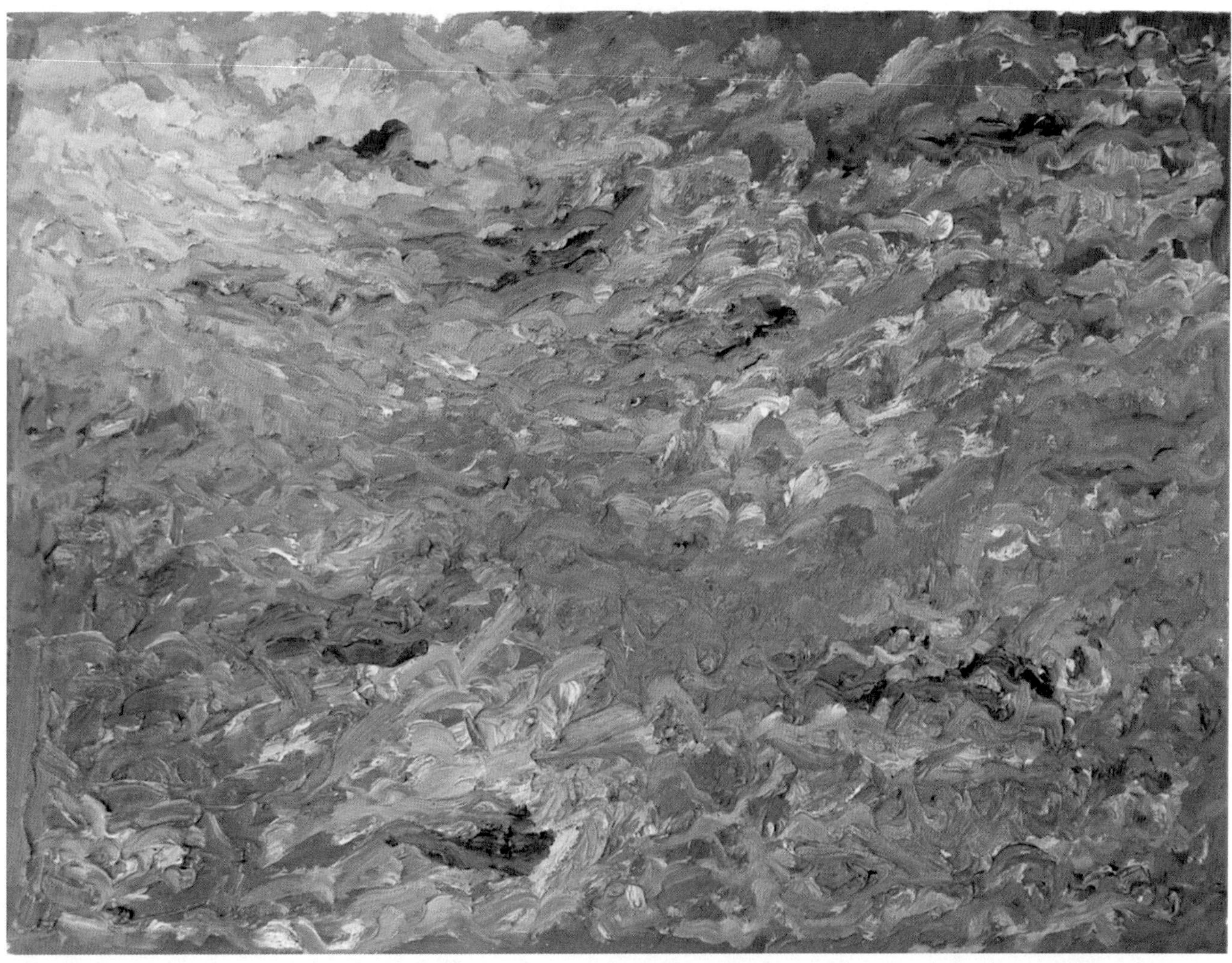

Reality is the way. Things appear to be. Actuality is the way. Things actually are. It appears. Most people would like for their reality to match their actuality. However, it appears. Our realities and actualities do not always match.

The totality exists. For that reason, we are part of the totality. Ideas are thoughts, beliefs, and expectations about the totality. We value certain ideas. These certain ideas are our values. We use our values. We build within our minds. We build models of the totality. Our models are our realities. Our realities are our houses of ideologies. We are the high ideologues of our houses of ideologies. We can change our realities to what. We would like our realities to be.

Let us suppose. A person values an idea. The idea is. A godless totality exists. In that event, this totality without deities would necessarily exist in the person's reality. Reality would enable the person. The person would imagine. Something can be greater than God.

Let us suppose. A person values an idea. The idea is. God exists. In that event, this God would necessarily exist in the person's reality. Reality would enable the person. The person would imagine. Something can not be greater than God.

I build a model of the totality. I call it reality. My reality is the way. Things appear to be. My actuality is the way. Things actually are. Let us suppose. It appears. My reality is in accord with my actuality. In that event, I would not change my reality. Let us suppose. It appears. My reality is in conflict with my actuality. In that event, I would change my reality.

Metaphysical Naturalists say. 'Only the natural world exists'. By this statement, maybe they mean to say. Only the seed-body exists. Natural is a label for these things. Supernatural is a label for everything else.

It appears. Some atheistic negativists imagine scientists to be omniscient beings. The fact is. Scientists are far from being omniscient beings. Scientists know next to nothing about almost everything, just like everybody else.

Why does the world have to be either natural or supernatural; why not both? Let us suppose. An infinite divine eternal being exists. Let us suppose further. Scientists quantified infinity, qualified divinity, measured the longevity of eternity, and perceived the totality. In that event, the existence of the infinite divine eternal being would be considered natural and not supernatural.

Let us suppose. A Metaphysical Naturalist believes in the value of certain ideas. The certain ideas are. The seed-body of self exists. The seed-body of the world exists. Nothing else exists. The most optimistic myths are products of superstitious wishful thinking. In that event, we can not verify whether or not. These certain ideas are true. We can not verify whether or not. These certain ideas are false. We can verify. These certain ideas are both unverifiable and unfalsifiable. For that reason, these certain ideas are myths.

The Metaphysical Naturalist would be like me in the following way. We combine our truths, our theories, and our favored myths. We build within our minds. We build our models of the totality. Our models are our realities. Our realities are our Houses of Ideologies. We are the High Ideologues of our Houses of Ideologies. We can change our realities to what. We would like our realities to be.

Let us suppose. A person tells me of their own belief in the value of pessimistic myths. In that event, I would be unable to take the person's word for it. I have been deceived too many times by too many people about too many important things. I would have to wonder: Does the person actually believe in the value of these pessimistic myths?

Let us suppose. I am convinced. The person actually does believe in the value of these pessimistic myths. Let us suppose further. I ask the person. Why choose to believe in the value of these pessimistic myths? Why not choose to believe in the value of the most optimistic myths? Let us suppose finally. The person responds with an affirmation. The person affirms an ability to know. These pessimistic myths are truths. In that event, the person knows next to nothing about almost everything. The person values a lie. The lie is. These pessimistic myths are truths. The person devalues a truth. The truth is. These pessimistic myths are myths.

Atheists value pessimistic myths. These pessimistic myths include. Life has very definite book ends; birth and death. On either side of those bookends is oblivion.

I value the most optimistic myths. The most optimistic myths include. We are seed, body, soul, and spirit. The life of the seed-body has very definite book ends; birth and death. The life of the soul-spirit has no definite book ends. The life and immunity of the soul-spirit is, eternal and divine. On the other side of the bookends of the seed-body, are an infinite number, diversity, and variety of lives to live.

Bodies create unconscious minds. Souls order the chaos of unconscious minds. We confine our awareness of the totality to our conscious minds. We become individuals. We know next to nothing about almost everything. The drama of life and death entertains. We enjoy the entertainment.

Atheists believe in the value of pessimistic myths. The pessimistic myths include. Self is only a seed and a body. Self has only one life to live. Self has only one body to give. The totality is without deities. They choose to have a low esteem of self. They choose to have a low esteem of the world.

Atheists know next to nothing about almost everything, just like everybody else. Some atheists go about a task. The task is. They attempt to convince us. They know something more. For that reason, they say. We should. Be like them. Believe in the value of these pessimistic myths. Choose to have a low esteem of self. Choose to have a low esteem of the world. Some atheists claim. To do otherwise, would be irrational, illogical, and or insane.

I value truths. Our seed-bodies make senses and perceptions available to us. Our senses and perceptions enable us. We can verify. Truths are true. We can verify. Lies are false. However, we can not verify whether or not. Myths are true. We can not verify whether or not. Myths are false. Myths are both unverifiable and unfalsifiable. The fact is. A myth is a myth.

It appears. Optimism correlates with happiness and good health. Pessimism correlates with sorrow, fear, anger, and disease. The totality makes possible an infinite number, diversity, and variety of myths. The correct myths are unknown.

Let us suppose. A person desires happiness and good health. In that event, the person should believe in the value of the most optimistic myths. To do otherwise would be illogical, irrational, and or insane.

I believe in the value of the most optimistic myths. My belief in the value of the most optimistic myths enables me. I balance the emotional forces of my mind. Emotional balance in my mind is conducive to happiness and good health in my life. Happiness and good health in my life is conducive to success and prosperity in my business.

CHAPTER 59. PROJECTION THEORY

Projection theory enables me. I predict. Some people believe in the value of pessimistic myths. These people tend to project. They gather truths about their set of living arrangements. They project their truths into their imaginations. They use their imaginations. They make myths. Their myths suggest their truths. Why do they tend to do this? Projection theory enables me. I offer an explanation. The explanation is. They value certain ideas. These certain ideas are their values. They wish to use their senses and perceptions to confirm their belief in the value of their ideas. Many of their ideas are truths. Their senses and perceptions enable them. They can verify. Truths are true. For that reason, they can use their senses and perceptions to confirm their belief in the value of their truths. Many of their values are myths. Their senses and perceptions do not enable them. They can not verify whether or not. Myths are true. They can not verify whether or not. Myths are false. Myths are both unverifiable and unfalsifiable. For that reason, they can not use their senses and perceptions to confirm their belief in the value of myths. However, their myths can suggest their truths. The act of suggesting their truths can enable them. They can use the act of suggesting their truths to confirm their belief in the value of their myths.

Let us suppose. The truths were. A few paranoid oppressive violent people ruled over domestic territories. The few paranoid oppressive violent people were at war with outsiders. The outsiders ruled over foreign territories. People lived within the domestic territories. A system of reward and punishment existed. The system compelled the people. The people observed and obeyed the will of the few paranoid oppressive violent people. The people disregarded and disobeyed the will of the outsiders. In that event, projection theory would enable me. I would predict. Some of these people would have believed in the value of pessimistic myths. These people would have tended to project. These people would have used their senses and perceptions. Searched their surroundings. Gathered truths about their set of living arrangements. These people would have projected their truths into their imaginations. They would have made myths. Their myths would have suggested their truths. The act of suggesting their truths would have enabled these people. These people would have used the act of suggesting their truths to confirm their belief in the value of their myths.

Let us suppose. Their myths were. A good entity rules in Heaven. The good entity is at war with an evil entity. The evil entity rules over the Earth. A system of divine eternal reward and abominable infernal punishment exists. The system compels the faithful. The faithful must observe and obey the will of the good entity. The faithful must disregard and disobey the will of the evil entity. In that event, the act of suggesting their truths would not make their myths into truths. Their myths would remain myths. However, projection theory would enable me. I would predict. The act of suggesting their truths would have enabled these people. These people would have used the act of suggesting their truths to confirm their belief in the value of their myths.

Let us suppose. The truths were. The needs and aspirations of the few paranoid oppressive violent people included. Achieve and maintain authority, power, order, and control. For that reason, the few paranoid oppressive violent people gained influence over religious authority figures. Religious authority figures gained influence over communities of faithful believers. Communities of faithful believers gained influence over members. Members affirmed an ability to know. The few paranoid oppressive violent people are representatives of the good entity here on planet Earth. The few paranoid oppressive violent people are divinely ordained to rule over domestic territories. The will of the few paranoid oppressive violent people is, in fact, the will of the good entity. The few paranoid oppressive violent people are at war with outsiders. The outsiders are representatives of the evil entity here on planet Earth. The outsiders are not divinely ordained to rule over foreign territories. The will of the outsiders is, in fact, the will of the evil entity. In that event, Projection theory would enable me. I would predict. Their myths suggested their truths. The act of suggesting their truths enabled these people. These people were able to use the act of suggesting their truths to confirm their belief in the value of their myths.

Let us suppose. Time passes. The few paranoid oppressive violent people no longer rule over domestic territories. A democracy rules over domestic territories. The democracy supports a large middle class. The large middle class forms a secular pluralistic society. The secular pluralistic society supports the freedoms and rights of people. In that event, the people would be subject to a new set of living arrangements.

Let us suppose. Communities of faithful believers still exist. Members still believe in the value of these pessimistic myths. In the minds of members, confirmation of their belief in the value of these pessimistic myths means. Members are correct in their belief in the value of these pessimistic myths. Members wish to be correct. For that reason, these members wish to use their senses and perceptions. Gather truths about their set of living arrangements and find. These pessimistic myths suggest their truths. Members would like the act of suggesting their truths to enable them. They would like to be able to use the act of suggesting their truths to confirm their belief in the value of these pessimistic myths. However, the absence of an autocracy complicates things. The absence of psychotic extremes of poverty and wealth complicates things. The absence of a religious elitist society complicates things. The absence of slaveries and wrongs complicates things.

Let us suppose further. Some members don't like these complications. The members blame the democracy, the large middle class, the secular pluralistic society, freedoms and rights, for all manner of social ills. The members tout a return to a universal belief in the value of these pessimistic myths as the remedy. The members wish to replace the democracy with an autocracy. The members wish to replace the large middle class with psychotic extremes of poverty and wealth. The members wish to replace the secular pluralistic society with a religious elitist society. The members wish to replace freedoms and rights with slaveries and wrongs.

Let us suppose even further. Loud voices spread out across the land. The loud voices shout from the mountain tops about their belief in the value of these pessimistic myths. The loud voices affirm an ability to know. These pessimistic myths are truths. The loud voices attract communities of faithful believers. Members become candidates. The candidates campaign for political office. Communities of faithful believers support their campaigns. Their campaigns attract the support of the majority of voters. The majority of the voters elect the candidates. The candidates become politicians. The politicians enact policies. The policies enable a few people. The few people concentrate wealth, income, and power into their own hands. The few people rule over domestic territories. Success attracts competition. The concentration of wealth, income, and power into the hands of the few people makes the competition to rule homicidal, genocidal, and even suicidal at times. The few people become a few paranoid oppressive violent people.

Let us suppose finally. The few paranoid oppressive violent people replace democracy with autocracy. The few paranoid oppressive violent people replace the large middle class with psychotic extremes of poverty and wealth. The few paranoid oppressive violent people replace the secular pluralistic society with a religious elitist society. The few paranoid oppressive violent people replace freedoms and rights with slaveries and wrongs. In that event, projection theory predicts. Members would. Use their senses and perceptions. Search their surroundings. Gather truths about their set of living arrangements and find. These pessimistic myths suggest their truths. The act of suggesting their truths would enable these members. These members could use the act of suggesting their truths. They could confirm their belief in the value of these pessimistic myths. These members could do so without complications.

Let us suppose. Members affirm an ability to know. The good entity chose prophets. The good entity revealed visions of the future to the prophets. Religious authority figures wrote down the exclusive divine revelations of spiritual knowledge as words in a set of sacred scrolls. The religious authority figures know how to translate and interpret the words. The religious authority figures say. The visions of the future are. These are the end times. Armageddon is imminent. Armageddon is a necessary final horrible war. After Armageddon occurs, the good entity will have a final victory over the evil entity. In that event, projection theory predicts. The visions of the future make predictions about the final outcome of the competition to rule. The predictions are. A horrible war will occur. After the horrible war, the few paranoid oppressive violent people will have a final victory over the outsiders.

The few paranoid oppressive violent people rule over domestic territories. The outsiders rule over foreign territories. So in effect, this means. The prediction is. After the horrible war, the few paranoid oppressive violent people will rule the world.

The identities of insiders and outsiders are a matter of point of view. The locations of domestic and foreign territories are also a matter of point of view. For that reason, the few paranoid oppressive violent people in every territory can claim to be the representatives of the good entity for whom the visions of the future predict final victory.

Let us suppose. Members affirm an ability to know. The good entity revealed further visions of the future to the prophets. Religious authority figures say. The further visions of the future are. After the good entity has a final victory over the evil entity, the good entity will judge all people. The good entity will use a system of divine eternal reward and abominable infernal punishment. The good entity will find. Some people observed and obeyed the will of the good entity. The good entity will reward those people. The good entity will elevate those people to a place of divine eternal bliss. The good entity will find. Some people disregarded and disobeyed the will of the good entity. The good entity will punish those people. The good entity will throw those people into a place of abominable infernal torment. In that event, projection theory predicts. The visions of the future make predictions about the future behaviors of the few paranoid oppressive violent people. The predictions are. After the few paranoid oppressive violent people have a final victory over the outsiders, the few paranoid oppressive violent people will judge all people. The few paranoid oppressive violent people will use a system of reward and punishment. The few paranoid oppressive violent people will find. Some people observed and obeyed the will of the few paranoid oppressive violent people. The few paranoid oppressive violent people will reward those people. The few paranoid oppressive violent people will elevate those people to a place of safety and refuge. The place of safety and refuge will be a haven on Earth. The few paranoid oppressive violent people will find. Some people disregarded and disobeyed the will of the few paranoid oppressive violent people. The few paranoid oppressive violent people will punish those people. The few paranoid oppressive violent people will throw those people into a place of danger and exposure. The place of danger and exposure will be hell on Earth. Some of those people will perform slave labor under horrendous conditions until they die of disease or starvation. Some of those people will be murdered upon arrival.

Projection Theory enables me. I predict. Some people believe in the value of pessimistic myths. These people tend to project. These people use their senses and perceptions. They gather truths about their set of living arrangements. These people tend to project their truths into their imaginations. They use their imaginations. They make myths. Their myths suggest their truths. For that reason, their myths are pessimistic myths.

A myth is. A spiritual conflict between good and evil divides the spiritual realm. The myth suggests a truth. The truth is. A primal conflict between predator and prey divides our body-consuming biosphere.

A myth is. A good entity rules in Heaven. The myth suggests a truth. The truth is. A few paranoid oppressive violent people ruled over domestic territories.

A myth is. The good entity is at war with an evil entity. The myth suggests a truth. The truth is. The few paranoid oppressive violent people were at war with outsiders.

A myth is. An evil entity rules over the Earth. The myth suggests a truth. The truth is. The outsiders ruled over foreign territories.

A myth is. A system of divine eternal reward and abominable infernal punishment exists. The myth suggests a truth. The truth is. A system of reward and punishment existed.

A myth is. The laws of a deity exist. The myth suggests a truth. The truth is. The laws of the state existed.

A myth is. The laws of a deity and or deities govern the behavior and fate of matter and energy in the known universe. The myth suggests a truth. The truth is. Laws of cause and effect predict the behavior and fate of matter and energy in the known universe.

A myth is. A good entity chose prophets. The myth suggests a truth. The truth is. A few paranoid oppressive violent people chose prophets.

A myth is. The good entity revealed visions of the future to the prophets. The myth suggests a truth. The truth is. The few paranoid oppressive violent people revealed predictions about the final outcome of the competition to rule to the prophets.

A myth is. The visions of the future include. A great tribulation will occur. The myth suggests a truth. The truth is. The predictions about the final outcome of the competition to rule include. Population overshoot, depletion of natural resources, pollution, abrupt climate change, and habitat loss will occur.

A myth is. The visions of the future include. The evil entity will have a son. The son of the evil entity will be an anti-christ. The anti-christ will rise to power. The myth suggest a truth. The truth is. The predictions about the final outcome of the competition to rule include. An outsider will have a son. The son of the outsider will be a powerful foreign adversary. The powerful foreign adversary will rise to power.

A myth is. The visions of the future include. Armageddon will follow. Armageddon is a necessary final horrible war. After Armageddon, the good entity will have final victory over the evil entity. The myth suggest a truth. The truth is. The predictions about the final outcome of the competition to rule include. A horrible war will follow. After the horrible war, the few paranoid oppressive violent people who concentrate wealth, income, and power into their own hands and rule over domestic territories, will have final victory over the outsiders.

A myth is. The visions of the future include. The good entity will judge all people. The myth suggests a truth. The truth is. The predictions about the final outcome of the competition to rule include. The few paranoid oppressive violent people will judge all people.

A myth is. The visions of the future include. The good entity will find. Some people observed and obeyed the will of the good entity. The good entity will reward those people. The good entity will elevate those people to a place of divine eternal bliss. The myth suggests a truth. The truth is. The predictions about the final outcome of the competition to rule include. The few paranoid oppressive violent people will find. Some people observed and obeyed the will of the few paranoid oppressive violent people. The few paranoid oppressive violent people will reward those people. The few paranoid oppressive violent people will elevate those people to a place of safety and refuge. The place of safety and refuge will be a haven on Earth.

A myth is. The visions of the future include. The good entity will find. Some people disregarded and disobeyed the will of the good entity. The good entity will punish those people. The good entity will throw those people into a place of abominable infernal torment. The myth suggests a truth. The truth is. The predictions about the final outcome of the competition to rule include. The few paranoid oppressive violent people will find. Some people disregarded and disobeyed the will of the few paranoid oppressive violent people. The few paranoid oppressive violent people will punish those people. The few paranoid oppressive violent people will throw those people into a place of danger and exposure. The place of danger and exposure will be a hell on Earth. Some of those people will be enslaved under horrendous conditions until they drop dead of disease and or starvation. Some of those people will be murdered upon arrival.

A myth is. A savior exists. The savior loves you. The myth suggests a truth. The truth is. People often form life-long relationships with a spouse. Let us suppose. A person is willing. The person accepts a spouse into their heart. In that event, the spouse would exist. The spouse would love the person.

A myth is. Punishments for breaking the laws of a deity and or deities exist. The myth suggests a truth. The truth is. Disease and death exist.

A myth is. Rewards for obeying the laws of the deity and or deities exist. The myth suggests a truth. The truth is. Life and immunity exist.

A myth is. Spiritual stratification exists. The myth suggests a truth. The truth is. Socioeconomic stratification exists.

A myth is. A place of abominable infernal torment exists. The myth suggests a truth. The truth is. The fiery interior of the Earth exists.

A myth is. A place of divine eternal bliss exists. The myth suggests a truth. The truth is. The sky exists.

A myth is. A deity exists. The myth suggests a truth. The truth is. The moon exists.

A myth is. A deity exists. The myth suggests a truth. The truth is. The sun exists.

A myth is. A deity exists. The myth suggests a truth. The truth is. The universe exists.

A myth is. A godless totality exists. The myth suggests a truth. The truth is. We know a finite amount about an infinite subject.

Project Theory enables me. I predict. Some people believe in the value of pessimistic myths. These people tend to project. They gather truths about their set of living arrangements. They project their truths into their imaginations. They use their imaginations. They make myths. Their myths suggest their truths. For that reason, their myths are pessimistic myths. The act of suggesting their truths enables these people. These people can confirm their belief in the value of their pessimistic myths. The most optimistic myths do not suggest their truths. The act of not suggesting their truths does not enable them. They can not confirm a belief in the value of the most optimistic myths. For those reasons, they value pessimistic myths. They devalue the most optimistic myths.

We know next to nothing about almost everything. The totality makes possible an infinite number, diversity, and variety of myths. Optimism correlates with happiness, good health, and prosperity. For that reason, the logical, rational, sane choice to make when orienting the self to the world and explaining the world to the self is a belief in the value of the most optimistic myths.

CHAPTER 60. A SIX-PART MODEL

Let us suppose. A person proclaims a belief in the value of pessimistic myths. These pessimistic myths are. A good entity rules in Heaven. The good entity is at war with an evil entity. The evil entity rules over the Earth. We are sinners. Our seed-bodies were supposed to live forever in perfect youth and everlasting good health. However, the evil entity had the power. The evil entity tempted our ancestors. Our ancestors disobeyed the will of the good entity. Sin entered the world. With sin came death. In the future, the good entity will have final victory over the evil entity. The good entity will resurrect the dead. The good entity will give each person a seed-body of perfect form and function. The good entity will judge all people. The good entity will use a system of divine eternal reward and abominable infernal punishment. Some people will have observed and obeyed the will of the good entity. The good entity will reward those people. The good entity will elevate those people to a place of divine eternal bliss. Some people will have disregarded and disobeyed the will of the good entity. The good entity will punish those people. The good entity will cast down those people to a place of abominable infernal torment. In that event, I can not take the person's word for it. I have been deceived too many times by too many people on too many important things. I have to wonder: Does the person actually believe in the value of these pessimistic myths?

Let us suppose. The person convinces me. The person actually believes in the value of these pessimistic myths. Let us suppose further. I ask the person. Why do you choose to believe in the value of these pessimistic myths? Why don't you choose to believe in the value of the most optimistic myths? Let us suppose finally. The person responds with an affirmation. The person affirms an ability to know. These pessimistic myths are truths. In that event, the person knows next to nothing about almost everything. The person values a lie. The lie is. These pessimistic myths are truths. The person devalues a truth. The truth is. These pessimistic myths are myths.

Let us suppose. The person claims an ability to know. The good entity does not want to punish people for lack of knowledge about the will of the good entity. For that reason, the good entity chose messengers. The good entity revealed the will, words, way, and laws of the good entity to the messengers. Religious authority figures wrote down the exclusive divine revelations of spiritual knowledge as words in a set of sacred scrolls. Religious authority figures know how to translate and interpret these words. The only hope of salvation from an afterlife of abominable infernal torment is. Do what religious authority figures say. Religious authority figures will guide the faithful to an afterlife of divine eternal bliss. In that event, the person is the authority. The person makes up the person's own mind about self. The person makes up the person's own mind about the world. The person is the architect. The person values certain ideas. These certain ideas are the person's values. The person uses the person's own values. The person builds within the person's own mind. The person builds a model of the totality. The person calls it reality. The person's reality is the person's own House of Ideology. The person is the High Ideologue of the person's own House of Ideology. I respect the person's authority.

This model of the totality consists of six parts. The six parts are; Infernus, Earth, and Heaven; the evil entity, self, and the good entity. Infernus is the place of abominable infernal torment. Earth is the stage for the spiritual conflict between good and evil. Heaven is the place of divine eternal bliss. The evil entity rules over the Earth. Self and all other life forms are participants in the spiritual conflict between good and evil. The good entity rules in Heaven.

CHAPTER 61. THEOCRACY OF PLUTOCRACY

A plutocrat is a wealthy ruler. A plutocracy is a government, or state, wherein; the wealthy, high income, powerful people rule. Wealth, income, and power enables them. Plutocrats can exercise their influence over religious authority figures, communities of faithful believers, and members. Plutocrats can edit and assemble a set of sacred scrolls to their own liking. Plutocrats can lay out the theocracy of plutocracy.

Myths play a vital role in society. Myths help prop up society. Social norms dictate. People use myths. Myths enable people. People can justify ethical and legal systems. Ethical and legal systems enable society. Society can maintain order. Myths can overlay society with an appealing veneer of justification. People can convert a perception of an utterly mysterious, confusing, chaotic, and uncontrollable reality into the perception of an orderly, sane, and purposeful reality.

The theocracy of plutocracy enables the plutocracy. Plutocrats can transfer meaning or information from mythical subjects to actual subjects. Plutocrats can compare the similar features of the mythical subjects and actual subjects. Plutocrats can create reasoning or explanations for actual subjects from reasoning or explanations for parallel mythical subjects.

After thinking many years about politics, I have come to define liberal politics and conservative politics as follows: Liberal politics liberate the many from a power structure. Conservative politics conserve the power structure. The power structure concentrates wealth, income, and power into the hands of a few paranoid oppressive violent people.

Let us suppose. The few paranoid oppressive violent people believe in the value of truths. The few paranoid oppressive violent people believe in the value of pessimistic myths. The pessimistic myths include. Self has only one life to live. Self has only one body to give. Self is only a seed and a body. In that event, their values would act as forces upon their emotions. The most powerful emotional forces of sorrow, fear, and anger would follow from their discovery of a truth. The truth is. It appears. One day the seed body of self will die. Their belief in the value of these pessimistic myths would not enable them. They would be unable to balance the emotional forces of their minds. For that reason, their hearts would be filled with sorrow, fear, and anger.

Let us suppose further. The few paranoid oppressive violent people think, believe, and predict. The accumulation of wealth, income, and power into their own hands will enable them. They will be able to balance the emotional forces of their minds.

Let us suppose finally. The few paranoid oppressive violent people gain influence over religious authority figures. Religious authority figures gain influence over communities of faithful believers. Communities of faithful believers gain influence over members. Members affirm an ability to know. A system of divine eternal reward and abominable infernal punishment exists.

The system compels the faithful. The faithful must observe and obey the will of the good entity. The will of the good entity is, in fact, the will of the few paranoid oppressive violent people. In that event, the few paranoid oppressive violent people would find. They are slave owners. Religious authority figures are their slave drivers. Members are their spiritual slaves. For that reason, the few paranoid oppressive violent people would count communities of faithful believers as part of their wealth, income, and power. It would be logical to infer. The will of the good entity would be. Communities of faithful believers must. Expand the wealth, income, and power of the few paranoid oppressive violent people. That means. Members must. Behave like racist fascist warmongers. Channel all sexual energy into sex for procreative purposes. Prohibit sex for occupational, recreational, and homosexual purposes. Prohibit sex education. Work all of the hours of the day from dawn to dusk. Practice sexual fascism: Fight against anybody who is not doing the same thing. Practice spiritual fascism: Fight against anybody who is not believing in the same way. Work, fight, and outnumber competition. Run a race to Armageddon. Glorify Armageddon as a necessary final horrible war. Aggrandize the evil entity as ruler of the Earth. Affirm an ability to know. Armageddon is a good thing. Armageddon means. The good entity will have final victory over the evil entity. Judgment day is nigh. The good entity will reward the faithful for their racist fascist warmongering behaviors. The good entity will elevate the faithful to a place of divine eternal bliss. The good entity will punish the unfaithful for their friendly tolerant peacemaking behaviors. The good entity will cast down the unfaithful to a place of abominable infernal torment.

Let us suppose. Religious authority figures say. The few paranoid oppressive violent people are representatives of the good entity. The few paranoid oppressive violent people are divinely ordained to rule over domestic territories. The will of the few paranoid oppressive violent people is, in fact, the will of the good entity. Universal submission to the will of the good entity would be a Heaven on Earth.

Let us suppose further. A Heaven on Earth sounds pretty good to communities of faithful believers. For that reason, members are collaborators. Members help the few paranoid oppressive violent people. Members hope. The few paranoid oppressive violent people will concentrate wealth, income, and power into their own hands. The few paranoid oppressive violent people will have final victory over the outsiders. The few paranoid oppressive violent people will bring about universal submission to the will of the good entity. In that event, the few paranoid oppressive violent people would find. They can determine. What is good? They can determine. What is evil? They can play the dual role of the good entity and the evil entity. They can play the role of the good entity for communities of faithful believers in domestic territories. They can play the role of the evil entity for communities of faithful believers in foreign territories. They can achieve and maintain authority, power, order, and control over communities of faithful believers. By extension, the few paranoid oppressive violent people can achieve and maintain authority, power, order, and control over the many people of our global culture.

Let us suppose. Members plan to work, fight, and outnumber competition. In that event, there is nothing proprietary about this plan. Outsiders can also plan to work, fight, and outnumber competition. The outsiders might even consider doing so a matter of survival.

Let us suppose. Everybody struggles to work, fight, and outnumber competition. In that event, human population would surge to ever higher numbers. Natural resources would become ever more scarce. An ever more complex and sophisticated technological infrastructure would become necessary to support the survival of the many people. This complex and sophisticated technological infrastructure would be vulnerable to devastating terrorist attacks. Vulnerability would result in risks of liability for many people.

Let us suppose. The few paranoid oppressive violent people offer protection from terror in exchange for wealth, income, and power. The few paranoid oppressive violent people create a demand for protection by terrorizing the outsiders. In that event, the few paranoid oppressive violent people extort wealth, income, and power from the many people in a shakedown of epic proportions. The few paranoid oppressive violent people prey upon the many people of our global culture.

Let us suppose. In terror, people are induced by a beast of a military-industrial complex. People buy the latest technology at this year's arms shows. Let us suppose further. The beast of a military-industrial complex becomes ever more powerful. In that event, the living conditions of many people would deteriorate.

Let us suppose. The living conditions of many people deteriorate for a long enough time. In that event, many people would be living in abject poverty in a desolate war zone. Diseases would run rampant. Famine would become a fact of everyday life.

Let us suppose. Religious authority figures affirm an ability to know. Before Armageddon occurs, the rapture will occur. The good entity will reward the faithful for their racist fascist warmongering behaviors. The good entity will transport living members of communities of faithful believers to Heaven. In that event, communities of faithful believers may come to wish for this horrible war.

Let us suppose. A few paranoid oppressive violent people profit from the sale and manufacture of the products and services of a beast of a military-industrial complex. Let us suppose further. Communities of faithful believers would be quite willing to march off to their own deaths in this horrible war. In that event, this willingness to go to this horrible war might be to the liking of the few paranoid oppressive violent people. That is, of course, provided the horrible war isn't a war fought against the few paranoid oppressive violent people.

Let us suppose. A few paranoid oppressive violent people rule an underworld of cities and bunkers. Let us suppose further. The few paranoid oppressive violent people designed the cities and bunkers to withstand a catastrophe on the scale of a super-volcano eruption or global nuclear war. In that event, I would wonder. Who wins in a race to Armageddon? Will the few paranoid oppressive violent people win in a race to Armageddon? Will the few paranoid oppressive violent people take refuge in an underworld? Will the few paranoid oppressive violent people await an opportunity to bloom as a seed of the next overworld? Will the many people lose in a race to Armageddon? Will the many people behave like lemmings whose breeding cycle has run its course?

Let us suppose. A few paranoid oppressive violent people believe in the value of pessimistic myths. These pessimistic myths include. Self has only one life to live. Self has only one body to give. Self is only a seed and a body. In that event, no amount of wealth, income, and power would ever be enough to compensate the few paranoid oppressive violent people for their discovery of a truth. The truth is. It appears. One day, the seed-body of self will die. Enough would never be enough.

CHAPTER 62. OUR HABITAT

We live our lives in our habitat. Our habitat is a body-consuming biosphere. The body-consuming biosphere is on a crusted magma globe. The crusted magma globe is of limited dimensions. We play a game of survival and sacrifice. Let us suppose. Racism is wide spread. In that event, racists would race. The race would be a race to work, fight, and outnumber competition. The race to work, fight, and outnumber competition could easily lead to population overshoot, depletion of natural resources, pollution, abrupt climate change, and habitat loss. The finish line of the race would be a horrible war. The horrible war could easily precipitate human extinction.

Let us suppose. Population overshoot, depletion of natural resources, pollution, abrupt climate change, habitat loss, a horrible war, and human extinction occur. In that event, the few paranoid oppressive violent people would lose their wealth, income, and power. Communists would not take their wealth, income, and power away from them. Socialists would not take their wealth, income, and power away from them. Fundamentalists would not take their wealth, income, and power away from them. Population overshoot, depletion of natural resources, pollution, abrupt climate change, habitat loss, a horrible war, and human extinction would take their wealth, income, and power away from them.

I value truths. Scientists say. It appears. Life has existed on planet Earth for billions of years. During that time, the body-consuming biosphere has been home to many species. A species is a group of organisms. The group of organisms are related by interbreeding. The group of organisms shares a genetic heritage. The genetic heritage enables the group of organisms. The group of organisms can reproduce. The group of organisms can produce fertile offspring.

Let us suppose. A species dies out. The species completely disappears from the planet Earth. In that event, the species becomes an extinct species. Greater than ninety-nine percent of all species are now extinct species. Very few of those extinct species were hunted to extinction. The vast majority of extinct species went extinct due to a loss of habitat.

All life forms play a game of survival and sacrifice. A fit species has attributes. These attributes make it possible. The fit species can survive. The fit species can reproduce. A lacking species has attributes. These attributes do not make it possible. The lacking species can not survive. The lacking species can not reproduce. The genetic materials from the fit species survive. The genetic materials from the lacking species are sacrificed. The group of all species consists of fit species and lacking species.

Let us suppose. A loss of habitat occurs. A fit species loses its habitat. In that event, the fit species would become a lacking species. The lacking species would be lacking a habitat. Let us suppose. The lacking species does not find a habitat soon. In that event, the lacking species would soon become an extinct species.

A mass extinction event occurs when a large number of species go extinct within a relatively short period of geological time. Mass extinction events have occurred in the past due to catastrophic global changes. Mass extinction events have occurred in the past due to widespread environmental changes. These changes lead to a loss of habitat. Let us suppose. The loss of habitat occurs too rapidly. Most species do not have enough time. Most species can not evolve quickly enough. Most species can not adapt. In that event, the loss of habitat would lead to a mass extinction event.

It appears. Widespread environmental changes are underway right now. The sad, mad, and bad behaviors of human beings are an agent of the widespread environmental changes. The exponential growth of human population has led to the rapacious consumption of ever more scarce natural resources. We human beings are exceeding the carrying capacity of our habitat. The human species is entering into a state of population overshoot. Too many people are demanding too many resources from too little habitat. Forests have been cleared so as to make way for factory farms. Mining operations have blown the tops off of mountains in an effort to more profitably extract minerals. Industrial civilization has poisoned the soil, the water, and the air. The burning of fossil fuels has released huge quantities of carbon dioxide and methane. These gasses trap heat in the atmosphere. The atmosphere heats up. The ocean heats up. Ancient glaciers melt. This causes less sunlight to be reflected at the poles, and consequently, the oceans heat up even more.

It appears. After the last ice age, some eleven thousand years ago, global temperatures were just right for human beings. The global temperatures enabled human beings. Human beings cultivated grain-bearing plants. Human beings harvested and stored surplus quantities of grains. Doing so enabled human beings. Human beings gave rise to human civilization. Human civilization made possible our exponential population growth.

Grain-bearing plants grow in and are dependent upon a delicate web of species. The topsoil contains this delicate web of species. This is the habitat of the grain-bearing plants.

Abrupt climate change threatens the habitat of grain-bearing plants. Let us suppose. Grain-bearing plants lose their habitat. In that event, human beings would no longer be able to harvest and store surplus quantities of grains. Let us suppose. Human beings are no longer able to harvest and store surplus quantities of grains. In that event, human civilization would no longer be able to feed itself. Let us suppose. Human civilization is no longer able to feed itself. In that event, human civilization would collapse. Accordingly, abrupt climate change threatens to cause the collapse of human civilization.

Human beings are animals. Homo Sapien is the name of our species. Our species depends upon a delicate web of species for its survival. Let us suppose. The delicate web of species goes extinct. In that event, our species would go extinct. Abrupt climate change threatens us with extinction.

CHAPTER 63. TERRORISM

I oppose terrorism. Terrorism is the unlawful use or threatened use of violence against people and or property with an intention. The intention is. Intimidate or coerce people, societies, and or governments. Terrorism is the unlawful use or threatened use of violence against people and or property for ideological and or political reasons.

I oppose the use of my words as a license to kill people. Let us suppose. A person believes in the value of a lie. The lie is. A myth is a truth. In that event, I oppose the use of my words as authorization to kill such a person. The person is not the lie.

I oppose the use of my words as a license to destroy a building. Let us suppose. A community of faithful believers meets in a building. Let us suppose further. Members believe in the value of a lie. The lie is. A myth is a truth. In that event, I oppose the use of my words as authorization to destroy such a building. The building is not the lie.

I prefer the real challenge of using nothing more serious than the simple communication of ideas. I persuade people. Let us suppose. I persuade liars. In that event, liars would change themselves into truthful people. Let us suppose. A community of faithful believers meets in a building. Members believe in the value of a lie. The lie is. A myth is a truth. Let us suppose further. I persuade these liars. In that event, truthful people would meet in the building.

Our seed-bodies make senses and perceptions available to us. We use our senses and perceptions. We verify the truth of ideas. We verify the falsity of ideas. Each of us does so independently. Let us suppose. A person is able to verify the truth of an idea. Another person is unable to verify the truth of the idea. The other person is unable to verify the falsity of the idea. In that event, one person perceives the idea to be a truth. The other person perceives the idea to be a myth.

I know next to nothing about almost everything. I have written my words. Let us suppose. A person claims to have an ability to know. An idea is a truth. Let us suppose. From my point of view, the idea is a myth. In that event, please understand. Only the person can know for sure whether or not. The person is lying. The possibility of lying exists. For that reason, I direct my words at liars. They know who they are.

The lie is. A myth is a truth. Let us suppose. Religion, as practiced by liars, is a protection racket. Religious authority figures promise protection from anything bad happening after life. Let us suppose further. War, as practiced by a few paranoid oppressive violent people, is also a protection racket. The few paranoid oppressive violent people promise protection from anything bad happening during life. Let us suppose finally. The few paranoid oppressive violent people gain influence over religious authority figures. In that event, religious protection rackets would nest within military-industrial protection rackets.

Let us suppose. Religious authority figures lie. Let us suppose further. The few paranoid oppressive violent people, also lie. Let us suppose even further. Some people argue. The act of lying is justified in the interests of crime prevention. Let us suppose finally. Those same people are too heavily invested in the lie to change. In that event, they can not and or will not understand. Lying is a crime and a source of crime.

Let us suppose. Our minds have the power. We can make things manifest. Let us suppose further. A billion people believe in the value of pessimistic myths. Let us suppose finally. These pessimistic myths are. A good entity rules in Heaven. The good entity is at war with an evil entity. The evil entity rules over the Earth. In that event, the evil entity would manifest. A few paranoid oppressive violent people would concentrate wealth, income, and power into their own hands. Politicians would lie, steal, cheat, conquer, enslave, and kill. People would believe themselves to be demon possessed. People would believe other people to be demon possessed. People would exhibit sad, mad, and bad behaviors. These sad, mad, and bad behaviors would act as forces upon their bodies. The forces upon their bodies would be conducive to a state of disease in their bodies. These sad, mad, and bad behaviors would act as forces upon their habitats. The forces upon their habitats would be conducive to a state of disease in their habitats.

Let us suppose. Terrorism follows from religious extremism. In that event, the way to deal with this terrorism is. Reject a lie in all of its various forms. The lie is. These pessimistic myths are truths. Affirm an inability to know the unknowable. Accept a truth. The truth is. These pessimistic myths are myths. Promote tolerance. Acknowledge. The totality makes possible an infinite, number, diversity and variety of myths. Reject religious authority figures who repeat the lie in defense of their fraud, threat making, and extortion.

Let us suppose. People within secular states self-organize around freedom of speech, thought, and religious expression. People within secular states broadcast programming through mass communications media. Let us suppose further. People within fundamentalist states affirm an ability to know. A good entity rules in Heaven. The good entity is at war with an evil entity. The evil entity rules over the Earth. The minds of the many of our global culture are the property of the good entity. The broadcast of programming by the people of secular states is doing the work of the evil entity. The people of secular states are guilty of corrupting minds. The act of corrupting minds is an act of violence. The act of violence is done to the property of the good entity. The act of violence is a form of terrorism. Let us suppose finally. Some people within some fundamentalist states retaliate as terrorists with acts of violence against the people and property of secular states. In that event, a clash of cultures would occur. This clash of cultures could escalate into war, wherein; each side accuses the other of terrorism. Out of this war on terror comes a central moral question: Will states treat the minds of people as free or as the property of a good entity?

Let us suppose. A few paranoid oppressive violent people profit from supplying the demand for protection services. Let us suppose further. Terrorist activities create the demand for protection services. In that event, terrorism would have a tendency to become self-perpetuating.

Let us suppose. A few paranoid oppressive violent people terrorize the many people of the free states. The few paranoid oppressive violent people offer protection from terror in exchange for wealth, income, and power. In that event, they perpetrate a shakedown of epic proportions. Some people might call it a global war on terror.

Let us suppose. The goals of the global war on terror are not. End terror. Create security necessary for a lasting peace. The goals of the global war on terror are. Spread terror in war. Create insecurity necessary for a lasting war. Let us suppose further. Terror enables a few paranoid oppressive violent people. The few paranoid oppressive violent people create greater demand in the global marketplace for the sale and manufacture of the services and products of a beast of a military-industrial complex. Greater demand generates greater profits. In that event, greater profits would further concentrate wealth, income, and power into the hands of the few paranoid oppressive violent people.

Let us suppose. The many people of the state rely upon the mass media for news and entertainment. The many people of the state rely on politicians for representation in government. The few paranoid oppressive violent people own and operate the mass media. The few paranoid oppressive violent people own and operate the government. In that event, the few paranoid oppressive violent people could transmit fraudulent prewar intelligence as a means to an end of generating public support for the sale and manufacture of the services and products of a beast of a military-industrial complex. The act of transmitting fraudulent prewar intelligence would be an act of treason. Politicians would be unable and or unwilling to investigate the act of treason. The politicians would instead rally around the flag.

CHAPTER 64. IS IT WISE?

Is it wise for people to give their wealth, income, and power in exchange for a promise of protection? Is it wise to allow the wealth, income, and power of the people to concentrate into the hands of a few people? Lying, stealing, cheating, conquering, enslaving, and killing are sad, mad, and bad behaviors. Racist fascist warmongering behaviors are sad, mad, and bad behaviors. Let us suppose. These few people exhibit sad, mad, and bad behaviors. In that event, it would not be wise for people to give their wealth, income, and power in exchange for a promise of protection. It would not be wise to allow wealth, income, and power to concentrate within the hands of these few people. Truth telling, sharing, playing well with others, liberating, emancipating, and nurturing are glad behaviors. Friendly tolerant peacemaking behaviors are glad behaviors. Let us suppose. These few people exhibit glad behaviors. In that event, it would be wise for people to give their wealth, income, and power in exchange for a promise of protection. It would be wise to allow wealth, income, and power to concentrate into the hands of these few people.

Let us suppose. A few people have concentrated wealth, income, and power into their own hands. Let us suppose further. The many people gain influence over a state. The state heavily taxes the wealth, income, and property of these few people. Is heavy taxation a form of theft? Is taking ownership of the means of production away from these few people a form of theft? People band together for mutual protection. For that reason, a state forms. The only reason anybody owns anything is. A state authority says. This person owns this property. The state authority will take this person's side in any dispute over property rights. In exchange, the state authority expects. This person will. Pay tribute to the state authority. Pay property taxes, sales taxes, income taxes, estate taxes, vice taxes, and any other kind of taxes. Pledge allegiance to the state authority. Support the state authority in times of war. Let us suppose. This person does not pay their taxes. In that event, the state authority would no longer take this person's side in any dispute over property rights. The state authority might even confiscate property from this person as punishment. The state authority is the big bully. The big bully determines who owns what property. For that reason, the redistribution of wealth, income, and power by this state authority could not possibly be a form of theft. Heavy taxation could not possibly be a form of theft. Taking away ownership of the means of production from these few people could not possibly be a form of theft.

Theft inspires theft. Generosity inspires generosity. Theft robs the victim of the opportunity to be generous. Theft robs the thief of the opportunity to be grateful. Is it wise to expect generosity from people who believe in the value of pessimistic myths? Our values act as forces upon our emotions. Our emotions act as forces upon our behaviors. For those reasons, it would not be wise to expect generosity from people who believe in the value of pessimistic myths. However, it would be wise to expect generosity from people who believe in the value of the most optimistic myths.

Let us suppose. Terrorist activity creates demand in the marketplace for protection services.

A few paranoid oppressive violent people offer protection services. Terrorists and the few paranoid oppressive violent people collude in a shakedown of epic proportions. The few paranoid oppressive violent people sell the shakedown of epic proportions to the people of free societies as a 'global war on terror'. The terrorists sell the shakedown of epic proportions to religious extremists as a fight against an evil entity. In that event, profit becomes a motive for terrorism. However, the root cause of terrorism is. The few paranoid oppressive violent people have a low esteem of the totality. The terrorists have a low esteem of the totality.

Should I expect to win a 'war on terror' by giving all my income, wealth, and power to a few paranoid oppressive violent people in exchange for a promise of protection? Should I expect to win a 'war on terror' by creating terror in war? The 'war on terror' cannot be won by spreading terror in war. Spreading terror in war is a way to lose a war on terror. We lose a war on terror by spreading terror in war because we lose peoples, destroy properties, dissipate energies, and desolate our habitats. The 'war on terror' can be won by spreading humor in peace. Spreading humor in peace is a way to win a war on terror. We win a war on terror by spreading humor in peace because we gain new friends, create properties, recuperate energies, and restore our habitats.

Would a redistribution of wealth by the state provide to people a better means of defending themselves against terrorist attacks? Let us suppose. These people have the highest esteem of the totality. They value truths. They value the most optimistic myths. They balance the emotional forces of their minds. They are happy. They exhibit glad behaviors. In that event, this redistribution of wealth would likely work for the happiness, good health, and prosperity of these people. Let us suppose. These people have a low esteem of the totality. They value truths. They value pessimistic myths. They have an unbalance of the emotional forces of their minds. Their hearts are filled with sorrow, fear, and anger. They behave like racist fascist warmongers. In that event, this redistribution of wealth would likely not work for the happiness, good health, and prosperity of these people. The result would likely be exponential human population growth. Exponential human population growth would most likely be followed by increasing scarcity of breathable air, drinkable water, arable land, and available sunlight. Increasing scarcity would most likely be followed by a great deal more terrorism, war, destruction, suffering, sorrow, disease, stress, alienation, and abomination of death.

Let us suppose. A person argues. Life is a chemical reaction. The sun powers the chemical reaction. The chemical reaction feeds on itself. Seed bodies consume seed bodies. The game of survival and sacrifice selects for seed bodies of ever higher form and function. Certain people were willing and able to work, fight, and outnumber competition. Those people survived. Other people were unwilling and or unable to work, fight, and outnumber competition. Those people were sacrificed. The game of survival and sacrifice selected for human nature. Human nature motivates communities of faithful believers. For that reason, communities of faithful believers behave like racist fascist warmongers. This is a world of eternal struggle. Those who want to live, let them fight, and those who do not want to fight do not deserve to live. In that event, I would ask myself the question. What is wrong with that argument? I would answer. The argument is predicated on premises. These premises are. Self is only a seed and a body. Competition is the sole means of selecting for seed bodies of ever higher form and function. The soul-spirit plays no role in guiding the evolution of the form and function of seed-bodies. This person has no way of knowing whether or not. These premises are true. This person has no way of knowing whether or not. These premises are false. These premises are pessimistic myths. I value the most optimistic myths. For that reason, I think, believe, and predict. Life is, in part, a chemical reaction. Life is, in part, entertainment. The game of survival and sacrifice enables the soul spirit. The soul spirit selects for seed bodies of ever higher form and function. The soul-spirit plays a central role in guiding the evolution of the form and function of seed-bodies. The central role is. Our souls order the chaos of our minds. For that reason, cooperation is also a means of selecting seed bodies of ever higher form and function. Those who do not want to fight deserve to live. In fact, not fighting is often one of the surest ways of continuing to live.

Let us suppose. Religious authority figures propagate aggressive ideological traditions. These aggressive ideological traditions motivate communities of faithful believers. Members join a collective effort to work, fight, and outnumber the competition. In that event, the religious authority figures pander to the lowest moral instincts of human beings. They exacerbate the problem of exponential human population growth. They give their blessings to the behavior of racist fascist warmongers. Such religious authority figures recklessly endanger all life on planet Earth.

Let us suppose. A few paranoid oppressive violent people and their collaborators, admirers, and followers, think, believe, and predict. War is a means of purifying of the seed. This means of purifying the seed is necessary for the continued evolution of the body. In that event, they know next to nothing about almost everything. They value pessimistic myths. I value the most optimistic myths. A war of purification is not required for a species to evolve a seed-body of ever higher form and function. Our soul-spirit guides the evolution of our seed-bodies. Our soul-spirit can do so through cooperative means.

Let us suppose. A person argues. People exhibit sad, mad, and bad behaviors. The sad, mad, and bad behaviors threaten our habitat with disease. The concentration of wealth, income, and power into the hands of a few paranoid oppressive violent people suppresses the reproductive success of these people. Suppressing the reproductive success of these people preserves the health of our habitat. A need to preserve the health of our habitat justifies the concentration of wealth, income, and power into the hands of the few paranoid oppressive violent people. In that event, I would ask myself the question. What is wrong with this argument? I would answer. The argument is predicated on premises. The premises are. People are incapable of believing in the value of the most optimistic myths. People are incapable of having the highest esteem of self. People are incapable of having the highest esteem of the world. People are incapable of balancing the emotional forces of their minds. People are incapable of being happy. People are incapable of exhibiting glad behaviors. People are incapable of being healthy. People are incapable of preserving the health of our habitat. This person does not know whether or not. These premises are true. This person does not know whether or not. These premises are false. These premises are pessimistic myths. What else is wrong with this argument. The argument is predicated on a premise. The premise is. The concentration of wealth, income, and power into the hands of the few paranoid oppressive violent people suppresses the reproductive success of people. The fact is. Evidence suggests otherwise. Let us suppose. The few paranoid oppressive violent people find. They are slave owners. Religious authority figures are their slave drivers. Members are their spiritual slaves. In that event, it would be logical to infer. The few paranoid oppressive violent people would regard communities of faithful believers as part of their wealth. They would seek to expand their wealth. They would encourage members to behave like racist fascist warmongers. Be fruitful and multiply. Work all the hours of the day from dawn to dusk. Fight against anybody who is not doing the same thing. Fight against anybody who is not believing in the same way.

Let us suppose. People believe in the value of the most optimistic myths. People believe in the value of truths. In that event, the values of these people would act as forces upon the emotions of these people. Joy, faith, and love, would balance sorrow, fear, and anger. These people would balance the emotional forces of their minds. These people would be happy. The emotions of these people would act as forces upon the behaviors of these people. These people would exhibit glad behaviors. These glad behaviors would act as forces upon the bodies of these people. These forces would be conducive to a state of good health in the bodies of these people. These glad behaviors would act as forces upon the habitat of these people. These forces would be conducive to a state of good health in the habitat of these people. These people would prevent the global culture from falling victim to apocalyptic self-fulfilling prophecies. These people would spare the environment from destruction. These people would stop a global war on terror. These people would better meet human demands for the necessities of life: The necessities of life are breathable air, drinkable water, arable land, and available sunlight. These people would make sex for occupational, recreational, and homosexual purposes as honorable and acceptable as sex for procreative purposes. These people would make sex safer. These people would provide sex education to people. A need to suppress the reproductive success of people would disappear. Psychotic extremes of poverty and wealth would disappear.

CHAPTER 65. PERSECUTION COMPLEX

Let us suppose. A few people concentrate wealth, income, and power into their own hands. The few people compete. The few people rule over territories. Success attracts competition. The concentration of wealth, income, and power into the hands of these few people makes the competition to rule homicidal, genocidal, and even suicidal at times. These few people become a few paranoid oppressive violent people.

Let us suppose. The needs and aspirations of these few paranoid oppressive violent people include. Achieve and maintain authority, power, order, and control. For that reason, the few paranoid oppressive violent people gain influence over religious authority figures. Religious authority figures gain influence over communities of faithful believers. Communities of faithful believers gain influence over members.

Let us suppose. These members use their senses and perceptions. Gather truths about their set of living arrangements and find. The few paranoid oppressive violent people rule over domestic territories. The few paranoid oppressive violent people are at war with outsiders. The outsiders rule over foreign territories. A system of reward and punishment exists. The system compels the members. The members observe and obey the will of the few paranoid oppressive violent people. The members disregard and disobey the will of the outsiders.

Let us suppose. These members believe in the value of pessimistic myths. The pessimistic myths are. A good entity rules in Heaven. The good entity is at war with an evil entity. The evil entity rules over the Earth. A system of divine eternal reward and abominable infernal punishment exists. The system compels the faithful. The faithful observe and obey the will of the good entity. The faithful disregard and disobey the will of the evil entity.

Let us suppose. Members find. Their pessimistic myths suggest their truths. For that reason, these members think, believe, and predict. The few paranoid oppressive violent people are representatives of the good entity here on planet Earth. The few paranoid oppressive violent people are divinely ordained to rule over domestic territories. The will of the few paranoid oppressive violent people is, in fact, the will of the good entity. The outsiders are representatives of the evil entity here on planet Earth. The outsiders are not divinely ordained to rule over foreign territories. The will of the outsiders is, in fact, the will of the evil entity.

Let us suppose. The members think, believe, and predict. The good entity chose prophets. The good entity revealed visions of the future to the prophets. Religious authority figures wrote down the exclusive divine revelations of spiritual knowledge as words in a set of sacred scrolls. Religious authority figures know how to translate and interpret these words.

Let us suppose. Religious authority figures affirm an ability to know. The visions of the future reveal. Armageddon will occur. Armageddon is a necessary final horrible war. The good entity will have final victory over the evil entity. The good entity will judge all people. The good entity will find. Some people observed and obeyed the will of the good entity. The good entity will reward these people. The good entity will elevate these people to a place of divine eternal bliss.

The good entity will find. Some people disregarded and disobeyed the will of the good entity. The good entity will punish these people. The good entity will throw these people into a place of abominable infernal torment.

Let us suppose. Religious authority figures affirm an ability to know. The good entity does not wish to punish people for lack of knowledge about the will of the good entity. For that reason, the good entity chose messengers. The good entity revealed to the messengers the will, words, way, and laws of the good entity. Religious authority figures wrote down these exclusive divine revelations of spiritual knowledge as words in the set of sacred scrolls.

Let us suppose. Members think, believe, and predict. Religious authority figures know how to translate and interpret these words. Religious authority figures will guide the faithful to a place of divine eternal bliss.

Let us suppose. The religious authority figures say. Our only hope of salvation from a place of abominable infernal torment is. Observe and obey the will of the good entity. The will of the good entity is, in fact, the will of the few paranoid oppressive violent people. Do what the few paranoid oppressive violent people say.

Let us suppose. The few paranoid oppressive violent people find. Authority, power, order, and control enables them. They can. Make members into their slaves. Make religious authority figures into their slave drivers. Make themselves into slave masters.

Let us suppose. An autocracy rules over domestic territories. This autocracy supports psychotic extremes of poverty and wealth. These psychotic extremes of poverty and wealth form a religious elitist society. This religious elitist society supports slaveries and wrongs.

Let us suppose finally. Some people would venture to disagree with members. In that event, I would advise those people. Before doing so, take pause. Make a rigorous examination of the reasons for the disagreement. Assess the possible risks and costs of the act of revealing the disagreement to communities of faithful believers. Study history. A study of history reveals. Intolerant communities of faithful believers often regarded outsiders as representatives of the evil entity. Intolerant communities of faithful believers often judged outsiders to be unfit to rule over foreign territories. Intolerant communities of faithful believers often regarded the will of the outsiders as the will of the evil entity. Intolerant communities of faithful believers often condemned outsiders as a dangerous threat to the future of society. Intolerant communities of faithful believers often condemned outsiders as evil people, infidels, blasphemers, heretics, and or witches. The few paranoid oppressive violent people have had outsiders crucified, burned, hung, impaled, disemboweled, beheaded, drowned, banished, exiled, excommunicated, persecuted, tortured, intimidated, interrogated, assaulted, abused, injured, mutilated, and or alienated. The few paranoid oppressive violent people have deprived outsiders of property and or status. The few paranoid oppressive violent people have put outsiders to death.

Let us suppose. A democracy rules over domestic territories. This democracy supports a large middle class. This large middle class forms a secular pluralistic society. This secular pluralistic society supports freedoms and rights. In that event, I advise those people, who would venture to disagree with members. Don't be intimidated by intolerant communities of faithful believers. Members proudly affirm an ability to know. These pessimistic myths are truths. The truth is. These members know next to nothing about almost everything.

The truth is. It appears. These pessimistic myths suggest truths. These truths were true when the myths were made. These truths were true when the words were written down in a set of sacred scrolls. The truths were about the seed body and the material plane. The myths are about the soul spirit and the spiritual realm. The truths are pessimistic. For that reason, the myths are pessimistic. A myth is. A good entity exists. This myth suggests a truth. The truth is. A few paranoid oppressive violent people existed. A myth is. The will of the good entity exists. This myth suggests a truth. The truth is. The will of the few paranoid oppressive violent people existed. A myth is. Universal submission to the will of the good entity would be Heaven on Earth. This myth suggests a truth. The truth is. Universal submission to the will of the few paranoid oppressive violent people was a spiritual slavery. A myth is. An evil entity exists. This myth suggests a truth. The truth is. Outsiders existed. A myth is. The will of the evil entity exists. This myth suggests a truth. The truth is. The will of the outsiders existed. A myth is. The good entity reigns in Heaven. This myth suggests a truth. The truth is. The few paranoid oppressive violent people ruled over domestic territories. A myth is. The evil entity rules over the Earth. This myth suggests a truth. The truth is. Outsiders ruled over foreign territories. A myth is. The good entity is at war with the evil entity. This myth suggests a truth. The truth is. The few paranoid oppressive violent people were at war with the outsiders.

The act of suggesting these truths does not make these pessimistic myths into truths. These pessimistic myths remain myths. Truths are rare. Myths are infinitely abundant. However, it appears. The act of suggesting these truths enables members. Members can confirm their belief in the value of these pessimistic myths.

It appears. These pessimistic myths suggest predictions about the future. A myth is. Armageddon will occur. The prediction about the future is. A horrible war will occur. A myth is. The good entity will have final victory over the evil entity. The prediction about the future is. The few paranoid oppressive violent people will have final victory over the outsiders. A myth is. The good entity will judge all people. The prediction about the future is. The few paranoid oppressive violent people will judge all people. A myth is. The good entity will find. Some people observed and obeyed the will of the good entity. The good entity will reward those people. The good entity will elevate those people to a place of divine eternal bliss. The prediction about the future is. The few paranoid oppressive violent people will find. Some people observed and obeyed the will of the few paranoid oppressive violent people. The few paranoid oppressive violent people will reward those people. The few paranoid oppressive violent people will elevate those people to a place of safety and refuge. These people will be safe from violent abuse. The place of safety and refuge will be a haven on Earth. A myth is. The good entity will find. Some people disregarded and disobeyed the will of the good entity. The good entity will punish these people. The good entity will throw these people into a place of abominable infernal torment. The prediction about the future is. The few paranoid oppressive violent people will find. Some people disregarded and disobeyed the will of the few paranoid oppressive violent people. The few paranoid oppressive violent people will punish those people. The few paranoid oppressive violent people will throw those people into a place of danger and exposure. Some of these people will work as slaves under horrendous conditions until they die of disease or starvation. Some of these people will be murdered upon arrival. The place of danger and exposure will be Hell on Earth.

From these suggestions, it is logical to infer. Members of intolerant communities of faithful believers are collaborators in search of a tyrant. They would replace democracy with autocracy. They would replace a large middle class with psychotic extremes of poverty and wealth. They would replace a secular pluralistic society with a religious elitist society. They would replace freedoms and rights with slaveries and wrongs. Let us suppose. They did so. In that event, they wouldn't feel one ounce of sympathy for outsiders. Outsiders would be enslaved under horrendous conditions. Outsiders would be killed in places of danger and exposure.

These members value certain ideas. These certain ideas are their values. Their values act as forces upon their emotions. Listen to their voices. Can you hear the sorrow, fear, and anger? They value truths. The most powerful emotional forces of sorrow, fear, and anger follow from the discovery of a truth. The truth is. It appears. One day, the seed-body of self will die. They value pessimistic myths. The three most commonly valued pessimistic myths are. Self has only one life to live. Self has only one body to give. Self is only a seed and a body. Their belief in the value of these pessimistic myths does not enable them. They are unable to balance the emotional forces of their minds. For that reason, their hearts are filled with sorrow, fear, and anger. Their emotions act as forces upon their behaviors. For that reason, they exhibit sad, mad, and bad behaviors. Lying, stealing, cheating, conquering, enslaving, and killing are sad, mad, and bad behaviors. Racist fascist warmongering behaviors are sad, mad, and bad behaviors.

They are practitioners of discovery religions. Discovery religions are built upon a lie. The lie is. These pessimistic myths are truths. They wish to build civilizations upon the lie. Let us suppose. They succeed in doing so. In that event, these civilizations would be weak and unstable.

Belligerent nationalism has been tried before. See World War One. See the interwar years. See World War Two. See ethnic cleansing. See war against humanity. See concentration camps. See mass murder. Never Forget.

CHAPTER 66. OUR SOUL-SPIRIT IS CAPABLE

I believe in the value of truths. The truth is. I know next to nothing about almost everything. The truth is. A myth is a myth.

We live in a body-consuming biosphere. The body-consuming biosphere is on a crusted magma globe. Let us suppose. A person is standing on the surface of the crusted magma globe. In that event, it appears. The person is standing on a material plane. The crusted magma globe has limited dimensions. For that reason, it appears. Scarcity exists on the material plane.

Some people have a low esteem of self and a low esteem of the world. These people value certain ideas. These certain ideas are their values. Their values act as forces upon their emotions. They value truths. The most powerful emotional forces of sorrow, fear, and anger follow from the discovery of a truth. The truth is. It appears. One day, the seed-body of self will die. They value pessimistic myths. The three most popular pessimistic myths are. Self has only one life to live. Self has only one body to give. Self is only a seed and a body. Their belief in the value of pessimistic myths does not enable them. They are unable to balance the emotional forces of their minds. For that reason, their hearts are filled with sorrow, fear, and anger.

Very often, these people think, believe, and predict. The accumulation of wealth, income, and power into their own hands will enable them. They will be able to balance the emotional forces of their minds. For that reason, they seek to concentrate wealth, income, and power into their own hands. However, no amount of wealth, income, and power will ever be great enough to compensate them for their discovery of a truth. The truth is. It appears. One day, the seed-body of self will die. For that reason, their attempts to balance the emotional forces of their minds are destined to be desperate and failing attempts.

Let us suppose. A few of these people are successful. They concentrate, wealth, income, and power into their own hands. Let us suppose further. They continue to have a low esteem of self and a low esteem of the world. In that event, enough would never be enough. Their hearts would continue to be filled with sorrow, fear, and anger. Their emotions would act as forces upon their behaviors. They would exhibit sad, mad, and bad behaviors. Racist fascist warmongering behaviors are sad, mad, and bad behaviors. Lying, stealing, cheating, conquering, enslaving, and killing are sad, mad, and bad behaviors. The success of the few people would attract competition. The concentration of wealth, income, and power into the hands of the few people would make the competition to rule homicidal, genocidal, and even suicidal at times. The few people would become a few paranoid oppressive violent people. The end result would be. A few paranoid oppressive violent people would exhibit sad, mad, and bad behaviors because their hearts are filled with sorrow, fear, and anger. For that reason, I do not collaborate with these people. I have the highest esteem of myself. I have the highest esteem of my world. I provide good examples of how to do so.

Let us suppose. A few paranoid oppressive violent people gain influence over religious authority figures. Religious authority figures gain influence over communities of faithful believers. Communities of faithful believers gain influence over members. In that event, these members would align their values with the needs and aspirations of the few paranoid oppressive violent people. The needs and aspirations of the few paranoid oppressive violent people are. Achieve and maintain authority, power, order, and control.

Our minds have the power. We can make things manifest. We build within our minds. We build models of the totality. We build these models in accordance with our values.

Let us suppose. A billion people believe in the value of pessimistic myths. In that event, the billion people would manifest finite scarcity. Finite scarcity would inspire theft. A few paranoid oppressive violent people would concentrate wealth, income, and power into their own hands. Politicians would lie, steal, cheat, conquer, enslave, and kill. People would exhibit sad, mad, and bad behaviors. Sad, mad, and bad behaviors would act as forces upon their bodies. These forces would be conducive to a state of disease in their bodies. Sad, mad, and bad behaviors would act as forces upon their habitats. These forces would be conducive to a state of disease in their habitats.

Let us suppose. A billion people believe in the value of the most optimistic myths. In that event, the billion people would manifest infinite abundance. Abundance would inspire generosity. The few would give generously to the many. Politicians would tell the truth, share, play well with others, liberate, emancipate, and nurture. The people would exhibit glad behaviors. Glad behaviors would act as forces upon their bodies. These forces would be conducive to a state of good health in their bodies. Glad behaviors would act as forces upon their habitats. These forces would be conducive to a state of good health in their habitats.

Let us suppose. Legal constructs concentrate wealth, income, and power into the hands of a few people. Let us suppose further. A billion people make infinite abundance manifest. In that event, the billion people would exhibit glad behaviors. Glad behaviors would inspire generosity. The few people would liberate the billion people from the legal constructs. Politicians would liberate the billion people from the legal constructs. The billion people would liberate themselves from the legal constructs.

I believe in the value of the most optimistic myths. Our spirit endows each and every creature with a seed, body, soul, and spirit. Our seed bodies are fractal infernal and temporal. Our soul spirit is divine and eternal. Our soul-spirit is able. Our soul-spirit accepts the conduct of any given creature as entertainment. From the abundance of an infinite being follows an abundance of finite creatures. From the abundance of an infinite being follows the acceptance of the conduct of each finite creature as entertainment.

CHAPTER 67. USED AS A TOOL

Let us suppose. Our common needs and aspirations are. Achieve and maintain happiness, good health, and prosperity. Optimism correlates with happiness and good health. Pessimism correlates with sorrow, fear, anger, and disease. Happiness and good health in our lives correlates with success and prosperity in our businesses. Sorrow, fear, anger, and disease in our lives correlates with failure and hardship in our businesses.

Let us suppose further. A few paranoid oppressive violent people use pessimistic myths as a tool. The tool enables them. The few paranoid oppressive violent people satisfy their needs and aspirations. Their needs and aspirations include. Achieve and maintain authority, power, order, and control. In that event, the few paranoid oppressive violent people put their own needs and aspirations above our common needs and aspirations.

Let us suppose. The few paranoid oppressive violent people gain influence over religious authority figures. Religious authority figures gain influence over communities of faithful believers. Communities of faithful believers gain influence over members. Members think, believe, and predict. These pessimistic myths are truths. A good entity rules in Heaven. The good entity is at war with an evil entity. The evil entity rules over the Earth. A system of divine eternal reward and abominable infernal punishment exists. The system compels the faithful. The faithful observe and obey the will of the good entity. In that event, projection theory enables me. I think, believe, and predict. These pessimistic myths suggested truths. These truths were true when the myths were made. The truths were true when the words were written down in a set of sacred scrolls. The truths were. A few paranoid oppressive violent people ruled over domestic territories. The few paranoid oppressive violent people were at war with outsiders. The outsiders ruled over foreign territories. A system of reward and punishment existed. The system compelled the insiders. The insiders observed and obeyed the will of the few paranoid oppressive violent people.

Let us suppose. Members affirm an ability to know. The good entity chose messengers. In that event, projection theory enables me. I think, believe, and predict. These messengers used their senses and perceptions. Searched their surroundings. Gather truths about their set of living arrangements. These messengers projected their truths into their imaginations. They used their imaginations. These messengers made these pessimistic myths. These pessimistic myths suggested their truths. The act of suggesting their truths did not make these pessimistic myths into truths. These pessimistic myths remained myths. However, it would appear. These members did believe in the value of truths. For that reason, the act of suggesting their truths did enable these members. These members found confirmation of their belief in the value of these pessimistic myths.

Let us suppose. Members think, believe, and predict. The good entity chose prophets. The good entity revealed visions of the future to the prophets. Religious authority figures wrote down these exclusive divine revelations of spiritual knowledge as words in a set of sacred scrolls. Religious authority figures know how to translate and interpret these words. Religious authority figures say. The visions of the future reveal. A great tribulation will occur.

An anti-christ will rise to power. Armageddon will follow. Armageddon is a necessary final horrible war. After Armageddon occurs, the good entity will have final victory over the evil entity.

Let us suppose further. These religious authority figures go on to say. These are the end times. Armageddon is imminent. Judgment day is nigh. The good entity is on our side. The will of the good entity is. The faithful must go to war against the outsiders. A big reward awaits the faithful after they march to their own deaths in war.

Let us suppose finally. Members believe in the value of these pessimistic myths. In that event, their belief in the value of these pessimistic myths would not enable them. They would be unable to balance the emotional forces of their minds. For that reason, their hearts would be filled with sorrow, fear, and anger. They would exhibit sad, mad, and bad behaviors. Their sad, mad, and bad behaviors would threaten the health of our habitats and the health of our seed bodies. On the other hand, their belief in the value of these pessimistic myths would. Build camaraderie, high morale, and a shared sense of purpose. The camaraderie, high morale, and shared sense of purpose would make them a formidable fighting force. The few paranoid oppressive violent people would find. They can use pessimistic myths as a tool. They can use the tool to enslave. They can use the tool to plant sorrow, fear, and anger in hearts. They can harness the sorrow, fear, anger in hearts. They can order the faithful to march off to their own deaths in war. They can defend their own private business interests. They can expand their own wealth, income, and power. They can profit from the sale and manufacture of war.

Let us suppose. Members think, believe, and predict. The evil entity has the power. The evil entity can influence the thoughts and actions of ordinary people. Ordinary people can not trust their own abilities to think and act for themselves. Ordinary people must trust religious authority figures to think and act for them. Ordinary people can not trust their own abilities to make up their own minds. Ordinary people must trust religious authority figures to make up their minds for them. In that event, communities of faithful believers psychologically corner members into doing what religious authority figures say.

Let us suppose. Religious authority figures say. The will of the good entity is, in fact, the will of the few paranoid oppressive violent people. In that event, the few paranoid oppressive violent people would find. They can make members into their slaves. They can make religious authority figures into their slave drivers. They can make themselves into slave owners.

The will of the few paranoid oppressive violent people suggests a standard of conduct. Let us suppose. The standard of conduct promotes racist fascist warmongering behaviors. Let us suppose further. Conformity to the standard of conduct becomes a matter of national patriotic duty. In that event, nonconformists may find themselves. Outcast from communities of faithful believers. Condemned by religious authority figures. Treated like traitors by the few paranoid oppressive violent people. Conformists may find themselves. Welcomed by communities of faithful believers. Praised by religious authority figures. Treated like patriots by the few paranoid oppressive violent people.

Let us suppose. Members think, believe, and predict. A good entity chose messengers. The good entity revealed karmic laws of cause and effect to the messengers. Religious authority figures wrote down these exclusive divine revelations of spiritual knowledge as words in a set of sacred scrolls. Religious authority figures know how to translate and interpret these words. Religious authority figures say. We have souls. Our souls incarnate within our seed-bodies. The karmic laws of cause and effect govern the behavior, fate, and destiny of our souls. The karmic laws of cause and effect suggest a standard of conduct. Some people did conform their behaviors to the standard of conduct during previous lifetimes. Those souls have low karmic debt. For that reason, those souls were born with high socio-economic, political, and or cultural status within society during this lifetime. Some people did not conform their behaviors to the standard of conduct during previous lifetimes. Those souls have high karmic debt. For that reason, those souls were born with low socio-economic, political, and or cultural status within society during this lifetime.

Let us suppose finally. Members think, believe, and predict. Souls can make amends. Souls can conform their behaviors to the standard of conduct during this lifetime. Souls can lower their karmic debt. Thereby, souls can be born with higher status within society during future lifetimes. In that event, the few paranoid oppressive violent people would find. They can aggrandize themselves. They can dictate the details of this standard of conduct.

CHAPTER 68. SPIRITUAL CONFLICT

Let us suppose. Religious authority figures say. The good entity chose messengers. The good entity revealed the will, words, way, and laws of the good entity to the messengers. Religious authority figures wrote down the exclusive divine revelations of spiritual knowledge as words in a set of sacred scrolls. Religious authority figures know how to translate and interpret the words.

Religious authority figures say. An evil entity had the power. The evil entity tempted our ancestors. Our ancestors disregarded and disobeyed the will of the good entity. Sin entered the world. With sin came death. Ordinary people are sinful. For that reason, the good entity does not commune with ordinary people. Personal divine revelations of spiritual knowledge will not confirm the exclusive divine revelations of spiritual knowledge. Ordinary people must trust religious authority figures to make up their minds for them.

Let us suppose further. Members believe in the value of these pessimistic myths. In that event, members would. Malign themselves. Malign their world. Malign their ancestors. The few paranoid oppressive violent people would find. They can. Strip members of their authority to make up their own minds. They can make members feel unworthy of a more equitable distribution of wealth, income, and power.

Let us suppose. A symbiotic relationship connects the fates and destinies of ideological traditions, citizens, and states. A game of survival and sacrifice enables the soul spirit. The soul spirit selects for ideological traditions, citizens, and states. In that event, a defeat of a state would be a defeat of its ideological traditions. A defeat of a state would be a defeat of its citizens. A victory of a state would be a victory of its ideological traditions. A victory of a state would be a victory of its citizens.

Aggressive ideological traditions promote a collective effort to work, fight, and outnumber competition. Some aggressive ideological traditions originated before the establishment of ancient paternalistic theocracies. Let us suppose. A few paranoid oppressive violent people, religious authority figures, communities of faithful believers, and members, propagate aggressive ideological traditions. Let us suppose further. The few paranoid oppressive violent people, the religious authority figures, the communities of faithful believers, and the members, survive the test of time. In that event, these aggressive ideological traditions would survive the test of time.

Let us suppose. Citizens of a state devote themselves to the interests of the state. Let us suppose further. The citizens of the state think, believe, and predict. These aggressive ideological traditions have worked for citizens and the state in the past. These aggressive ideological traditions are working for citizens and the state in the present. These aggressive ideological traditions will work for citizens and the state in the future. In that event, devotion to the interests of the state would lead these citizens. These citizens would continue to propagate these aggressive ideological traditions.

Let us suppose. Aggressive ideological traditions offer entertainment, education, and leadership. This entertainment, education, and leadership conserves power structures. These power structures concentrate wealth, income, and power into the hands of the few paranoid oppressive violent people. For that reason, these aggressive ideological traditions are conservative.

Let us suppose further. The aggressive ideological traditions come to dominate the global culture. In that event, the few paranoid oppressive violent people, the religious authority figures, the communities of faithful believers, and the members would face challenges. The limited dimensions of our body-consuming biosphere would challenge their exponential population growth. The many people would experience greater scarcity while the few paranoid oppressive violent people would experience greater wealth, income, and power. The exponential population growth of communities of faithful believers would force members to go further out on to a technological limb in order to survive. Out on this technological limb, members would be even more vulnerable to terrorist attack. Their race to work, fight, and outnumber competition could lead to population overshoot, resource depletion, pollution, abrupt climate change, and habitat loss. Their race to work, fight, and outnumber competition could turn into a race to Armageddon. Armageddon could precipitate human extinction.

Let us suppose. Members think, believe, and predict. A sacrificed demigod will return as a warrior in a second coming. The warrior will fight in the end times to achieve a final victory. The final victory will be against the evil entity. The good entity will reward the faithful for their racist fascist warmongering behaviors. The good entity will rapture the faithful up to Heaven before Armageddon unfolds upon those sinners who are "left behind". In that event, they would know next to nothing about almost everything. Members would use these pessimistic myths. Members would dismiss the idea of a savior whose messages are of love, compassion, and forgiveness.

My messages are of love, compassion, and forgiveness. Instead of a discovery religion, I offer a mystery religion. Instead of a low esteem of the totality, I offer the highest esteem of the totality. Instead of conservative education, entertainment, and leadership, I offer liberal education, entertainment, and leadership. Instead of spiritual laws of a good entity, I offer spiritual laws of infinite love, divine forgiveness, eternal freedom, and unifying grace. Instead of racist fascist warmongering behaviors, I offer friendly tolerant peacemaking behaviors. Instead of a prohibition of sex for occupational, recreational, and homosexual purposes, I offer an allowance of sex for occupational, recreational, and homosexual purposes. Instead of opposition to sexual education, I offer support for sexual education. Instead of a belief in the value of pessimistic myths, I offer a belief in the value of the most optimistic myths. Instead of pessimistic myths about the existence of a spiritual conflict between good and evil, I offer the most optimistic myths about the existence of spiritual unity between Mother God and all of her Soul Children. Instead of pessimistic myths about the existence of exclusive divine revelations of spiritual knowledge, I offer a most optimistic myth about the existence of continuous spiritual communion between soul and spirit.

CHAPTER 69. UNITED VERSUS DIVIDED

Let us suppose. Members affirm an ability to know. In the beginning, a good entity ruled over the Earth. In the end, the good entity will rule over the Earth again. In the present and on into the unforeseeable future, an evil entity rules over the Earth. The evil entity has a name. The name is Satan. In that event, these members would be "Satan Aggrandizers".

Let us suppose. Members value a lie. The lie is. These pessimistic myths are truths. Let us suppose further. Communities of faithful believers wage an organized campaign of negativism against anybody who devalues the lie. In that event, I might become a target of these communities of faithful believers.

Let us suppose. Billions of people affirm an ability to know. These pessimistic myths are truths. In that event, the minds of billions of people would have the power. They would make things manifest. The evil entity would manifest. A few paranoid oppressive violent people would concentrate wealth, income, and power into their own hands. Politicians would lie, steal, cheat, conquer, enslave, and kill. Billions of people would exhibit sad, mad, and bad behaviors. These sad, mad, and bad behaviors would be conducive to a state of disease in their bodies. These sad, mad, and bad behaviors would be conducive to a state of disease in their habitats.

I don't want billions of people to suffer a state of disease in their bodies. I don't want billions of people to suffer a state of disease in their habitats. For that reason, I educate, entertain, and lead by example. I align my values with our common needs and aspirations. Our common needs and aspirations are. Achieve and maintain happiness, good health, and prosperity.

These pessimistic myths are all about the existence of a divided spiritual realm. Pessimism correlates with sorrow, fear, anger, and disease in our lives. Sorrow, fear, anger, and disease in our lives correlates with failure and hardship in our businesses. I do not desire unhappiness, disease, failure, and hardship. For that reason, I do not believe in the value of these pessimistic myths.

The most optimistic myths are about the existence of a unified spiritual realm. Optimism correlates with happiness and good health in our lives. Happiness and good health in our lives correlates with success and prosperity in our businesses. I desire happiness, good health, and prosperity. For that reason, I believe in the value of the most optimistic myths. The most optimistic myths include. Spiritual unity exists between all beings even when a conflict between predator and prey makes the drama of life and death an entertaining experience.

In a material sense, conflict limits both predator and prey. Risk of liability limits both predator and prey. The form and function of seed-bodies limits both predator and prey. The attributes of seed-bodies limit both predator and prey. The limited dimensions of the body-consuming biosphere limit both predator and prey. Life forms compete for energy, space, and time in the body-consuming biosphere. The competition limits both predator and prey.

Let us suppose. Members use their senses and perceptions. Search their surroundings. Gather truths about their set of living arrangements, and find. It appears. Laws of nature, state, and the universe predict the behavior and fate of matter and energy in the known universe. The behavior of life forms is strangely attracted to a standard of conduct. The standard of conduct follows from the act of observing and obeying these laws. Let us suppose further. Members project these truths into their imaginations. They use their imaginations. They make pessimistic myths. The pessimistic myths include. The laws of the good entity exist. In that event, these communities of faithful believers would be worshiping nature, the state, and the universe as the good entity. They would be worshiping the creation rather than the creator.

Let us suppose. Members use their senses and perceptions. Search their surroundings. Gather truths about their set of living arrangements, and find. It appears. A divided material plane exists. A primal conflict between predator and prey divides the body-consuming biosphere. Let us suppose further. Members project their truths into their imaginations. They use their imaginations. They make pessimistic myths. The pessimistic myths include. A divided spiritual realm exists. A good entity is at war with an evil entity. In that event, these pessimistic myths would suggest their truths. The act of suggesting their truths would not make these pessimistic myths into truths. These pessimistic myths would remain myths. However, Projection theory enables me. I predict. The act of suggesting their truths would enable these members. These members would find confirmation of their belief in the value of these pessimistic myths.

Let us suppose. Members use their senses and perceptions. Search their surroundings. Gather truths about their set of living arrangements, and find. A few paranoid oppressive violent people rule over domestic territories. The few paranoid oppressive violent people are at war with outsiders. The outsiders rule over foreign territories. A system of reward and punishment exists. The system compels members. Members observe and obey the will of the few paranoid oppressive violent people. Members disregard and disobey the will of the outsiders. Let us suppose further. These members project their truths into their imaginations. They use their imaginations. They make pessimistic myths. The pessimistic myths include. A good entity rules in Heaven. The good entity is at war with an evil entity. The evil entity rules over the Earth. A system of divine eternal reward and abominable infernal punishment exists. The system compels the faithful. The faithful observe and obey the will of the good entity. The faithful disregard and disobey the will of the evil entity. Let us suppose still further. Members find. Their pessimistic myths suggest their truths. For that reason, these members think, believe, and predict. The few paranoid oppressive violent people are divinely ordained to rule over domestic territories. The few paranoid oppressive violent people are representatives of the good entity. The will of the few paranoid oppressive violent people is, in fact, the will of the good entity. The outsiders are not divinely ordained to rule over foreign territories. The outsiders are representatives of the evil entity. The will of the outsiders is, in fact, the will of the evil entity. Let us suppose finally. Members regard me as an outsider. In that event, the members would most likely consider me, my ideas, and or my actions to be evil.

Let us suppose. The members do consider me, my ideas, and or my actions to be evil. In that event, the members might actually persecute me.

These members are beautiful. Danger often accompanies beauty. For that reason, I admire their beauty from a safe distance. I seek contact with like-minded individuals. I avoid contact with those people who would label me 'evil'.

CHAPTER 70. A BIG MISTAKE

We live in a body-consuming biosphere. The body-consuming biosphere is not a static system. The body-consuming biosphere is a complex chaotic dynamic system. A primal conflict between predator and prey divides the body-consuming biosphere. Life forms play a game of survival and sacrifice. Seed bodies consume seed bodies. Over time, the soul spirit selects for seed bodies of ever higher form and function.

States, ideological traditions, and communities of faithful believers also play a game of survival and sacrifice. Over time, the soul spirit selects for states, ideological traditions, and communities of faithful believers.

Let us suppose. Communities of faithful believers don't usually micromanage members. Members are semi-autonomous. Members are otherwise intelligent. Members can think for themselves in most instances. Let us suppose further. Most of what the religious authority figures say is very appealing to members. The religious authority figures say. The will of the good entity is. Be fruitful and multiply. Work all of the hours of the day from dawn to dusk. Fight against anybody who is not doing the same thing. Fight against anybody who is not believing in the same way. Let us suppose finally. Members observe and obey the will of the good entity. In that event, it would be logical to infer. The act of being fruitful and multiplying would make superior numbers possible. The act of working all of the hours of the day from dawn to dusk would make superior labor possible. The act of fighting against anybody who is not doing the same thing, would make military superiority possible. The act of fighting against anybody who is not believing in the same way, would make superior morale possible. The act of observing and obeying the will of the good entity would make superior performance possible. Let us suppose. The communities of faithful believers outperform the competition. In that event, the survival of these communities of faithful believers would best ensure the survival of their belief in the value of these pessimistic myths.

Would their belief in the value of these pessimistic myths also best ensure the survival of these communities of faithful believers? Let us suppose. These communities of faithful believers did not survive. In that event, their belief in the value of these pessimistic myths would not survive. For that reason, a relationship does exist between their belief in the value of these pessimistic myths and the survival of communities of faithful believers. Their belief in the value of these pessimistic myths would enable communities of faithful believers. These communities of faithful believers would work, fight, and outnumber competition. Survival of these communities of faithful believers would best ensure the survival of their belief in the value of these pessimistic myths.

However, their values would act as forces upon their emotions. Most likely, they would value truths. The most powerful emotional forces of sorrow, fear, and anger would follow from their discovery of a truth. The truth is. It appears. One day, the seed body of self will die. Most likely, they would value the three most commonly valued pessimistic myths. The three most commonly valued pessimistic myths are. Self has only one life to live. Self has only one body to give. Self is only a seed and a body. Their belief in the value of these pessimistic myths would not enable them. They would be unable to balance the emotional forces of their minds. For that reason, their hearts would be filled with sorrow, fear, and anger. Their emotions would act as forces upon their behaviors. These communities of faithful believers would gain influence over members. Members would exhibit sad, mad, and bad behaviors. Lying, stealing, cheating, conquering, enslaving, and killing are sad, mad, and bad behaviors. Racist fascist warmongering behaviors are sad, mad, and bad behaviors. Their sad, mad, and bad behaviors would act as forces upon their bodies. The forces would be conducive to a state of disease in their bodies. Their sad, mad, and bad behaviors would act as forces upon their habitats. The forces would be conducive to a state of disease in their habitats. For that reason, in the long run, their belief in the value of these pessimistic myths would not best ensure the survival of these communities of faithful believers.

Let us suppose. We built a civilization upon a lie. The lie is. These pessimistic myths are truths. In that event, the act of building the civilization upon a lie would be a big mistake. It would be a big mistake, because our values would not be aligned with our common needs and aspirations. Our common needs and aspirations are. Achieve and maintain happiness, good health, and prosperity. Optimism correlates with happiness, good health, and prosperity. Pessimism correlates with sorrow, fear, anger, disease, and failure.

Our minds have the power. We can cause things to manifest. Let us suppose. In the name of doing the will of a good entity, members focus their mental energies on pessimistic myths. The pessimistic myths are. An evil entity rules over the Earth. We are sinners. These are the end times. In that event, these members would. Hate the world. Hate themselves. Manifest an end of the world scenario.

Let us suppose. These members really do. Hate the world. Hate themselves. Manifest an end of the world scenario. Let us suppose further. These members think, believe, and predict. A great big reward awaits them after they march off to their own deaths in war. In that event, they would behave like members of a megafauna death cult.

Let us suppose. The truth is. A megafauna death cult has spread out across the land. A few paranoid oppressive violent people profit from the sale and manufacture of war. The few paranoid oppressive violent people gain influence over religious authority figures. These religious authority figures shout from the mountain tops. These religious authority figures declare their belief in the value of these pessimistic myths. This megafauna death cult has members. They value truths. They value these pessimistic myths. Their values act as forces upon their emotions. Their hearts are filled with sorrow, fear, and anger. For that reason, these members exhibit sad, mad, and bad behaviors. This megafauna death cult has pro-life crusaders. These pro-life crusaders demand. Women must carry all pregnancies to term. These members use their pro-life positions as fig leaves. These members attempt to cover the nakedness of their own sad, mad, and bad behaviors. In that event, their sad, mad, and bad behaviors would have consequences. These members would not escape the consequences of their sad, mad, and bad behaviors.

I value truths. Scientists say. One million species of animals and plants are hurtling towards extinction. It appears. Their sad, mad, and bad behaviors have been leading humanity down a path towards extinction. We can see the possibility of abrupt climate change, habitat loss, and Armageddon on the horizon. Abrupt climate change, habitat loss, and Armageddon, could easily bring about human extinction. Human extinction may be the cost of their sad, mad, and bad behaviors.

Let us suppose. Religious authority figures say. Don't worry. A good entity rules in Heaven. The good entity is at war with an evil entity. The evil entity rules over the Earth. The good entity revealed visions of the future to prophets. Religious authority figures wrote down the exclusive divine revelations of spiritual knowledge as words in a set of sacred scrolls. Religious authority figures know how to translate and interpret the words. Religious authority figures say. The visions of the future reveal. A great tribulation will occur. A final necessary horrible war will be fought. Abrupt climate change, habitat loss, and Armageddon are the fulfillment of prophecy. The fulfillment of prophecy is a prelude to a final victory. The good entity will have the final victory over the evil entity. The good entity will judge all people. The good entity will find. Members of the megafauna death cult observed and obeyed the will of the good entity. The good entity will reward members. The good entity will elevate members to a place of divine eternal bliss. The good entity will find. Outsiders disregarded and disobeyed the will of the good entity. The good entity will punish the outsiders. The good entity will throw the outsiders into a place of abominable infernal torment. In that event, it would be logical to infer. Members would want the good entity to reward them. Members would want the prophecies to be fulfilled. For that reason, members would want abrupt climate change, habitat loss, and Armageddon. Abrupt climate change, habitat loss, and Armageddon, could easily bring about human extinction. Human extinction may be the cost of their sad, mad, and bad behaviors.

These visions of the future would suggest predictions about our behaviors. The predictions about our behaviors are. A horrible war will be fought. A few paranoid oppressive violent people will have final victory over the outsiders. The few paranoid oppressive violent people will judge all people. The few paranoid oppressive violent people will find. Some people observed and obeyed the will of the few paranoid oppressive violent people. The few paranoid oppressive violent people will reward those people. Those people will be elevated to a place of safety and refuge. The place of safety and refuge will be a haven on Earth. The few paranoid oppressive violent people will find. Some people disregarded and disobeyed the will of the few paranoid oppressive violent people. The few paranoid oppressive violent people will punish those people. Those people will be thrown into a place of danger and exposure. The place of danger and exposure will be hell on Earth. Some of those people will be enslaved under horrendous conditions until they drop dead of disease and or starvation. Some of those people will be murdered upon arrival.

The identities of insiders and outsiders are a matter of point of view. The locations of domestic and foreign territories are also a matter of point of view. For that reason, the few paranoid oppressive violent people in every territory can claim to be the representatives of the good entity for whom the visions of the future predict final victory.

Is the totality as evil as some communities of faithful believers would have me believe? Is a pessimistic model of the totality a tool? Does the tool enable the few paranoid oppressive violent people? Do the few paranoid oppressive violent people enslave communities of faithful believers? Is it necessary to destroy the self-esteem of a people to rule over the people? Is it necessary to destroy the world esteem of a people to rule over the people?

Let us suppose. A few paranoid oppressive violent people decide. It is necessary to destroy the self-esteem of a people to rule over the people. It is necessary to destroy the world esteem of a people to rule over the people. In that event, their values would not be aligned with our common needs and aspirations. Our common needs and aspirations are. Achieve and maintain happiness, good health, and prosperity. Their values would be aligned with their own needs and aspirations. Their own needs and aspirations include. Achieve and maintain authority, power, order, and control.

Let us suppose. Members will do whatever religious authority figures say. Religious authority figures say. Our only hope of salvation is. Observe and obey the will of the good entity. The will of the good entity is, in fact, the will of the few paranoid oppressive violent people. Do what the few paranoid oppressive violent people say. In that event, the few paranoid oppressive violent people would find. Authority, power, order, and control enables them. The few paranoid oppressive violent people can. Make themselves into slave owners. Make religious authority figures into their slave drivers. Make communities of faithful believers into their slaves.

Let us suppose. A person believes in the value of the most optimistic myths. The most optimistic myths include. Self has an infinite number, diversity, and variety of lives to live. Self has an infinite number, diversity, and variety of bodies to give. Self is seed, body, soul, and spirit. Slavery to a paranoid oppressive violent few won't save us. We are saved. We have been saved. We always will be saved. In that event, I would ask myself. How would the few paranoid oppressive violent people gain influence over such a person? Would they exhibit glad behaviors? Truth telling, sharing, playing well with others, liberating, emancipating, and nurturing are glad behaviors. Friendly tolerant peacemaking behaviors are glad behaviors.

Evil is an abstract idea. It appears. Some people use the idea of evil. They vilify and demonize prey. They promote a low esteem of the totality. They justify double standards. They justify their own predatory behaviors.

A pessimistic myth is. An evil entity exists. This pessimistic myth suggests a truth. The truth is. Outsiders exist. The act of suggesting this truth does not make this pessimistic myth into a truth. This pessimistic myth remains a myth.

Does the evil entity exist? I value the most optimistic myths. I devalue pessimistic myths. For that reason, my answer is no. The evil entity does not exist. However, the pessimistic myth does suggest a truth. The truth is. Outsiders exist.

Let us suppose. A few paranoid oppressive violent people gain influence over religious authority figures. These religious authority figures gain influence over communities of faithful believers.

These communities of faithful believers gain influence over members. These members affirm an ability to know. We are not strong enough on our own to conform to the will of the good entity. The good news is. The good entity had a son. The son of the good entity is a savior. The savior has the power. The savior can pay for our sins. All we need do is. Believe in the power of the savior. Ask the savior to dwell within our hearts. The savior will enable us. We will be able to do the will of the good entity. We will be able to do what religious authority figures say. The savior offers us an afterlife of divine eternal bliss. Universal submission to what religious authority figures say would be a Heaven on Earth. These are the end times. Spreading the good news about the savior is more important now than ever. In that event, these members would know next to nothing about almost everything. They would value a lie. The lie is. These pessimistic myths are truths. They would devalue a truth. The truth is. These pessimistic myths are myths.

A pessimistic myth is. A savior exists. This pessimistic myth suggests a truth. The truth is. A spouse exists. The act of suggesting this truth does not make this pessimistic myth into a truth. This pessimistic myth remains a myth.

Does the savior exist? I value the most optimistic myths. I devalue pessimistic myths. For that reason, my answer is no. The savior does not exist. However, the pessimistic myth does suggest a truth. The truth is. People often form life-long relationships with a spouse. Let us suppose. A person is willing to accept the spouse into their heart. In that event, the spouse would exist. For that reason, the savior would exist.

Let us suppose. Members made an affirmation. The affirmation is. A savior has the power. The savior can pay for our sins. Let us suppose further. I made the same affirmation. In that event, the act of making the same affirmation would not be enough. I would be making the same affirmation without actually being a believer.

Let us suppose. Members pray for guidance from a savior. Let us suppose further. I pray for guidance from the savior. Let us suppose finally. I receive guidance. In that event, I would have to ask myself. Am I receiving this guidance from the savior? Am I receiving this guidance from myself?

I know next to nothing about almost everything. My senses and perceptions are limited. I occupy specific points in energy, space, and time. Let us suppose. Members seek to win my soul for a savior. Members invite me. I enter a special building. I attend a service. Members perform a special ritual. I participate in the special ritual. I hear some music. I hold hands with members. I sing some songs. I recite some magic words. Members encourage me to ask for a savior to 'dwell inside my heart'. Let us suppose further. I ask a savior to 'dwell inside my heart'. In that event, the act of asking a savior to 'dwell inside my heart' would not be enough. I would have spoken the words and sung the songs without actually being a believer.

Let us suppose. Communities of faithful believers seek to win my soul for a savior. Let us suppose further. The savior enables them. They introduce me to the savior in person. I see where the savior was mortally wounded and miraculously healed. I hear the savior tell me a story. This story answers my question. My question is. What has this savior been doing with himself since floating away on a cloud after his resurrection? Let us suppose finally. I believe the story. In that event, I would be a believer.

Let us suppose. Members affirm an ability to know. A savior is the 'one true God'. In that event, it should be no problem for the savior. The savior should be able to appear to me in person. Not only that, the savior should be able to appear, seemingly by magic, like a genie, to anyone, anywhere, at any time.

Let us suppose. According to their own myths, the savior is not a god. The savior is a demigod. A demigod is an entity born out of the union of a god and a woman. In that event, the savior is born of the union of seed-body and soul-spirit. In that regard, we are all just like the savior.

Let us suppose. Members speak of a marriage. The marriage is between the savior and communities of faithful believers. The savior is the groom. The communities of faithful believers are the bride. In that event, this pessimistic myth would suggest a truth. The truth is. People often form a life-long relationship with a spouse. Does the spouse exist? I value truths. For that reason, my answer is. Let us suppose. A person is willing to accept the spouse into their heart. In that event, the spouse would exist.

I value truths. It appears. One day, the seed-body of self will die. I value the most optimistic myths. The most optimistic myths include. Life forms are born with divine eternal souls. All divine eternal souls transcend the diseases and deaths of their seed-bodies. Infinite abundance enables Mother God. Mother God bestows infinite love, divine forgiveness, eternal freedom, and unifying grace upon all of her Soul Children. We are saved. We have been saved. We always will be saved. For that reason, I need not ask in prayer. Savior, will you dwell in my heart? I need not go about the business of winning souls for the Savior.

CHAPTER 71. A CONTINUING SERIES OF WARS

Let us suppose. The only reason anybody owns anything is. A state authority says. A person owns a property. The state authority will take the person's side in any dispute over property rights. Let us suppose further. In exchange, the person must pay tribute to the state authority. Otherwise, the state authority might not take the person's side in any dispute over property rights. The state authority might even confiscate the property from the person. In that event, whom ever gains influence over the state authority decides. What tribute will be paid? How much tribute will be paid by each person?

Let us suppose. A state exists. Many people live in the state. The state grants certain rights and privileges to its citizens. In return, citizens are expected to obey their country's laws and defend it against its enemies. Let us suppose further. A few paranoid oppressive violent people have a low esteem of self. The few paranoid oppressive violent people have a low esteem of the world. Their hearts are filled with sorrow, fear, and anger. They exhibit sad, mad, and bad behaviors. They concentrate wealth, income, and power into their own hands. The few paranoid oppressive violent people achieve and maintain authority, power, order, and control. The few paranoid oppressive violent people dominate the state. They profit from the sale and manufacture of a continuing series of wars. Let us suppose still further. The state has a foreign policy. The few paranoid oppressive violent people conduct this foreign policy. This foreign policy creates enemies for the many people of the state. These enemies are all over the world. Let us suppose even still further. These enemies threaten to go to war against the state. These enemies threaten to make terrorist attacks against the many people who are living in the state. Let us suppose finally. The few paranoid oppressive violent people make use of these threats. The few paranoid oppressive violent people offer promises to the many people of the state. The few paranoid oppressive violent people promise protection from these threats in exchange for wealth, income, and power. In that event, their promises of protection would be worthless. The few paranoid oppressive violent people would be extorting wealth, income, and power from the many people of the state. Doing so would require. These threats be clear and present.

Let us suppose. The many people of the state have wealth, income, and property. The state imposes direct taxes on the wealth, income, and property. Let us suppose further. The many people of the state regard the direct taxes as thinly veiled extortion payments. In that event, the direct taxes would most likely be unpopular with the many people of the state.

Let us suppose. The few paranoid oppressive violent people regard the direct taxes as too inflexible and too limiting. In that event, the direct taxes would most likely be unpopular with the few paranoid oppressive violent people.

Let us suppose. The few paranoid oppressive violent people decide. The right way to finance a continuing series of wars is. Create a central bank. Let us suppose further. The few paranoid oppressive violent people dominate the state. In that event, the state would create a central bank. A privately owned central bank would be a beast of a military-industrial complex.

Let us suppose. The state gives a central bank authority, power, order, and control over the manufacture, sale, and distribution of a currency. Let us suppose further. The state creates legal tender laws. The legal tender laws require the citizens. The citizens must use the currency as money. In that event, the many people of the state would use the currency as money.

Money is in effect, an intermediate good. The many people of the state use the intermediate good for trading. The purpose of money is to facilitate the transfer of value over space and time. The many people of the state use the currency to exchange wealth, income, and property geographically. The many people of the state use the currency to provide for future payment. The use of the currency makes possible a division of labor. A division of labor is also known as specialization. Everyone's standard of living would suffer without specialization.

Let us suppose. The intermediate good for trading is gold. The central bank makes the gold into a currency. The many people of the state use the currency. Let us suppose finally. The state has a limited supply of gold. In that event, the supply of gold limits the money supply.

Let us suppose. The limited money supply makes financing a continuing series of wars difficult. In that event, the few paranoid oppressive violent people must find a new intermediate good.

Let us suppose. The new intermediate good for trading is paper. The central bank prints some numbers, letters, and images on paper. The central bank makes this paper into a currency. The many people of the state use this currency. Let us suppose further. The state has a near limitless supply of paper. In that event, the supply of the commodity does not limit the money supply. The near limitless money supply makes financing a continuing series of wars far easier for the few paranoid oppressive violent people.

In addition, let us suppose. The central bank enables the state. The state can finance spending programs on credit. In that event, the credit would enable the few paranoid oppressive violent people. The few paranoid oppressive violent people would be able to finance a continuing series of wars on credit.

Let us suppose. The many people in the state exchange a paper currency for valuable goods and services. They compare the value of this paper currency to the value of these goods and services. They find. This paper currency lacks value. For that reason, they resist the use of this paper currency. Let us suppose further. The state responds to this resistance. The state makes a guarantee. The guarantee is. The many people of the state can exchange this paper currency for a fixed quantity of another commodity. Let us suppose finally. The another commodity is gold. The many people of the state compare the value of this gold to the value of these goods and services. They find. This gold has value. In that event, the state would tie the value of this paper currency to the value of gold. The state would make this paper currency more acceptable.

Let us suppose. The central bank expands the money supply. The central bank loans money to the state. The money enables the state. The state continues to fight in times of war. The state taxes the wealth, income, and property of the many people in the state. In that event, the state need not increase taxes. The loan may be paid off over time.

Let us suppose. Private banks exist. These private banks have shareholders. These shareholders buy the debt from the central bank. In that event, these shareholders would profit. These shareholders would collect interest and fees. These shareholders would turn the state into an income stream.

Let us suppose. Politicians don't have to consult citizens or tax them directly to fund government programs. Politicians can implement whatever programs they wish. Let us suppose further. The many people demand welfare from the government. A few paranoid oppressive violent people demand warfare from the government. The government responds with spending programs. The central bank expands the money supply. Let us suppose finally. Politicians declare to the many people of the state. The central bank is no longer able. The central bank will not honor a previous guarantee. The previous guarantee is. The many people of the state can exchange this paper currency for a fixed quantity of another commodity. From now on, this paper currency is legal tender. This paper currency is backed only by the state's ability to collect taxes and other revenue in the future. In that event, this paper currency would no longer be backed by a fixed quantity of a commodity such as gold. This paper currency would become fiat money.

Let us suppose. The state enters into the digital age. Paper is no longer required. The central bank can create money by manipulating numbers. In that event, the state may now have the central bank issue an endless supply of fiat money.

Let us suppose. The central bank expands the money supply. In that event, more money would be chasing after the same amounts of goods and services. More money chasing after the same amounts of goods and services would lead to inflation of the asking price for the goods and services. Inflation would enable the central bank. The central bank would embezzle the purchasing power of savings. The many people would see the value of their savings decay over time.

Let us suppose. Inflation drives up the price of labor. The many people of the state make more income. The many people find themselves paying a larger percentage of their income to taxes. Let us suppose further. The many people of the state do not wish to be thrown in jail for tax evasion. In that event, they would end up paying a larger percentage of their income to taxes.

Let us suppose. A beast of a military industrial complex loans money to a state. The money enables the state. The state pays for massive spending programs. The state goes into debt. Let us suppose further. The many people of the state wish to preserve the full faith and credit of the state. Let us suppose finally. The many people of the state are able. In that event, the many people of the state would make a massive interest payment on an even more massive national debt.

Let us suppose. The many people of a state make a massive interest payment on an even more massive national debt. Let us suppose further. Enough is never enough. The few paranoid oppressive violent people desire more wealth, income, and power. The state makes drastic hikes in spending for warfare. The state makes equally drastic tax cuts for the wealthy. Large budget deficits create a massive national debt. The state uses an ever greater portion of tax revenue to make interest payments. Domestic spending programs are cut. The national debt keeps growing. In exchange for their tax dollars, the many people of the state get a receipt for a massive interest payment and a promise of protection. In that event, the few paranoid oppressive violent people would transform the state. The state would become an instrument of fiscal enslavement. The promise of protection would be worthless.

Let us suppose. A few paranoid oppressive violent people frequently invoke dubious threats to national security. The few paranoid oppressive violent people use war and military spending. They justify taking a lion's share of tax revenue. In that event, the state would redistribute wealth, income, and power into the hands of the few paranoid oppressive violent people.

CHAPTER 72. THE RISE OF A STATE

Let us suppose. A continuing series of wars leads to the rise of a state. The state dominates all other states within the global culture. Let us suppose further. This dominant state uses military power. This dominant state forces foreign states. These foreign states become submissive states. These submissive states serve the national interests of this dominant state. Let us suppose still further. This dominant state gives authority to a beast of a military industrial complex. This beast of a military industrial complex produces an unlimited supply of currency. Let us suppose finally. This dominant state uses shows of military force. This dominant state persuades these submissive states. These submissive states agree. Sales of key export commodities shall be made only in exchange for the currency of this dominant state. In that event, this dominant state would succeed in buying key export commodities with the unlimited supply of currency.

A reserve currency is a currency held by central banks in significant quantities. Let us suppose. These submissive states have central banks. The central banks demand a currency. This dominant state supplies the currency. The act of supplying the currency enables these submissive states. These submissive states can buy and sell key export commodities. In that event, the need to buy and sell would make the currency of this dominant state into a world reserve currency.

An ever-growing expansion of the money supply has inflationary effects. Let us suppose. This use of military force creates artificial demand for this world reserve currency. In that event, this artificial demand might shield the many people of the dominant state from these inflationary effects.

Extortion, intimidation, and violent abuse only work for a dominant state as long as the dominant state maintains military superiority. Let us suppose. A dominant state fails to maintain military superiority. In that event, other states would not be shocked and awed enough by shows of military power to submit. Other states would agree. This dominant state is now a formerly dominant state. Sales of key export commodities would not be made only in exchange for the currency of this formerly dominant state. States would not export vital commodities in exchange for easily produced currency of this formerly dominant state. States would no longer buy debt in exchange for exports of valuable goods and services. The currency of this formerly dominant state would no longer be a world reserve currency.

Let us suppose. The currency of this formerly dominant state is no longer a world reserve currency. Let us suppose further. Massive interest payments on an even more massive national debt burden the many people of this formerly dominant state. In that event, the many people of this formerly dominant state would no longer be protected. The inflationary effects of a greatly expanded money supply would become evident. The many people of this formerly dominant state would experience a significant loss of buying power and a lower standard of living.

Let us suppose. The currency of this formerly dominant state has a last source of value. The source of value is the collection of a direct tax. The collection of a direct tax confiscates the value of labor and property. This value of labor and property props up the value of the currency. Let us suppose further. A continuing series of wars were to prevent a collection of a direct tax. In that event, the currency of this formerly dominant state would lose its last source of value.

Let us suppose. The currency of this formerly dominant state loses its last source of value. Let us suppose further. The many people of this formerly dominant state have savings. These savings are denominated in the irredeemable currency of the formerly dominant state. In that event, the many people of this formerly dominant state would see their savings approach a negligible value.

Let us suppose. Two or more states enter into a war. In that event, I would ask myself the question. What would be accomplished by such a war?

Let us suppose. The many people in each territory contribute to the war effort. These civilians live in cities and work in factories. These cities and these factories keep armies supplied with food, weapons and ammunition. Let us suppose further. At least one state authority considers these civilians, cities, and factories to be legitimate military targets. Let us suppose finally. At least one army attacks these targets. The at least one army uses unconventional biological, chemical, and or nuclear weapons in addition to conventional weapons. In that event, these weapons could potentially kill millions of people.

Let us suppose. One army eventually prevails. In that event, the opposing armies, states, plutocrats, ideological authorities, and peoples would capitulate. Some people would lose everything. Their property would be destroyed. Their property rights might be lost. Their lives might be taken. Their names might be reviled.

Let us suppose. Battles occur at various sites. Let us suppose further. War desolates the local environments around the various sites. In that event, the few paranoid oppressive violent people may profit from reconstruction projects.

Let us suppose. The two or more states enter into a prolonged war of attrition. In that event, millions of people could lose their lives. The few paranoid oppressive violent people might profit from the sale and manufacture of the products and services of a beast of a military industrial complex.

Let us suppose. The two or more states enter into a prolonged truce for years without peace. In that event, a few paranoid oppressive violent people might profit from the sale and manufacture of the products and services of a Cold War.

Let us suppose. The few paranoid oppressive violent people fight war according to rules of engagement. One of these rules of engagement is. The few paranoid oppressive violent people don't attack one another directly. Instead, the few paranoid oppressive violent people retreat from the front lines of war. In that event, the few paranoid oppressive violent people would send collaborators into harm's way.

Let us suppose. The few paranoid oppressive violent people gain influence over conservative ideological authorities. These conservative ideological authorities gain influence over communities of faithful believers. These communities of faithful believers gain influence over members. These members claim an ability to know. Outsiders rule over foreign territories. National resources should be sacrificed. Lives should be sacrificed. This state must go to war against these outsiders. In that event, these members would be collaborators. The few paranoid oppressive violent people would send these members into harm's way. These members would march off to their own deaths in war.

Let us suppose. The few paranoid oppressive violent people rule over domestic territories. These domestic territories have standing armies. In that event, soldiers of the standing armies would be collaborators. The few paranoid oppressive violent people would send the soldiers of the standing armies into harm's way. The soldiers of the standing armies would march off to their own deaths in war.

Let us suppose. Spiritual liberation is an attribute of a state. The many people of this state liberate each other with a truth. The truth is. These pessimistic myths are myths. Let us suppose further. Slavery to a few paranoid oppressive violent people is an attribute of another state. The many people of this state enslave each other with a lie. The lie is. These pessimistic myths are truths. Let us suppose finally. These states go to war against each other. In that event, spiritual liberation would become a threat to spiritual slavery. Spiritual slavery would become a threat to spiritual liberation.

Let us suppose. A dominant state sets up strongmen dictators in submissive states. These strong man dictators enable this dominant state. This dominant state enslaves the many people who are living in these submissive states. The many people who are living in these submissive states serve the interests of the many people who are living in this dominant state. This dominant state knocks down these strongmen dictators over and over again. In that event, this dominant state would be leading the many people of our global culture into a cycle of violence. Free states and slave states would be entering into a continuing series of wars.

Let us suppose. The military industrial complex demonstrates the latest technology at the arms shows of the year. The few paranoid oppressive violent people proclaim. The latest technology will enable the state. The state can achieve its military objectives. The state can have final victory over the outsiders. Let us suppose further. The many people of the state value their continued security, safety, and status within our global culture. The many people of the state find. The latest technology is valuable. Let us suppose finally. The few paranoid oppressive violent people profit from the sale and manufacture of a continuing series of wars. The few paranoid oppressive violent people find. The latest technology is valuable. In that event, the state would purchase the latest technology at the arms shows of the year. The military industrial complex would grow stronger. The beast of a military industrial complex would drain money, morale, and resources from the many people of the state. The few paranoid oppressive violent people would concentrate wealth, income, and power into their own hands. The lives of the many people would fall prey to the military industrial complex. The military industrial complex would divide the many people of our global culture by race, clan, creed, and kind.

Let us suppose. A few paranoid oppressive violent people have a low esteem of self. The few paranoid oppressive violent people have a low esteem of the world. Their hearts are filled with sorrow, fear, and anger. They exhibit sad, mad, and bad behaviors. They concentrate wealth, income, and power into their own hands. The few paranoid oppressive violent people achieve and maintain authority, power, order, and control. The few paranoid oppressive violent people dominate the states of our global culture. They profit from the sale and manufacture of a continuing series of wars. The many people allow authority, power, order, and control over the states of our global culture to concentrate into the hands of the few paranoid oppressive violent people. Let us suppose further. I question the act of allowing authority, power, order, and control over the states of our global culture to concentrate into the hands of a few paranoid oppressive violent people. In that event, I would be confronted with a realization. This realization would be. It appears. Laws of cause and effect predict the behavior and fate of matter and energy in the known universe. The few paranoid oppressive violent people have acquired a mastery of these laws of cause and effect. They applied their mastery. They satisfied their needs and aspirations. Their needs and aspirations are. Achieve and maintain authority, power, order, and control over the many people of our global culture. The few paranoid oppressive violent people have put into action causes. These causes had the effect of giving them authority, power, order, and control over the many people of our global culture. They made themselves rulers. From an analysis of these facts, I develop a great respect for the few paranoid oppressive violent people. Freedom means. They can. Love and or hate. Fear and or faith. Truth and or lie. Save and or crucify.

CHAPTER 73. OUR MANY CONSCIOUS MINDS

I am the truth seeker. I am the myth maker. I am the authority. I find the freedom. I express my own point of view. Let us suppose. People acknowledge. The totality makes possible an infinite number, diversity, and variety of myths. In that event, a cultural environment of tolerance would follow.

The four motivations theory enables me. I predict. The motivations of seed-bodies are. Create and survive. The totality limits the dimensions of our body-consuming biosphere. For that reason, the motivations of seed-bodies run up against limits. These limits create competition.

A primal conflict between predator and prey feeds off of this competition. Like all life forms, people play dual roles of predator and prey. Some people play their roles in 'a civilized lawful way'. Some people play their roles in 'an uncivilized lawless way'. Either way, this primal conflict between predator and prey divides our body-consuming biosphere.

Our seed-bodies produce our unconscious minds. Our souls order the chaos of our unconscious minds. Our souls create our conscious minds. Our conscious minds are many. Our many conscious minds enable us. We can search for solutions to these problems.

Let us suppose. We find solutions to these problems. We overcome the limited dimensions of our body-consuming biosphere. We change our models of the totality. We gather new truths. We formulate new theories. We believe in the value of the most optimistic myths. We solve the problem of achieving and maintaining happiness, good health, and prosperity. We solve the problem of achieving and maintaining a global culture of sufficient technological sophistication. In that event, we would support the continued existence of our species. We would make possible the continued expansion of our numbers.

Let us suppose. Natural or man-made disasters bring about catastrophic change. The catastrophic change renders our technological limbs broken. In that event, our global culture would suffer the consequences of broken technological limbs. The consequences of broken technological limbs would be. People would be unable to adapt to catastrophic change. People would die.

Let us suppose. Our technological limbs remain intact. With each new technological breakthrough, new sets of plutocrats emerge. Let us suppose further. People spread life as we know it to the planets of our stars, to the stars of our galaxy, and to the galaxies of our universe. In that event, an ancient dream of going to Heaven would be realized as a technological scheme.

I believe in the value of truths. The truth is. It appears. The human species is in danger of going extinct. However, I believe in the value of the most optimistic myths. The most optimistic myths are all about infinite abundance. For that reason, I feel no urgency or give importance to this negativity.

However, I enjoy being human on planet Earth. I would like to do it again sometime. For that selfish reason, I made a plan. My plan is. Add value to people. Change behaviors with nothing more serious than the simple communication of ideas. Save humanity by changing behaviors. Save humanity from extinction.

Our common needs and aspirations are. Achieve and maintain happiness, good health, and prosperity. Let us suppose. We align our values with our common needs and aspirations. We believe in the value of truths. We believe in the value of the most optimistic myths. We balance the emotional forces of our minds. We are happy. We exhibit glad behaviors. In that event, our glad behaviors would act as forces. These forces would be conducive to a state of good health in our bodies. These forces would be conducive to a state of good health in our habitats.

Optimism correlates with happiness and good health. Pessimism correlates with sorrow, fear, anger, and disease. Let us suppose. We align our values with our common needs and aspirations. In that event, we would choose optimism.

I believe in the value of the most optimistic myths. For that reason, I think, believe, and predict. Most people will choose optimism. Most people will value the most optimistic myths. Most people will reject pessimism. Most people will devalue pessimistic myths. We will liberate each other from a spiritual slavery. This spiritual slavery follows from a lie. The lie is. These pessimistic myths are truths. A civilization built upon this lie would be weak and unstable. For that reason, we will abandon institutions of spiritual slavery. We will awaken to a freedom of choice. This freedom of choice follows from a truth. The truth is. These most optimistic myths are myths. A civilization built upon this truth would be strong and stable. For that reason, we will embrace institutions of spiritual emancipation. Almost all people will have the highest esteem of self. Almost all people will have the highest esteem of the world.

We will celebrate each other with a love. We will recognize. We are the authorities. We form opinions about ourselves. We form opinions about the world. We are the architects. We value certain ideas. These certain ideas are our values. We use our values. We build within our minds. We build models of the totality. Our models are our realities. Our realities are our Houses of Ideologies. We will identify ourselves as the High Ideologues of our Houses of Ideologies. Each of us will identify as the High Ideologue of a House of Ideology. We will change our realities to what. We would like are our realities to be. Nearly everybody will think, believe, and predict. Continuous spiritual communion between soul and spirit exists. Our belief in the value of continuous spiritual communion will enable us. We will receive inspiration, intuition, and good judgment. We will persevere. We will overcome obstacles. We will progress towards victory. We will transform the politics, economies, and religions of our global culture. Extortion, intimidation, and fear of military power will play a lesser role. Friendship, liberation, and faith in divine power will play a greater role.

Let us suppose. The current dominant state uses extortion, intimidation, and fear of military force. Let us suppose further. A transformation of the politics, economics, and religions of our global culture is made difficult by the extortion, intimidation, and fear of military force. Let us suppose still further. Throughout history, extortion, intimidation, and fear of military power have played a greater role in the politics, economics, and religions of our global culture. Friendship, liberation, and faith in divine power have played a lesser role. Let us suppose even still further. Dominant states have used extortion, intimidation, and fear of military force. Dominant states acquired valuable goods and services from submissive states virtually free of charge or at a great discount. Let us suppose finally. The many people of the current dominant state recognize. No state in the history of states has ever achieved and maintained a lasting military superiority. In that event, the many people of the current dominant state would be wise to acknowledge a possibility. The possibility is. Some day the many people of the current dominant state might find themselves and their families subject to the politics, economics, and religions of the many people of a new dominant state.

Let us suppose. Extortion, intimidation, and fear of military power create a socioeconomic stratification of our global culture. Let us suppose further. The many people of the current dominant state acknowledge. The socioeconomic stratification of our global culture creates gross inequities. Psychotic extremes of poverty and wealth are an attribute of these gross inequities. Let us suppose finally. People work together. They advance their shared political, social, and artistic ideas. They transform the politics, economies, and religions of our global culture. Friendship, liberation, and faith in divine power play a greater role. Extortion, intimidation, and fear of military power play a lesser role. In that event, the many people of the current dominant state would be in a unique position to lead such a movement.

CHAPTER 74. SPIRITUAL LIBERATION

I respect the freedom of others. Others make up their own minds about the totality. I offer an example. The example shows how. I take love of self and world to its highest esteem. I take Healthy Agnostic Positivistic Nationalistic Spiritization of self and world to its logical extreme. I best satisfy my needs and aspirations. My needs and aspirations are. Achieve and maintain happiness, good health, and prosperity.

Let us suppose. I have followers. Let us suppose further. My followers devote their energy, space, and time. They join communities of faithful believers. Let us suppose still further. I lead the communities of faithful believers by example. In that event, we would. Align our values with our common needs and aspirations. Believe in the value of truths. Believe in the value of the most optimistic myths. Balance the emotional forces of our minds. Be happy. Exhibit glad behaviors. Take love of self and world to its highest esteem. Take Healthy Agnostic Positivistic Nationalistic Spiritization of self and world to its logical extreme. Have the highest esteem of the totality.

Ideas are thoughts, beliefs, and expectations about the totality. My seed-body makes senses and perceptions available to me. My senses and perceptions enable me. I can use my senses and perceptions. I can correctly sort ideas into three simple categories. The three simple categories are truths, myths, and lies. Truths are ideas. I can verify. Truths are true. Truths are verifiable. Lies are ideas. I can verify. Lies are false. Lies are falsifiable. Myths are ideas. I can not verify whether or not. Myths are true. I can not verify whether or not. Myths are false. Myths are both unverifiable and unfalsifiable. I reject a lie. The lie is. A myth is a truth. I do not claim. The most optimistic myths are truths. I accept a truth. The truth is. The most optimistic myths are myths.

Spiritual slavery follows from a lie. The lie is. A myth is a truth. Spiritual liberation follows from a truth. The truth is. A myth is a myth. Spiritual celebration follows from a love of self and world. The love of self and world is taken to its highest esteem. Spiritual identification follows from a belief in the value of the most optimistic myths. The most optimistic myths include. We are Soul Children. We have an infinite number, diversity, and variety of lives to live. We have an infinite number, diversity, and variety of bodies to give. We are seed, body, soul, and spirit.

I write about my model of the totality. I use words. Seed-bodies produce unconscious minds. The unconscious minds limit the composition and interpretation of words. Souls order the chaos of unconscious minds. Our souls create conscious minds. Conscious minds make possible the composition and interpretation of words. Let us suppose. In the future, a language and culture grows, evolves, and changes. In that event, the composition and interpretation of words may change.

I provide liberal leadership, education, and entertainment. Liberal leadership, education, and entertainment liberates the many people from power structures. The few paranoid oppressive violent people promote conservative leadership, education, and entertainment. Conservative leadership, education, and entertainment conserves these power structures. These power structures concentrate wealth, income, and power into the hands of a few paranoid oppressive violent people.

Let us suppose. Our liberal leadership, education, and entertainment enables us. We align our values with our needs and aspirations. We believe in the value of truths. We believe in the value of the most optimistic myths. We balance the emotional forces of our minds. We are happy. In that event, we would be in the best possible position. We would exhibit glad behaviors. Our glad behaviors would enable us. We would best satisfy our common needs and aspirations. Our common needs and aspirations are. Achieve and maintain happiness, good health, and prosperity.

I affirm. I have an inability to know. I can not possess knowledge about the non-existence of deities. I claim. This inability to know leads me to a belief. This belief is. At least one deity could exist. I desire happiness and good health. Optimism correlates with happiness and good health. For that reason, I believe in the value of the most optimistic myths. These most optimistic myths include. The totality is an infinite divine eternal being. I am an agnostic theist: I acknowledge. The totality makes possible an infinite number, diversity, and variety of myths. I reject a lie. The lie is. These most optimistic myths are truths. I reject the lie in all of its various forms. I accept a truth. The truth is. These most optimistic myths are myths.

The presence of evidence in the form of the universe provides premises. We can use these premises. We can make valid logical inductive inferences. We can arrive at conclusions. These conclusions are ideas. Ideas are thoughts, beliefs, and expectations about the totality. We value certain ideas. These certain ideas are our values. Let us suppose. Our senses and perceptions do not enable us. We can not verify the veracity of some of our values. We can not verify the falsity of these same values. In that event, some of our values would be myths.

Validity is the quality of being logical or factually sound. The validity of myths follows from two definitions of the word valid. The two definitions are a logical definition and a pragmatic definition.

The logical definition of the word valid is: having a sound basis in logic or fact; reasonable or cogent. The logical definition of the word valid leads to a conclusion. The conclusion is. The totality makes possible an infinite, number, diversity, and variety of myths. Each myth is an equally valid possibility.

The pragmatic definition of the word valid is: producing the desired results. Let us suppose. The desired results are happiness and good health. Let us suppose further. Optimism correlates with happiness and good health. Pessimism correlates with sorrow, fear, anger, and disease. In that event, the pragmatic definition of the word valid would lead to a conclusion. The conclusion is. Optimistic myths are more valid. Pessimistic myths are less valid or even invalid.

Emotional balance in my mind is conducive to happiness and good health in my life. I desire happiness and good health in my life. For that reason, I believe in the value of truths. I believe in the value of the most optimistic myths. I balance the emotional forces of my mind.

I lead by example. I lead us to do the following;

1. Love a Healthy Agnostic Positivistic Nationalistic Spiritization of self and world. Take Healthy Agnostic Positivistic Nationalistic Spiritization of self and world to its logical extreme. Take love of self and world to its highest esteem.

2. Seek truths. Base the truths on the existence of discovery. Make theories. Base the theories on the existence of scientifically reproducible discoveries. Gather these truths and these theories. Believe in the value of these truths. Believe in the value of these theories. These truths and these theories suggest a material standard of conduct. Derive this material standard of conduct. Adhere to this material standard of conduct. Produce physiological balance. Achieve and maintain good health.

3. Make myths. Base these myths on what is possible within the realm of mystery. Identify the most optimistic myths. Believe in the value of these most optimistic myths. These most optimistic myths suggest a spiritual standard of conduct. Derive this spiritual standard of conduct. Adhere to this spiritual standard of conduct. Produce emotional balance. Achieve and maintain happiness.

4. Combine these truths, these theories, and these most optimistic myths. Build a model of the totality. This model of the totality suggests a comprehensive standard of conduct. Derive this comprehensive standard of conduct. Adhere to this comprehensive standard of conduct. Achieve and maintain happiness, good health, and prosperity.

CHAPTER 75. UNIVERSE WORSHIP

I believe in the value of the most optimistic myths. The most optimistic myths are all about infinite abundance. For that reason, I think, believe, and predict. The totality is an infinite divine eternal being. The infinite divine eternal being is everything, everywhere, at all times. The universe is a creation. The spirit is the creator.

I value truths. Scientists say. It appears. The universe exists. The known universe includes matter and energy. Laws of cause and effect predict the behavior and fate of the matter and energy. A natural standard of conduct follows logically from the laws of cause and effect. Life forms tend to conform to the natural standard of conduct. The act of behaving in conformity with the natural standard of conduct is most likely to result in survival.

Let us suppose. Some people discover these truths. These people project the discovery of these truths into their imaginations. They use their imaginations. They make myths. Their myths are. At least one deity does exist. A supernatural standard of conduct does exist. In that event, projection theory would enable me. I would predict. Their myths would suggest these truths. The act of suggesting these truths would not make their myths into truths. Their myths would remain myths. The act of suggesting these truths would enable these people. These people would confirm their belief in the value of these myths. For that reason, these theists would worship the at least one deity. These theists would behave in conformity with the supernatural standard of conduct.

Let us suppose. Other people discover these truths. These other people project the discovery of these truths into their imaginations. They use their imaginations. They make myths. Their myths are. The at least one deity does not exist. Only a godless totality does exist. The supernatural standard of conduct does not exist. Only a natural standard of conduct does exist. In that event, projection theory would enable me. I would predict. Their myths would suggest these truths. The act of suggesting these truths would not turn their myths into truths. Their myths would remain myths. However, the act of suggesting these truths would enable these other people. These other people would confirm their belief in the value of their myths. For that reason, these atheists would worship the universe. These atheists would behave in conformity with the natural standard of conduct.

Let us suppose. Some theists conform to their supernatural standard of conduct. Their supernatural standard of conduct suggests the natural standard of conduct. For that reason, some atheists respect these theists. Let us suppose further. Some atheists conform to the natural standard of conduct. The natural standard of conduct suggests the supernatural standard of conduct. For that reason, some theists respect these atheists. In that event, it would be logical to infer. Mutual respect would enable these people. These people would be able to form alliances. They could base these alliances upon an idea. The idea is. Lessons, predictions, and laws emanate from leaders, prophets, and teachers of the at least one deity. These lessons, predictions, and laws, embellish, ornament, and reinforce other lessons, predictions, and laws.

These other lessons, predictions, and laws, emanate from leaders, scientists, and teachers of nature, the state, and the universe.

CHAPTER 76. MY RESPONSE

My response is. I support the freedom of people. We are free. We build our models of the totality. We ornament our models with myths. We choose our own myths.

Freedom of speech, freedom of the press, and freedom of religion are attributes of a free society. I support freedom of speech, freedom of the press, and freedom of religion.

I oppose official sanctification of Fascist Atheistic Perfectionistic Nationalistic Negativism. I offer an alternative. The alternative is. Healthy Agnostic Positivistic Nationalistic Spiritization of self and world. I love Healthy Agnostic Positivistic Nationalistic Spiritization of self and world. I take my love of Healthy Agnostic Positivistic Nationalistic Spiritization to its logical extreme. I take a love of self and world to its highest esteem.

Ideas are thoughts, beliefs, and expectations about the totality. We value certain ideas. These certain ideas are our values. I value truths. Scientists say. It appears. Optimistic values correlate with happiness. Optimistic values correlate with improved health. Optimistic values correlate with improved health-related behavior. I desire happiness and good health. For that reason, I value optimistic myths. The most optimistic values produce the most desirable results. For that reason, I value the most optimistic myths.

I align my values with our common needs and aspiration. Our common needs and aspirations are. Achieve and maintain happiness, good health, and prosperity. I strive to rise to a position of authority, power, order, and control. I make significant contributions to society. I lead other people by example, in words, and in deeds. Let us suppose. I grow in wealth, income, power, and influence. In that event, other people would follow my example.

Hatred of Fascist Atheistic Perfectionistic Nationalistic Negativism begets hatred. I lead other people away from this hatred. Love of Healthy Agnostic Positivistic Nationalistic Spiritization begets love. I lead other people towards this love. I am against the hatred of Fascist Atheistic Perfectionistic Nationalistic Negativism. I am for love of Healthy Agnostic Positivistic Nationalistic Spiritization. I love Healthy Agnostic Positivistic Nationalistic Spiritization of self and world. I take Healthy Agnostic Positivistic Nationalistic Spiritization of self and world to its logical extreme and love happens.

Let us suppose. Love happens. In that event, an inspired celebration of liberation would occur. The inspired celebration of liberation would free the minds of people from ignorance, guilt, inhibition, and disgrace. The inspired celebration of liberation would enable people. People deserve their rights, dignity, freedom, and respect. People would demand their rights, dignity, freedom, and respect.

Let us suppose. We love each other. We feed, clothe, house, nurture, educate, and care for ourselves and others in peace. Let us suppose further. We do not hate each other. We do not starve, strip, pillage, rape, indoctrinate, and dispose of each other in war. In that event, love would happen.

The hatred of Fascist Atheistic Perfectionistic Nationalistic Negativism is the opposite of the love of Healthy Agnostic Positivistic Nationalistic Spiritization. Let us suppose. A few paranoid oppressive violent people gain influence over a state. This state propagates Fascist Atheistic Perfectionistic Nationalistic Negativism. Many people live in this state. Some of these people negate Fascist Atheistic Perfectionistic Nationalistic Negativism. These people are led by the soul-spirit. They arrive at their own love of Healthy Agnostic Positivistic Nationalistic Spiritization. In that event, I would have allies in this state!

We have already won the victory! Our minds are in control of our seed-bodies. Our souls are in control of our minds. The infinite divine eternal being is everything, everywhere, at all times! Let us suppose. All life on the planet Earth goes extinct. In that event, the spirit would have an infinite abundance of love, divine forgiveness, eternal freedom, and unifying grace in store for each and every one of our souls.

CHAPTER 77. DYNAMIC INFLUENCE DIAGRAM

The four structures are seed, body, soul, and spirit. The four structures combine to make up the content and the form; of finite self, infinite world, and an infinite number, diversity, and variety; of other finite creatures. From these four structures follow four motivations. The four motivations are. Create, survive, perfect, and revive. These four motivations reinforce four spiritual orientations. The four spiritual orientations are gnostic theism, agnostic atheism, gnostic atheism, and agnostic theism.

Let us suppose. One of the four motivations dominates within the mind of a person. In that event, the person would tend to choose one of four worldviews. The four worldviews are creator worldview, survivor worldview, perfecter worldview, and reviver worldview.

The motivation of the seed is. Create. The seed creates the body. Let us suppose. The act of creating dominates within the mind of a person. In that event, the person would tend to choose creator worldview. Creator worldview includes myths. These myths include spirit and no soul. The person would tend to be gnostic theist. The body shall die. For that reason, from a choice of creator worldview comes an experience of inhibition of self, love of the world, and sad sorrow.

The motivation of the body is. Survive. The body consumes the body. The body survives. Let us suppose. The act of surviving dominates within the mind of a person. In that event, the person would tend to choose survivor worldview. Survivor worldview includes myths. The myths include no spirit and no soul. The person would tend to be agnostic atheist. The body shall die. For that reason, from a choice of survivor worldview comes an experience of inhibition of self, hate of the world, and mad fear.

The motivation of the soul is. Perfect. The soul perfects the body. Let us suppose. The act of perfecting dominates within the mind of a person. In that event, the person would tend to choose perfecter worldview. Perfecter worldview includes myths. These myths include soul and no spirit. The person would tend to be gnostic atheist. The body is imperfect. The habitat is imperfect. For that reason, from a choice of perfecter worldview comes an experience of freedom of self, hate of the world, and bad anger.

The motivation of the spirit is. Revive. The spirit revives the seed. Let us suppose. The act of reviving dominates within the mind of a person. In that event, the person would tend to choose reviver worldview. Reviver worldview includes myths. These myths include soul and spirit. The person would tend to be agnostic theist. The infinite spirit is an infinite divine eternal being. The infinite seed is an infinite number, diversity, and variety of large universes of the correct kind to support living infernal fractal entities. From a choice of reviver worldview follows an experience of freedom of self, love of the world, and glad joy.

States, ideological authorities, communities of faithful believers and individuals self-organize around the four worldviews. These four worldviews support a number, diversity and variety of ornamentations. The number, diversity, and variety of ornamentations is only limited by our creative abilities and powers of imagination. Differences in ornamentation create unique qualities, and features. These unique qualities and features enable people. People create identities for themselves. People are able to distinguish states, ideological authorities, communities of faithful believers, and individuals from one another.

I designed the Dynamic Influence Diagram. The Dynamic Influence Diagram illustrates how. The states, ideological authorities, communities of faithful believers, and individuals interact within a complex chaotic dynamic system. The complex chaotic dynamic system is the body consuming biosphere.

In its' simplest form, the Dynamic Influence Diagram contains four circles. The outer circle represents a subject motivation. The subject motivation is one of the four motivations. The subject motivation dominates within the minds of insiders. The insiders choose to believe in the value of a worldview. The worldview corresponds to the subject motivation. The three inner circles represent three object motivations. The three object motivations are the other three of the four motivations. The other three of the four motivations dominate within the minds of outsiders. The outsiders choose to believe in the value of worldviews. The worldviews correspond to the other three of the four motivations.

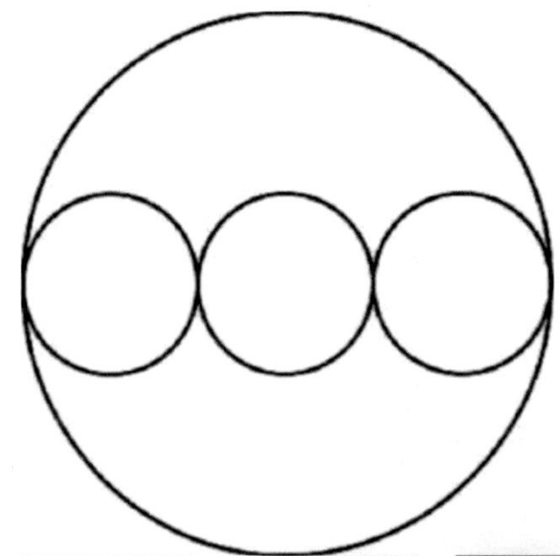

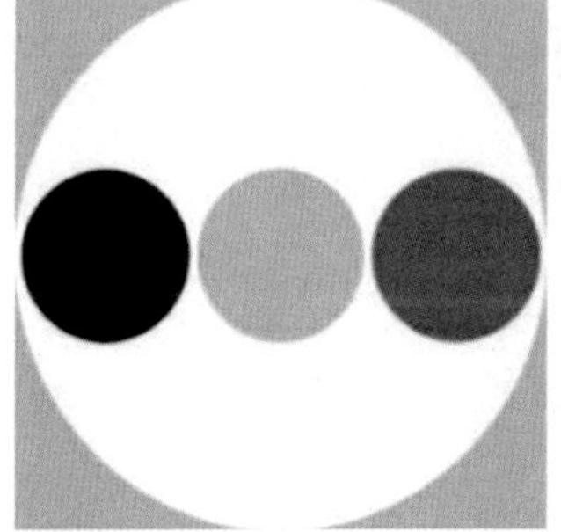

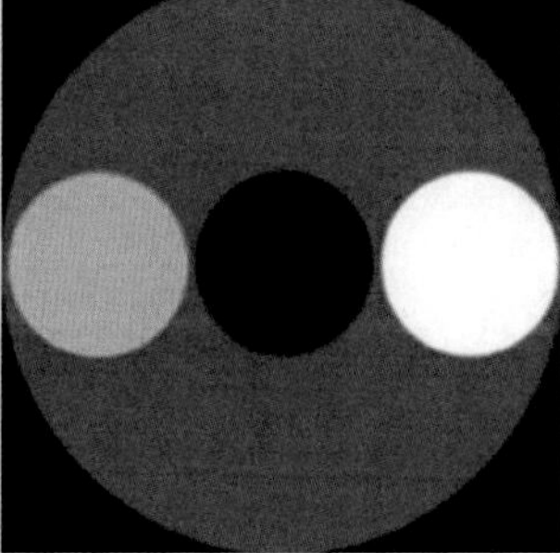

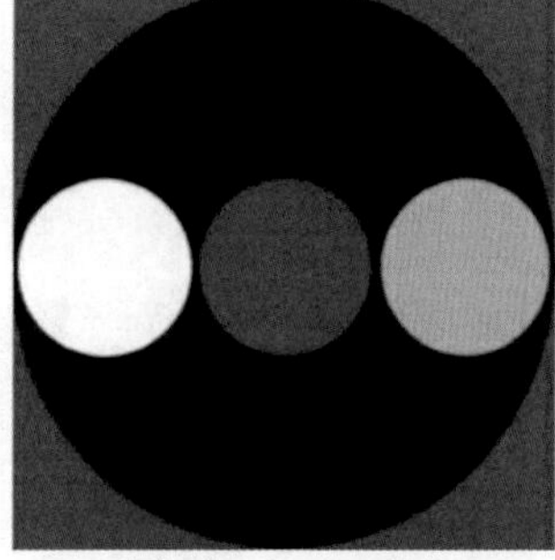

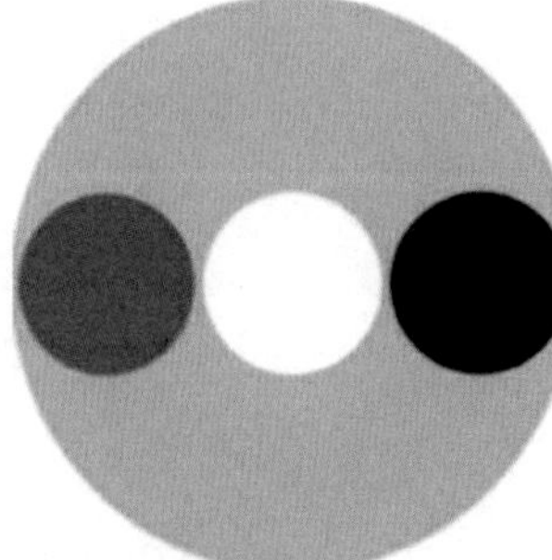

Color represents motivation and corresponding worldview. White represents the motivation of the seed and creator worldview. Red represents the motivation of the body and survivor worldview. Black represents the motivation of the soul and perfecter worldview. Gray represents the motivation of the spirit and reviver worldview.

People sort themselves into insiders and outsiders. Insiders choose a worldview. The insiders select the worldview from a group of worldviews. The group of worldviews consists of the four worldviews. The insiders form communities. The communities of insiders self-organize around the selected worldview. Outsiders choose a worldview. The outsiders select the worldview from a group of worldviews. The group of worldviews consists of the three remaining worldviews. The three remaining worldviews are the other three of the four worldviews. The outsiders form communities. The communities of outsiders self-organize around their selected worldviews.

The insiders interact with the outsiders. The outsiders interact with the insiders. The position of each of the three inner circles within the outer circles represents the interaction. The left position represents cooperation. The central position represents neutrality. The right position represents competition.

Gnostic theists and agnostic theists have a belief in common. Both believe in the existence of at least one deity. However, gnostic theists and agnostic theists do not have an affirmation in common. For that reason, they tend to be neutral.

Agnostic atheists and gnostic atheists have a lack of belief in common. Both lack a belief in the existence of deities. However, agnostic atheists and gnostic atheists do not have an affirmation in common. For that reason, they tend to be neutral.

Gnostic theists and gnostic atheists have an affirmation in common. Both affirm an ability to know. Both lack the humility to admit. They know next to nothing about almost everything. For that reason, they tend to cooperate.

Agnostic atheists and agnostic theists have an affirmation in common. Both affirm an inability to know. Both have the humility to admit. They know next to nothing about almost everything. For that reason, they tend to cooperate.

Gnostic theists and agnostic atheists have no affirmation in common. Gnostic theists and agnostic atheists have no belief in common. For that reason, they tend to compete.

Gnostic atheists and agnostic theists have no affirmation in common. Gnostic atheists and agnostic theists have no belief in common. For that reason, they tend to compete.

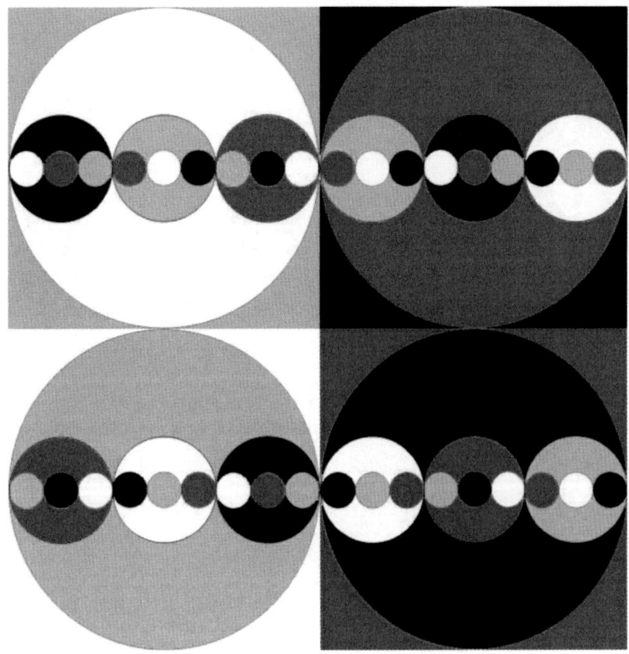

The Insiders are aware of the worldviews of the outsiders. The insiders are aware of the policies applied by the outsiders in their interactions with the insiders. The insiders use this awareness to predict the behavior of the outsiders. The outsiders are aware of the worldview of the insiders. The outsiders are aware of the policies applied by the insiders in their interactions with the outsiders. The outsiders use their awareness to predict the behavior of the insiders. However, the act of making predictions about the behavior of people can influence the behavior of the people. Sometimes people alter their behavior in anticipation of these predictions. Insiders don't always behave as predicted by outsiders. Outsiders don't always behave as predicted by insiders. I depict these ideas. I add three inner circles to each of the three inner circles. I create white, red, black and gray variations on the Dynamic Influence Diagram. Each of the variations has thirteen circles.

I add three more circles to each of these three inner circles. I create white, red, black and gray variations on the Dynamic Influence Diagram. Each of the variations has forty circles.

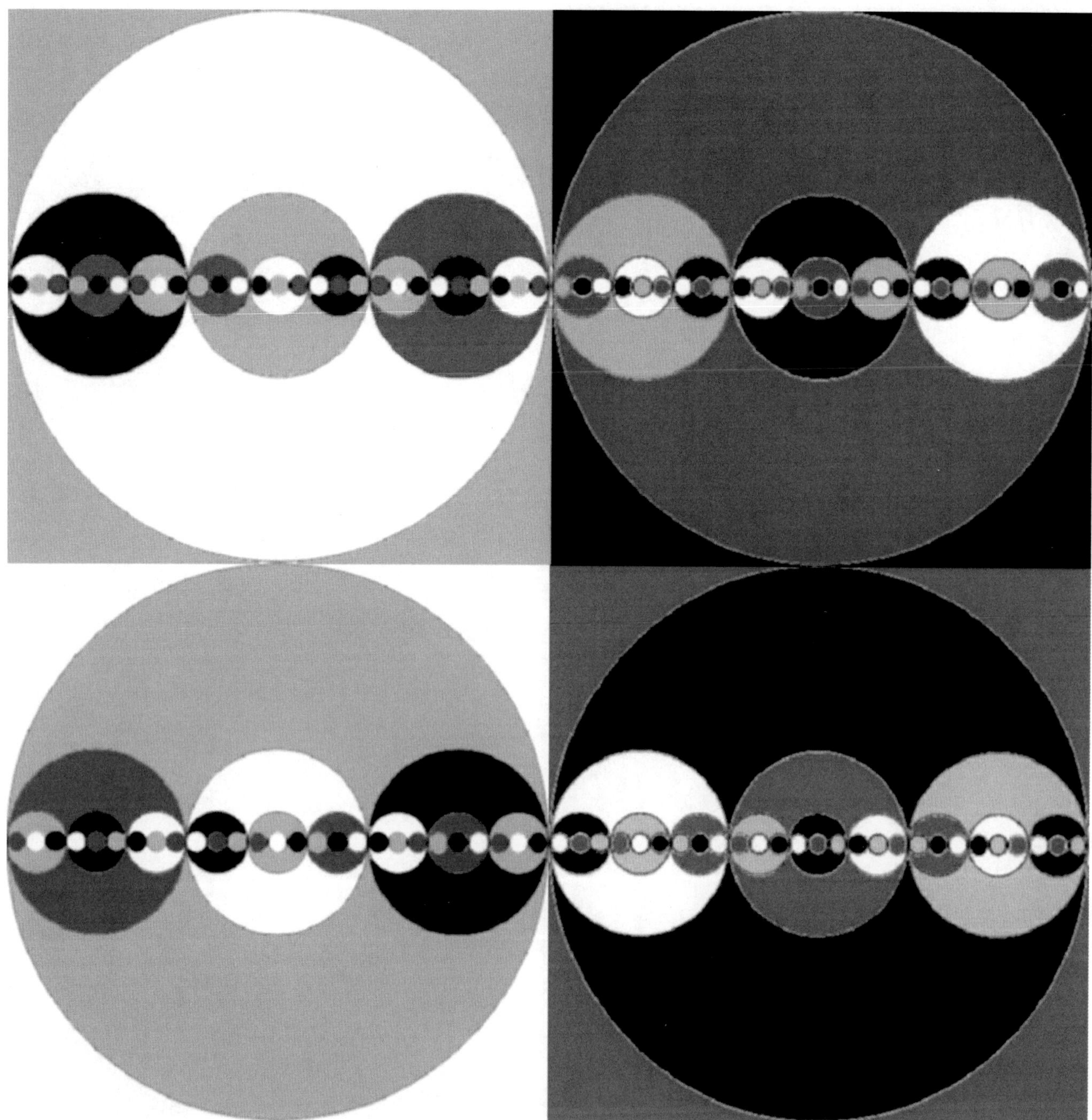

I can continue. I can create white, red, black and gray variations on the Dynamic Influence Diagram with one hundred and twenty-one circles, three hundred and sixty-four circles and so on. By way of this process, I create a Dynamic Influence Diagram with a fractal self-similarity between part and whole over the range of all scales of size.

I frame the Dynamic Influence Diagram with seven circles. The colors of the seven concentric circles correspond to the energies of the various colors of visible light. The energies of the various colors of visible light descend in order from highest to lowest in the following order; purple, blue, green, white, yellow, orange and red.

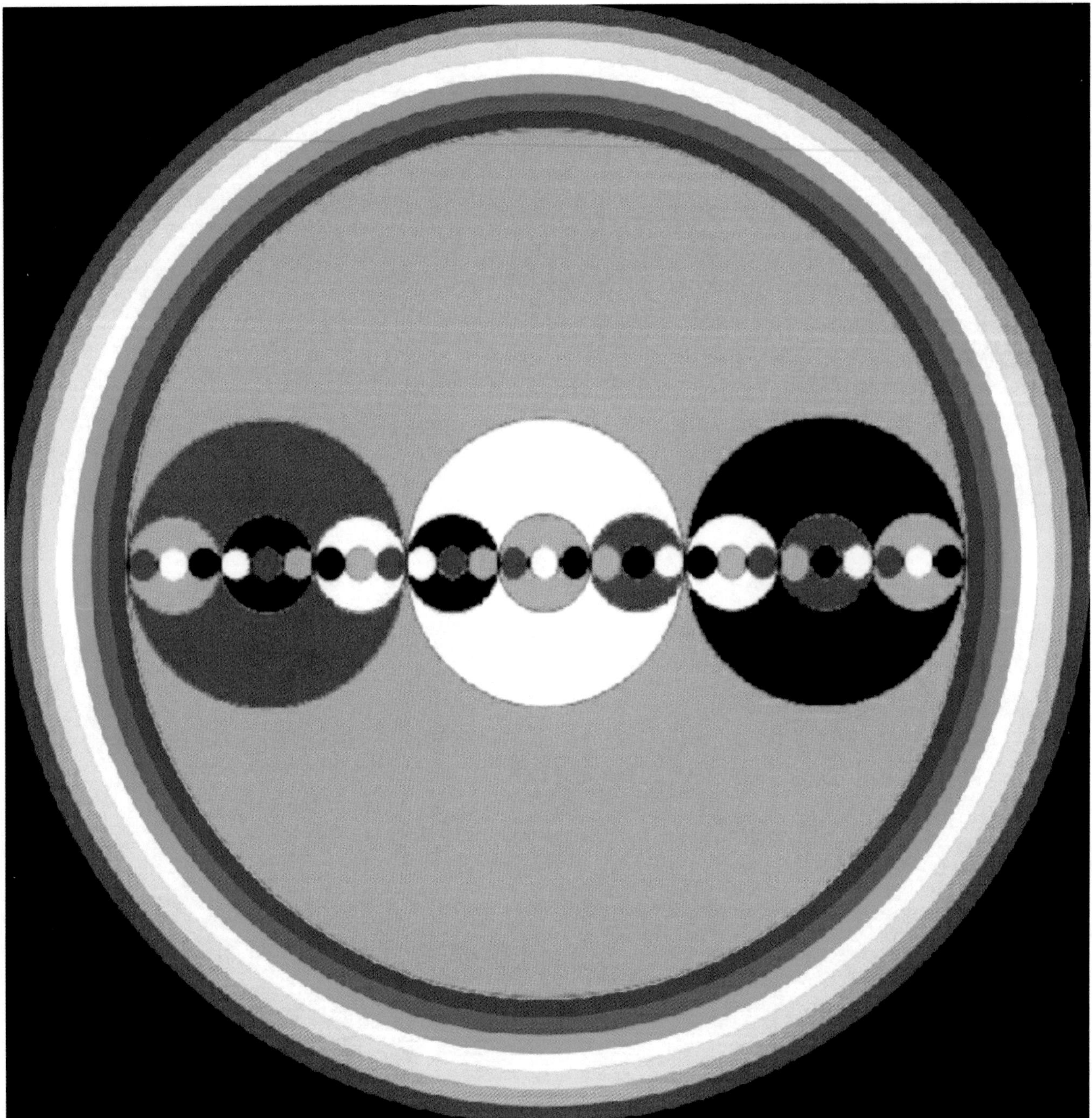

Prisms enable people. People can diffract sun light into its component color frequencies. Doing so results in the appearance of a rainbow spectrum. My arrangement of the colors within the design of the frame also makes a variation on the rainbow spectrum.

In the language of my emotional mind, I associate the rainbow with love and freedom. I value the most optimistic myths. Our spirit confers love and freedom upon all souls. As such, framing the Dynamic Influence Diagram with the rainbow-colored seven concentric circles produces conceptual balance. The Dynamic Influence Diagram with seven concentric rings of the frame surrounding the one outer circle, three inner circles, nine smaller inner circles and twenty-seven smallest inner circles contains forty-seven circles total. I whole-heartedly embrace the Dynamic Influence Diagram. I love it all. I love the sadness of the seed-body of our universe. I love the madness of the seed-body of self. I love the badness of the soul-spirit of self. I love the gladness of the soul-spirit of the world.

CHAPTER 78. I.D.E.O.L.O.G.Y. WAY

I value the most optimistic myths. The most optimistic myths include. Salvation has always been ours. We are saved. We have been saved. We always will be saved. Salvation is ours regardless of how. We behave during our brief lifetimes. Salvation is ours regardless of how. We build our models of the totality. Salvation is ours regardless of how. We adorn our models with myths. We are free in the love of the soul-spirit.

The love of the soul-spirit is infinitely abundant. A person could be guilty of any transgression during the person's brief lifetime. Their guilt would not in any way result in a loss of freedom; or a diminishment of love. Mother God gives love and freedom unconditionally to all of her Soul Children.

There is only one way. This one way is automatically followed by each soul. I describe this one way. I use a series of words in the English language. The series of words are Infinity Divinity Eternally One Love Our Gods Your Way. The series of words have initial letters. I arrange the initial letters in sequential order. I form an acronym. The acronym is IDEOLOGY way. An infinity divinity eternally one; frees us to love our gods in our own ways.

CHAPTER 79. INFINITE DIVINE ETERNAL BEING

I value certain ideas. These certain ideas are my values. I use my values. I build within my mind. I build a model of the totality. I adorn my model with the most optimistic myths. The most optimistic myths include. An infinite divine eternal being is everything, everywhere, at all times. The infinite divine eternal being enjoys entertainment. For that reason, the known universe exists.

I differentiate between this infinite divine eternal being; and the known universe. The infinite divine eternal being; is the mysterious creator. The known universe is a discovered creation. The known universe is limited in energy, space, and time. The infinite divine eternal being is limitless in energy, space, and time.

I differentiate between universal, state, and natural laws of cause and effect; and spiritual laws of love and freedom. Universal, state, and natural laws of cause and effect determine the fates and destinies of seed-bodies. Spiritual laws of love and freedom determine the fates and destinies of souls.

Spiritual laws are a product of speculation. We are free. Each of us makes up our own mind about spiritual laws. Each of us decides whether or not. Spiritual laws exist. Each of us decides whether or not. Spiritual laws apply in any given situation.

I am aware of my freedom. I decide how. I make up my mind. I believe in the value the most optimistic myths. The most optimistic myths include. Spiritual laws of love and freedom exist. These spiritual laws of love and freedom apply in every situation.

I think, believe, and predict. The conduct of our seed-bodies during our brief lifetimes is of no consequence to the fates and destinies of our souls. Upon the death of our seed-bodies, our souls choose. Our souls may travel through the totality. Our souls may arrive at another point in energy, space, and time. Our souls may live again as another life form. Our souls may also watch life go on from 'the other side'. Let us suppose. Some souls choose to watch life go on from 'the other side'. In that event, those souls join Mother God. The drama of life and death entertains. Mother God enjoys the entertainment. Our souls create the entertainment. Our choices are perfect expressions of spiritual laws of love and freedom.

I think, believe, and predict. Our spirit is both willing and able to provide infinite love, divine forgiveness, eternal freedom, and unifying grace to every soul in creation. We are life forms. We choose to be life forms. We base our choices on the magnitudes of our souls. We base our choices upon spiritual laws of love and freedom. The meaning of life is living. The purpose of living is the enjoyment of entertainment. Any kind of behavior is acceptable as entertainment.

This spiritual freedom does not guarantee material success. Material success requires me. I devote energy, space, and time to the study and analysis of standards of conduct. The standards of conduct are enforced by systems of reward and punishment. The systems of reward and punishment are established by universal, state, and natural laws of cause and effect.

I value truths. Scientists say. It appears. Universal laws of cause and effect predict the behavior, fate, and destiny of matter and energy in the known universe. The matter and energy, of the known universe, includes the matter and energy, of our seed-bodies. For that reason, it appears. Universal laws of cause and effect predict the behaviors, fates, and destinies of our seed-bodies.

State laws exist as a subset of universal laws. State laws of cause and effect predict the behavior, fate, and destiny of citizens. State laws govern the distribution and exploitation of resources. The resources exist within a state territory.

Let us suppose. A state exists. Citizens exist. State laws exist. These state laws function like a contract. The contract binds citizens and state together. Let us suppose further. This state exhibits behaviors. These behaviors best satisfy the common needs and aspirations of these citizens. These common needs and aspirations are. Achieve and maintain happiness, good health, and prosperity. Let us suppose finally. These citizens exhibit behaviors. These behaviors best satisfy the needs and aspirations of this state. These needs and aspirations are. Achieve and maintain authority, power, order, and control. In that event, these citizens would fulfill a set of civic duties. The set of civic duties would include. Uphold the laws of this state. Respect state authorities. Offer vows of loyalty to this state. Pledge allegiance. Pay tribute to this state. Defend this state in times of war. In exchange, this state would fulfill a set of duties. This set of duties would include. Provide citizens with services. Provide citizens with protection from foreign invasion and or terrorist attack. Determine who owns what property. Take the side of property owners in any dispute over property rights.

Laws of natural selection are a subset of universal laws. Laws of natural selection predict the outcome of the conflict between predator and prey in a body-consuming biosphere. Laws of natural selection establish a system. The system rewards fitness with survival and punishes lacking with sacrifice.

Selection is parental, communal, predatory, and sexual in nature. People make natural selections in favor of beauty, fertility, symmetry, intelligence, dexterity, strength, endurance, persistence, consciousness, ability, and activity. People make natural selections against ugliness, infertility, asymmetry, dullness, clumsiness, weakness, exhaustion, resignation, unconsciousness, disability, and passivity.

I desire good health. Universal, state, and natural laws of cause and effect suggest a material standard of conduct. I think, believe, and predict. The act of conforming my behaviors to the material standard of conduct will enable me. I can achieve and maintain good health. For that reason, I conform my behaviors to the material standard of conduct.

I desire happiness. Spiritual laws of love and freedom suggest a spiritual standard of conduct. I think, believe, and predict. The act of conforming my behaviors to the spiritual standard of conduct will enable me. I can achieve and maintain happiness. For that reason, I conform my behaviors to the spiritual standard of conduct.

I desire happiness, good health, and prosperity. I combine the material standard of conduct and the spiritual standard of conduct. The combination suggests a comprehensive standard of conduct. I think, believe, and predict. The act of conforming my behaviors to the comprehensive standard of conduct will enable me. I can achieve and maintain happiness, good health, and prosperity. For those reasons, I conform my behaviors to the comprehensive standard of conduct.

CHAPTER 80. A GAME OF SURVIVAL AND SACRIFICE

We live in a body-consuming biosphere. A primal conflict between predator and prey divides the body-consuming biosphere. We play the dual role of predator and prey. We play a game of survival and sacrifice. The game of survival and sacrifice enables the soul spirit. The soul spirit determines whether or not. Seed bodies survive the test of time.

States, communities of faithful believers, and ideological traditions also play a game of survival and sacrifice. The game of survival and sacrifice enables the soul spirit. The soul spirit determines whether or not. States, communities of faithful believers, and ideological traditions, survive the test of time.

Future generations will inherit ideological traditions. Those ideological traditions will enable ideological authorities. Ideological authorities will lead communities of faithful believers. Members will build models of the totality. These models of the totality will enable members. Members will compete in the game of survival and sacrifice.

Our survival is the most important factor in determining the survival of our ideological traditions. Let us suppose. In a competition, the survivors were aggressive ideological traditions. Aggressive ideological traditions aggressively motivated communities of faithful believers. Members worked, fought, and outnumbered competitors. The sacrifices were passive ideological traditions. Passive ideological traditions passively motivated communities of faithful believers. The competitors worked, fought, and outnumbered these communities of faithful believers. In that event, the survival of these aggressive ideological traditions can be understood by us today to be a product of this competition to survive.

Let us suppose. Members affirm an ability to know. A good entity commands the faithful. The faithful must observe and obey the will of the good entity. The will of the good entity is. Be fruitful and multiply. Work all the hours of the day from dawn to dusk. Fight against anybody who is not doing the same thing. Fight against anybody who is not believing in the same way. Let us suppose finally. These commands are effective. These commands motivate them. The members work, fight, and outnumber the competition. These members survive. Their belief in the value of these commands survives. In that event, these commands can be understood by us today to be the product of this competition to survive.

Let us suppose. Some communities of faithful believers are even more aggressive about outnumbering competition. Members enter into polygamous marriages. Members use fertility drugs. Members have litters of children. In that event, I wonder. How would room be made in this body consuming biosphere of limited dimensions for all of these new people?

Let us suppose. Members sacrifice outsiders to make room. In that event, the denunciation and sacrifice of outsiders can be understood by us today to be the product of this competition to survive.

The popularity of aggressive ideological traditions is a major contributing factor to the explosive growth of human population in recent history. This explosive growth of human population has enabled the soul spirit. The soul spirit has selected for a kind of human being. What kind of human being has been selected? I value truths. Scientists say. It appears. Over the last three thousand years of recorded history, human brains have lost a lemon size quantity of brain matter. Scientists do not know why our brains have shrunk. Scientists have suggested several possibilities in an effort to explain why. One possibility is. Human beings have been domesticated. Domesticated animals of a given species typically, though not necessarily, have smaller brains than wild animals of the same species. Another possibility is. Civilization made life easier for human beings. Human beings did not require as much brain power. Smaller brains do not require as much energy and resources. For that reason, our brains have shrunk.

My guess is. A few people concentrated wealth, income, and power into their own hands. The few people competed for territories to rule over. Success attracted competition. The concentration of wealth, income, and power into the hands of the few people made the competition to rule homicidal, genocidal, and even suicidal at times. For that reason, the few people became a few paranoid oppressive violent people. The few paranoid oppressive violent people selected for human beings who best satisfy the needs and aspirations of the few paranoid oppressive violent people. The needs and aspirations of the few paranoid oppressive violent people include. Achieve and maintain authority, power, order, and control. The few paranoid oppressive violent people selected for human beings who defer to outside authorities when making up their own minds. The act of allowing outside authorities to think for us requires less brain power than the act of thinking for ourselves. For that reason, our brains have shrunk in volume and mass.

Let us suppose. Members claim an ability to know. An aggressive ideological tradition survived. Survival is proof. The aggressive ideological tradition expresses the will of at least one deity. In that event, their line of reasoning would be faulty. The will of the soul spirit would be. These communities of faithful believers will survive. For that reason, their aggressive ideological traditions will also survive.

There is nothing proprietary about aggressive ideological traditions. Other aggressive ideological traditions have survived the test of time. Why are the words written down in one set of sacred scrolls right? Why are the words written down in every other set of sacred scrolls wrong? The totality makes possible an infinite number, diversity, and variety of myths. What happens when more than one aggressive ideological tradition appears in the global culture? What happens when competing communities of faithful believers self-organize around different words? Exponential population growth, pollution, depletion of natural resources, abrupt climate change, habitat loss, war, and human extinction, is that what happens?

We are facing an ordeal. Maybe those who vigorously defend their faith in an aggressive ideological tradition don't understand the ordeal. Human beings have been multiplying to the point of causing disease within a body. The body is our body-consuming biosphere. Population overshoot, pollution, global warming, deforestation, desertification, the desolation of large areas of land in war; dead zones in our oceans, and the melting of ancient glaciers are evidence of this disease as is the daily starvation of thousands of children aged zero to five.

Some people have used violence to resolve differences over ownership of increasingly scarce resources. Some people have used violence to resolve differences over matters of faith. The continuation of our historical use of violence to resolve our differences could cause the death of a body. The body is our body-consuming biosphere.

Let us suppose. I get a virus in my body. Let us suppose further. The virus multiplies to excess and causes disease. In that event, maybe I can take an anti-viral. Maybe the anti-viral can inhibit the multiplication of the virus and restore my body to a state of good health.

Let us suppose. Our body-consuming biosphere gets a liar in its body. Let us suppose further. The liar multiplies to excess and causes disease. In that event, maybe our body-consuming biosphere can take an anti-liar. Maybe the anti-liar can inhibit the multiplication of liars and restore the body-consuming biosphere to a state of good health. The anti-liar is a truth. The truth is. A myth is a myth.

CHAPTER 81. RECURRING THEMES

Planet Earth is a crusted magma globe. The material plane is the surface of the crusted magma globe. The crusted magma globe has limited dimensions. For that reason, the material plane is a place of limitations.

Projection theory enables me. I predict. Some people believe in the value of pessimistic myths. These people tend to project. They use their senses and perceptions. Search their surroundings. Gather truths about the limitations of the material plane. Project these truths into their imaginations. Use their imaginations. Make pessimistic myths about the limitations of the spiritual realm. These pessimistic myths have recurring themes.

One recurring theme is. These pessimistic myths include. A spiritual conflict between good and evil exists. A good entity rules in Heaven. The good entity is at war with an evil entity. The evil entity rules over the Earth. These pessimistic myths suggest truths. The truths include. A primal conflict between predator and prey exists. A few paranoid oppressive violent people rule over domestic territories. The few paranoid oppressive violent people are at war with outsiders. The outsiders rule over foreign territories.

Another recurring theme is. These pessimistic myths cast men and women in roles. These roles are essentially ruler and subject. In extreme cases, the roles are owner and property. These pessimistic myths suggest truths. The truths include. Men tend to be physically larger and stronger than woman. Men tend to be active and dominant during reproductive sexual activity. Women tend to be passive and submissive during reproductive sexual activity.

Let us suppose. Communities of faithful believers exist. Members affirm an ability to know. The good entity cast men and women in roles. These roles are essentially ruler and subject. These roles are owner and property. Let us suppose further. The moral high ground enables men. These men express the motivation of the seed more fully than would have otherwise been possible. In that event, doing so would enable members. Members would outnumber competitors. The act of outnumbering competitors would be conducive to the survival of their communities of faithful believers. The survival of their communities of faithful believers would be conducive to the survival of these roles. The survival of these roles could be understood by us today to be a product of this competition to survive.

Yet another recurring theme is. These pessimistic myths cast non-reproductive forms of sexual activity as a transgression against the will, words, way, and laws of at least one deity. Adultery, fornication, and promiscuity are prohibited. These pessimistic myths suggest truths. The truths include. The act of creating is the motivation of the seed. The act of surviving is the motivation of the body. Promiscuity is conducive to the spread of sexually transmissible diseases.

Let us suppose. Communities of faithful believers exist. Members affirm an ability to know. A good entity condemns as evil contraception, recreational sex, occupational sex, and any other non-reproductive form of sexual activity. The good entity makes threats of severe punishment. For that reason, members repress these sexual activities. Let us suppose further. Members practice ritualized mutilation of genitalia. Ritualized mutilation of genitalia reduces the perception of sexual pleasure. The reduced perception of sexual pleasure makes a command much easier to obey. The command is. Only engage in sexual activities for reproductive purposes. Let us suppose finally. Members accept mutilation of genitalia without resentment. In that event, less energy would be spent seeking pleasure through sex. More energy would be spent on the acts of working, fighting, and outnumbering competition. More energy spent on the acts of working, fighting, and outnumbering competition would most likely be conducive to the survival of their communities of faithful believers. The survival of their communities of faithful believers would most likely be conducive to the survival of ritualized mutilation of genitalia. The survival of ritualized mutilation of genitalia can be understood by us today to be a product of this competition to survive.

I do not incorporate any of the above reoccurring themes into my model of the totality. Yet, I think, believe, and predict. My model of the totality or something similar will survive. The survival of my model of the totality or something similar will enable us. We will best satisfy our common needs and aspirations. Our common needs and aspirations are. Achieve and maintain happiness, good health, and prosperity.

CHAPTER 82. CONCEPTUAL CHANGE

Our ancestors observed earthquakes, volcanic eruptions, lightning, thunder, tornados, hurricanes, floods, famines, plagues, movements of the sun, the moon, the planets, and the stars in the heavens and other awesome displays of power. Our ancestors left behind their written words. From the act of reading these written words, we learn. Many of our ancestors thought, believed, and predicted. These awesome displays of power demonstrated the activities of deities.

Their descendants also observe these awesome displays of power. Increasingly, their descendants think, believe, and predict. These awesome displays of power demonstrate predictable patterns, physical laws, and properties of the known universe.

It appears. Over time, the shadow of mystery has receded in the light of discovery. Myths and fantasies have receded in the light of truths and theories. Truths and theories have begun to take a larger role within the popular conception of the function of the known universe. Myths and fantasies have begun to take a smaller role within the popular conception of the function of the known universe. Deities play a role. The role has changed from an active, obvious, and discovered role; to a passive, hidden, and mysterious role.

The absence of evidence is not evidence of absence. The absence of evidence is evidence of the limitations of our senses and perceptions. Is evidence really absent? We know next to nothing about almost everything. For that reason, the discovery of truths and theories leaves open a possibility. The possibility is. An infinite divine eternal being sets in motion a large universe of the correct kind to support living infernal fractal entities. Once the universe is in motion, the infinite divine eternal being becomes passive, hidden, and mysterious from the point of view of the living infernal fractal entities.

The presence of evidence is not evidence of presence. The presence of evidence is evidence of the limitations of our senses and perceptions. Is evidence really present? The universe is presence of evidence. The presence of evidence in the form of the universe provides premises. We use these premises. We make valid logical inductive inferences. We arrive at conclusions. The conclusions are certain ideas. We value these certain ideas. These certain ideas are our values.

I value truths. Scientists say. It appears. Laws of cause and effect predict the behavior and fate of matter and energy in the known universe. Inorganic parts of our universe function according to the laws of cause and effect. Organic parts of the universe also function according to the laws of cause and effect. However, some part of the organic parts of the universe are made up of our seed-bodies.

I value the most optimistic myths. My seed-body is a probability possibility cloud. My soul-spirit observes my seed-body. The probability possibility cloud collapses down to one possibility. The one possibility becomes my conscious mind and free will. The role of my soul is. Ride my seed-body. Get inside my mind. Select my conscious mind. Exert my free will.

I value truths. The universe provides a stage. The universe does so according to its own rules. Upon this stage, we act in the drama of life and death. I value the most optimistic myths. The totality is an infinite divine eternal being. The infinite divine eternal being enjoys entertainment. The infinite divine eternal being derives entertainment from the drama of life and death. The infinite divine eternal being does so by way of continuous spiritual communion with our souls.

Video games often allow a user to control the conscious mind and free will of a computer-generated-virtual individual in a computer-generated-virtual reality. The user handles some functions. The software handles other functions automatically for the user. Such video games are roughly analogous in an infinitely less elaborate way to the universe. Some functions such as my conscious thought, feeling, and action are under the voluntary control of my soul. Other functions are under the involuntary control of laws of cause and effect.

Let us suppose. A person makes fantastic wishes. The person wishes for age reversal. The person wishes for the resurrection of a loved one who has died. The person wishes for eternal life, health, and youth in the flesh. Let us suppose further. A seed-body was never meant to survive beyond its' natural lifecycle. A perceptible violation of universal laws of cause and effect would be required to make such fantastic wishes come true. In that event, granting these fantastic wishes would be like going into the hardware of a computer and changing the software of a video game to affect the outcome. The result would be. The person would no longer be playing the same game.

The difference between playing a video game and playing the cosmic game is: When playing a video game, we are aware of a world outside of the video game. When playing the cosmic game, we are not aware of a world outside of the cosmic game. Our seed-bodies create unconscious minds. Our souls order the chaos of our unconscious minds. Thereby, our souls select our conscious minds. When playing the cosmic game, we confine our awareness of the totality to our conscious minds. Our souls exert our free wills. We gain the enjoyment of entertainment. We derive the entertainment. We ponder the existence of discovery and mystery. We act in the drama of life and death. We play the game of survival and sacrifice. We fight in the conflict of predator and prey. We take the test of success and failure. We experience the catharsis of comedy and tragedy. We feel the sensations of pleasure and pain. We select from a wide range of possibilities for thought, feeling, and action.

Let us suppose:

1. An infinite divine eternal being is the hardware of a computer.
2. The seed-body of self and the universe are the software;
3. And the soul-spirit of self, operates a user interface.
4. The user-interface controls the conscious mind and free will of self;

In that event, I wonder. How could I conceive of such ideas?

Let us suppose. The software is my seed-body and the universe. This software makes available a finite number, diversity, and variety of possibilities for thought, feeling, and action. My soul strings these possibilities together. A train of thought forms. Let us suppose further. The train of thought reveals these ideas to me. In that event, I conceive of these ideas by personal divine revelations of spiritual knowledge.

I think, believe, and predict. I have experienced such personal divine revelations of spiritual knowledge. I value these personal divine revelations of spiritual knowledge.

My personal divine revelations of spiritual knowledge are myths. The presence of evidence in the form of the universe provides premises. These premises enable us. We can make valid logical inductive inferences. We can make myths. The totality makes possible an infinite number, diversity, and variety of myths. Each of these myths is an equally valid possibility.

I interpret the universe as evidence in support of my most optimistic myths. The universe could also be interpreted as evidence in support of pessimistic myths. Both interpretations rely upon valid logical inductive inferences. I do not know whether or not. Either interpretation is correct. I do not know whether or not. Either interpretation is incorrect.

Let us suppose. I found objective evidence. I made logically valid deductive inferences. I arrived at a scientifically reproducible discovery. This scientifically reproducible discovery enabled me. I proved. My personal revelations of spiritual knowledge are true. In that event, my existence would not be nearly as entertaining as it is.

CHAPTER 83. I ANTHROPOMORPHIZE MY MODEL

Anthropomorphism is the attribution of human traits, emotions, or intentions to non-human entities. Projection theory enables me. I predict. Some of our ancestors believed in the value of pessimistic myths. These ancestors tended to project. They used their senses and perceptions. Searched their surroundings. Gathered truths about their set of living arrangements. They projected their truths into their imaginations. They used their imaginations. They made myths. Their myths suggested their truths. For that reason, some of our ancestors worshipped anthropomorphic gods.

Anthropomorphic gods are deities. People depict these deities with human characteristics or forms. Anthropomorphic gods often embody various aspects of human nature, emotions, and experiences. Throughout history, many cultures have conceived of their gods in anthropomorphic terms. They have attributed to their gods personalities, emotions, and physical appearances resembling those of humans.

One of the primary reasons for anthropomorphizing gods is. Make them more relatable to humans. By depicting gods with human traits, people can better understand and connect with their gods on a personal level. Anthropomorphic gods often serve as figures of worship. These figures of worship offer guidance, protection, and comfort to their followers.

In ancient Greek mythology, for example, the gods were depicted as having human-like appearances and personalities, albeit with superhuman powers. Zeus, the king of the gods, was often portrayed as a powerful and authoritative figure. Athena, the goddess of wisdom, was revered for her intelligence and strategic prowess.

Similarly, in Hinduism, many gods and goddesses are depicted in human form. Each represents different aspects of the universe. For instance, Vishnu, the preserver god, is often depicted with human-like features and emotions, such as compassion and kindness. Shiva, the destroyer god, embodies both benevolent and wrathful qualities.

Anthropomorphic gods can also serve as moral and ethical guides for believers. In Christianity, for instance, Jesus Christ is often viewed as both fully human and fully divine. He provides believers with a relatable figure. He embodies virtues such as love, compassion, and forgiveness.

However, anthropomorphizing gods can also raise philosophical questions about the nature of divinity and the relationship between humans and the divine. Some religious authority figures argue. Anthropomorphic depictions of gods limit our understanding of the divine. Anthropomorphic depictions reduce gods to human-like qualities. These human-like qualities may not fully capture the transcendence and complexity of the divine.

Despite these debates, the concept of anthropomorphic gods continues to play a significant role in religious and cultural traditions around the world. The significant role is. Act as symbols of divine power, moral exemplars, and or objects of worship. Anthropomorphic gods reflect humanity's enduring fascination with the divine. Anthropomorphic gods reflect our desire to comprehend the mysteries of the cosmos in certain terms. These certain terms are familiar and accessible to us.

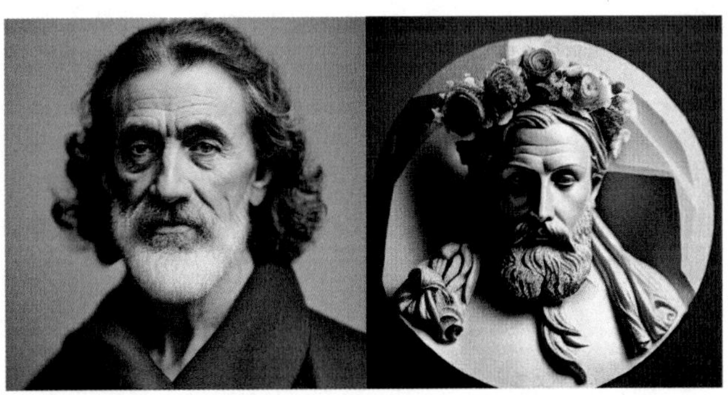

Criticism of anthropomorphic gods is almost as old as the myths and fantasies themselves. For example, Xenophanes was a 6th century B.C. poet, singer, philosopher, and critic of contemporary ethics and theology. Xenophanes specifically criticized the theology of Homer and Hesiod.

Ancient authors credited Homer and Hesiod with establishing Greek religious customs. Modern scholars refer to them as a major source on Greek mythology, farming techniques, early economic thought, archaic Greek astronomy, and ancient time-keeping.

Xenophanes had this to say.

THE NATURE OF THE GODS

Man made his gods and furnished them

with his own body, voice, and garments . . .

If a horse or lion or a slow ox

had agile hands for paint and sculpture,

the horse would make his god a horse,

the ox would sculpt an ox . . .

Our gods have flat noses and black skins

say the Ethiopians. The Thracians say

our gods have red hair and hazel eyes.

Xenophanes suggests. Ethnocentric preferences of communities of faithful believers are responsible for the popularity of earlier theological ideas. Afterwards, he states his own beliefs. Xenophanes submits. There is only a single God. This God is omniscient. This God bears no resemblance to any man in body or in thought. This God remains motionless in one place at all times.

His third point is. Human knowledge is limited. For that reason, man will never know the truth about the Gods.

KNOWLEDGE

The gods did not enrich man

with a knowledge of all things

from the beginning of life . . .

Yet man seeks, and in time

invents what may be better . . .

The truth is that no man ever was or will be

who understands the gods and all I speak of.

If you stumble on some rocks of the whole truth

you never know it. There is always speculation.

Xenophanes questioned the old beliefs. He presented his own beliefs as a hypothesis. Xenophanes broke down old beliefs. Xenophanes established a new more "scientific" method of logical thinking.

Xenophanes made his criticisms of anthropomorphic gods. His criticisms have been preceded by many other criticisms. His criticisms have been followed by many other criticisms. Yet, it appears. Anthropomorphic gods continue to be popular.

Let us suppose. Some people respect the traditions of their ancestors. Their ancestors worshipped anthropomorphic gods. In that event, the anthropomorphic gods would continue to be popular with these people.

A myth is. A savior exists. The savior loves you. The myth suggests a truth. The truth is. People often form life-long relationships with a spouse. Let us suppose. A person is willing. The person accepts a spouse into their heart. In that event, the spouse would exist. The spouse would love the person.

A myth is. A good entity rules in Heaven. The myth suggests a truth. The truth is. A few paranoid oppressive violent people ruled over domestic territories.

A myth is. The good entity is at war with an evil entity. The myth suggests a truth. The truth is. The few paranoid oppressive violent people were at war with outsiders.

A myth is. The evil entity rules over the Earth. The myth suggests a truth. The truth is. The outsiders ruled over foreign territories.

The big lie is. These pessimistic myths are truths. The truth is. These pessimistic myths suggest truths. The act of suggesting these truths does not make these pessimistic myths into truths. These pessimistic myths remain myths.

We know next to nothing about almost everything. The totality makes possible an infinite number, diversity, and variety of myths. Optimism correlates with happiness, good health, and prosperity. For that reason, the logical, rational, sane choice to make when orienting the self to the world and explaining the world to the self is a belief in the value of the most optimistic myths.

I value truths. I value the most optimistic myths. I use my values. I build within my mind. I build a model of the totality.

My model of the totality includes the most optimistic myths. The most optimistic myths include. The totality is an infinite divine eternal being. The infinite divine eternal being enjoys entertainment. The drama of life and death entertains. For that reason, the infinite divine eternal being manifests as an infinite four. The infinite four are an infinite seed, an infinite body, an infinite soul, and an infinite spirit. The infinite seed is an infinite number, diversity, and variety of large universes of the correct kind to support living infernal fractal entities. The infinite body is the seed-body of self and the seed-bodies of all of the other living infernal fractal entities. The infinite soul is the soul-spirit of self and the soul-spirits of all of the other living infernal fractal entities. The infinite spirit is the infinite divine eternal being.

I anthropomorphize my model. I anthropomorphize the infinite four. The Infinite Four are the family of Mo Go Fa Lo. The family of Mo Go Fa Lo consists of Mother God, Father Love, and the Soul Children. Mother God is the infinite soul-spirit. Father Love is the infinite seed-body. The union of Mother God and Father Love creates life. We are Soul Children.

CHAPTER 84. SOURCES OF GENDER IMAGERY

It appears. People anthropomorphize in various ways. I compare and contrast the various ways. Similarities and differences exist. I communicate, explain, and illustrate the similarities and differences. I diversify and vary presentation. I provide entertaining and educational spiritual leadership.

For some gnostic theists, their sources of gender imagery are pessimistic myths. Religious authority figures affirm an ability to know. These pessimistic myths are truths. These pessimistic myths include. A good entity rules in Heaven. They assign a masculine gender to this good entity. They assign a feminine gender to the communities of faithful believers.

I am an agnostic theist. My sources of gender imagery are also myths. I choose to draw upon myths anchored in Taoist traditions. I assign a masculine gender to the infinite seed-body. I assign a feminine gender to the infinite soul-spirit.

I believe in the value of truths. My seed-body makes senses and perceptions available to me. My senses and perceptions enable me. I can verify the veracity of a truth. The truth is. It appears. The matter and energy of the known universe exists.

The matter and energy of the known universe are part of the infinite seed-body. The matter and energy of the known universe have the quality of being obvious and discovered. The active yang principle of Taoist traditions has the quality of being masculine, obvious and discovered. For those reasons, I assign a masculine gender to the infinite seed-body.

I believe in the value of the most optimistic myths. My senses and perceptions do not enable me. I am unable to verify whether or not. The most optimistic myths are true. I am unable to verify whether or not. The most optimistic myths are false. The most optimistic myths are both unverifiable and unfalsifiable.

The infinite soul-spirit is an infinite divine eternal being. The infinite soul-spirit has the quality of being hidden and mysterious. The passive yin principle of Taoist Traditions has the quality of being feminine, hidden and mysterious. For those reasons, I assign a feminine gender to the infinite soul-spirit.

CHAPTER 85. THE IMPLICATIONS ARE

I think, believe, and predict. An infinite soul-spirit is passive, hidden, and mysterious. For that reason, I assign a feminine gender to the infinite soul-spirit. The act of assigning a feminine gender has implications. The implications are. I value a truth. The truth is. These most optimistic myths are myths. I devalue a lie. The lie is. These most optimistic myths are truths.

I acknowledge. I know next to nothing about almost everything. The totality makes possible an infinite number, diversity, and variety of myths. I desire happiness, good health, and prosperity. Optimism correlates with happiness, good health, and prosperity. For those reasons, I believe in the value of the most optimistic myths.

The most optimistic myths include. Our universe is one of an infinite seed-body of large universes of the correct kind to support living infernal fractal entities. The meaning of life is living. The purpose of living is entertainment. Before the birth of our seed-bodies, the infinite soul-spirit judged our universe. The infinite soul-spirit found. The drama of life and death entertains. Our universe entertains. For that reason, our infinite soul-spirit created the energy, space, and time of our universe. The infinite spirit became passive about the operation of our universe. The infinite soul became active within our universe. Our souls took control over the voluntary functions of our seed-bodies.

The universe is like a theatre. The surface of the earth is like a stage. We are actors in the drama of life and death. We create characters. We portray characters of our own creation as actors in the drama of life and death. The drama of life and death takes place in a body consuming biosphere. The body consuming biosphere exists on a crusted magma globe. A moon orbits the crusted magma globe. The crusted magma globe orbits a sun. The sun, the crusted magma globe, and the moon are reproducible; in a galaxy of stars; and a universe of galaxies. Collectively we direct the global drama of life and death. The infinite divine eternal being is the ultimate producer.

The most optimistic myths include. The infinite soul-spirit is happy, positivistic, hidden, mysterious, and feminine. Mother God is at peace with her Soul Children in a unified spiritual realm. Mother God provides to her Soul Children inspiration, intuition, and good judgment by way of continuous spiritual communion. Mother God bestows infinite love, divine forgiveness, eternal freedom, and unifying grace upon all of her Soul Children. Salvation has always been ours. We are saved. We have been saved. We always will be saved. We have an infinite number, diversity, and variety of lives to live. We have an infinite number, diversity, and variety of bodies to give. We are seed, body, soul, and spirit.

CHAPTER 86. YIN YANG SYMBOLISM

I combine four things. I complete my model of the totality. The four things are; the seed-body of the world, the seed-body of self, the soul-spirit of self, and the soul-spirit of the world. I find. Yin and yang symbolism is useful. I illustrate how. I assign passive and active qualities to the four things. I briefly review the original meanings given the yin and yang by Taoist. To summarize, the Tao Te Ching, Chapter 42 states:

The Tao is the One,
From the One come yin and yang:
From these two, creative energy;
From energy, ten thousand things;
The forms of all creation;

All life embodies the yin
And embraces yang,
Through their union
Achieving harmony.

Tao is the word for the cosmic whole. The way of the cosmic whole is the Tao. This cosmic whole is broken down into yin and yang. The essential difference between the Chinese conception of yin and yang and good and evil is. Good and evil are involved in an eternal conflict. Yin and yang are basically in eternal accord. Yin and yang are together in harmony. Yin and yang are complementary. Taoists elaborate on a complete system of opposites. Taoists characterize the yin principle as dark, hidden, passive, receptive, yielding, cool, soft, and feminine. Taoists characterize the yang principle as illuminated, evident, active, aggressive, controlling, hot, hard, and masculine.

Some Taoists go on to describe yin and yang as opposing forces of change. The opposing forces of change mean several things. A first thing is. All phenomena change into opposite phenomena in an eternal cycle of reversal. A second thing is. One principle produces the other. All phenomena have within them the seeds of their opposite. Sickness contains the seeds of health. Health contains the seeds of sickness. Wealth contains the seeds of poverty. Poverty contains the seeds of wealth, etc. A third thing is. One may not see an opposite phenomenon to be present. However, no phenomenon is completely devoid of its' opposite. Taoists call this "presence in absence."

The yin-yang symbol illustrates the Taoist concept of the opposing forces of change in the world. Red regions represent the active yang principle. Black regions represent the passive yin

principle. The disposition of black yin and red yang is symmetrical. The rotation of the yin-yang symbol suggests cyclical changes. When yin reaches its climax, it recedes in favor of yang. When yang reaches its climax, it recedes in favor of yin. This is the eternal cycle. Taoists add two circles to the yin yang symbol. One circle is red. This red circle represents the presence of this active yang principle within this passive yin principle. Another circle is black. This black circle represents the presence of this passive yin principle within this active yang principle. The addition of the two circles completes the yin-yang symbol. These circles illustrate. Within each principle is found the seeds of the other principle. The addition of these two circles brings the total number of elements to four. The yin-yang symbol consists of these four elements.

I value the most optimistic myths. For that reason, I assign an active quality to the involuntary functions of the seed-body of the world. I assign a passive quality to the voluntary functions of the seed-body of self. I assign an active quality to the soul-spirit of self. I assign a passive quality to the soul-spirit of the world.

I combine these four things. I complete my model of the totality. I have a way of assigning passive and active qualities to these four things. I illustrate the way. I use the four elements of the yin-yang symbol. The red yang region surrounds a black yin disk. I use the red yang region. I illustrate the way. I assign an active quality to the involuntary functions of the seed-body of the world. I use the black yin disk. I illustrate the way. I assign a passive quality to the voluntary functions of the seed-body of self. The black yin region surrounds a red yang disk. I use the red yang disk. I illustrate the way. I assign an active quality to the soul-spirit of self. I use the black yin region. I illustrate the way. I assign a passive quality to the soul-spirit of the world.

Let us suppose. Some people have a different way of assigning active and passive qualities to these four things. These people assign a passive quality to the seed-body of the world. These people assign an active quality to the seed-body of self. These people assign a passive quality to the soul-spirit of self. These people assign an active quality to the soul-spirit of the world. In that event, we would have ways of assigning passive and active qualities to the four things. Their way would be the opposite of my way.

I use the four elements of the yin-yang symbol. I illustrate the way. These people assign passive and active qualities to the four things. The black yin region surrounds the red yang disk. I use the black yin region. I illustrate the way. These people assign a passive quality to the seed-body of the world. I use the red yang disk. I illustrate the way. These people assign an active quality to the seed-body of self. The red yang region surrounds the black yin disk. I use the black yin disk. I illustrate the way. These people assign a passive quality to the soul-spirit of self. I use the red yang region. I illustrate the way. These people assign an active quality to the soul-spirit of the world.

We have two different and opposite ways of assigning passive and active qualities. I compare my way to their way. I assign an active quality to involuntary functions of the seed-body of the world. They assign a passive quality to the seed-body of the world. I assign a passive quality to the voluntary functions of the seed-body of self. They assign an active quality to the seed-body of self. I assign an active quality to the soul-spirit of self. They assign a passive quality to the soul-spirit of self. I assign a passive quality to the soul-spirit of the world. They assign an active quality to the soul-spirit of the world.

Four elements combine to complete the yin-yang symbol. I use the four elements. I depict two different and opposite ways of assigning active and passive qualities to four things. The four things are seed-body of the world, seed-body of self, soul-spirit of self, and soul-spirit of the world. I combine the four things. I complete my model of the totality.

CHAPTER 87. MOTHER GOD, FATHER LOVE, AND THE TAO

I value truths. The totality is everything, everywhere, at all times. I know next to nothing about almost everything. I value the most optimistic myths. The most optimistic myths are all about infinite abundance. For that reason, I think, believe, and predict. The totality is an infinite divine eternal being. The infinite divine eternal being is everything, everywhere, at all times.

This most optimistic myth about the existence of the infinite divine eternal being is similar to a myth about the existence of the Tao. From this infinite divine eternal being; comes the soul-spirit of the world, and the seed-body of the world. From the one Tao come the two; yin and yang. Taoists characterize the yin principle as dark, hidden, passive, receptive, yielding, cool, soft, and feminine. I assign a feminine gender and the name Mother God to the soul-spirit of the world. Taoists characterize the yang principle as illuminated, evident, active, aggressive, controlling, hot, hard, and masculine. I assign a masculine gender and the name Father Love to the seed-body of the world.

"The Tao that can be told is not the eternal Tao." So begins the Tao Te Ching of Lao Tzu, written some 2,500 years ago. Chapter 25 of the book begins with a brief passage.

Something mysteriously formed,
Born before heaven and earth.
In the silence and the void,
Standing alone and unchanging,
Ever present and in motion.
Perhaps it is the mother of ten thousand things.
I do not know its name.
Call it Tao.

The brief passage reveals to me. Some Taoists beliefs are similar to my own beliefs. Taoists say. The Tao is Mother of perhaps ten thousand things. I say. An infinite creator creates an infinite number, diversity, and variety of finite creatures. The infinite creator endows each finite creature with a soul-spirit and a seed-body. Accordingly, the infinite creator creates each finite creature in the image of the infinite creator. These finite creatures are the Soul Children of Mother God and Father Love.

Ten thousand things is not the same as an infinite number, diversity, and variety of finite creatures. Maybe the concept of infinity would not have been native to the thinking of Lao Tzu. I doubt the difference in the enumeration of things is significant.

How then, do Taoists describe the indescribable? How do Taoists fit the Tao into words? Is the Tao beyond words? Let us suppose. A person insists on a description. In that event, Taoists may describe the Tao. It is vast and active. It moves in great cycles. The Tao is the constant round of life and death. The Tao resides in us as we reside in the Tao. The Tao is the source as well as the end of our being. The Tao neither judges nor condemns but continually blesses, in all moments, with an unending cycle of change and renewal. The Tao has always been. The Tao will always be. The Tao is. The Tao actually has no need of us. Yet the Tao continually and forever sustains us. As Chuang-tzu says, 'It exists by and through itself,' it is self-generating, of itself so.

The Tao is the way. The Tao is the source, destination, purpose, and process. In imagining and exploring the Tao, the process and the destination are the same.

The notion of a Supreme Being is essential to Western religions. Taoist thought replaces the Supreme Being with a Supreme State of Being. The Supreme State of Being is an impersonal perfection. Only delusion separates all beings, including man, from this Supreme State of Being. The Supreme State of Being is not some unattainable something. The Supreme State of Being is not "out there". The Supreme State of Being is not far removed from the mundane affairs of humankind. The Supreme State of Being is an attainable something. We are part of the Supreme State of Being. The Supreme State of Being is a part of us. Living with a wrathful, personified deity is much harder than living with something so simple, so natural, and all-encompassing as the Tao. The Tao may reign but the Tao does not rule. The Tao is the pattern of things but not the enforcer.

I value the most optimistic myths. The most optimistic myths include. An infinite divine eternal being exists. Taoists value a myth. The myth is. A Supreme State of Being exists. Let us suppose. Gnostic Theists value a myth. The myth is. A Supreme Being exists. In that event, I think, believe, and predict. Taoist values would be closer to my values than would be the values of the Gnostic Theists.

The Tao does not judge. The Tao does not condemn. The Tao does not punish. Taoists teach. By refusing to go along with the majestic flow of the Tao, we punish ourselves. By refusing to go along with the majestic flow of the Tao, we cause ourselves all sorts of worries and problems.

Similarly, I teach by example. I value my truths. I base my truths on the existence of discovery. I value my theories. I base my theories on scientifically reproducible discoveries. My truths and my theories inform me. It appears. Laws of cause and effect predict the behavior and fate of matter and energy in the known universe.

These universal laws of cause and effect suggest a material standard of conduct. I think, believe, and predict. The act of conforming to this material standard of conduct best produces rewards. The rewards are good health. I desire good health. For that reason, I conform to this material standard of conduct.

Let us suppose. I deviate from this material standard of conduct. In that event, I would think, believe, and predict. I would punish myself. My punishment would be. I would be diseased.

I value my most optimistic myths. I base my most optimistic myths on what is possible within the realm of mystery. My most optimistic myths include. Spiritual laws of love and freedom govern the behavior, fate, and destiny of our souls. These spiritual laws of love and freedom suggest a spiritual standard of conduct. I think, believe, and predict. The act of conforming to this spiritual standard of conduct best produces rewards. The rewards are happiness. I desire happiness. For that reason, I conform to this spiritual standard of conduct.

Let us suppose. I deviate from this spiritual standard of conduct. In that event, I would think, believe, and predict. I would punish myself. My punishment would be. I would be unhappy.

I combine my truths, my theories, and my most optimistic myths. These are my values. I use my values. I build within my mind. I build my model of the totality. My model is my reality. My reality is my House of Ideology. I am the High Ideologue of my House of Ideology. I can change reality to what. I would like it to be.

I combine this spiritual standard of conduct and this material standard of conduct. I create a comprehensive standard of conduct. I think, believe, and predict. The act of conforming to this comprehensive standard of conduct best produces rewards. The rewards are happiness and good health. Happiness and good health are conducive to success and prosperity. I desire happiness. I desire good health. I desire success. I desire prosperity. For those reasons, I conform to this comprehensive standard of conduct. Let us suppose. I deviate from this comprehensive standard of conduct. In that event, I would think, believe, and predict. I would punish myself. My punishment would be. I would be unhappy, unhealthy, and or poor.

Taoists say. Everything is sacred, not just musty old "holy" books, or special buildings, or even special people. The special people have a job. The job is. They act as intermediaries between the sacred and the profane. To the followers of the way, there is no difference between the sacred and the profane. There is no escaping the Tao, or sacredness. The Tao is contained within everything as everything is contained within the Tao.

CHAPTER 88. MANDALA OF MY HOUSE OF IDEOLOGY

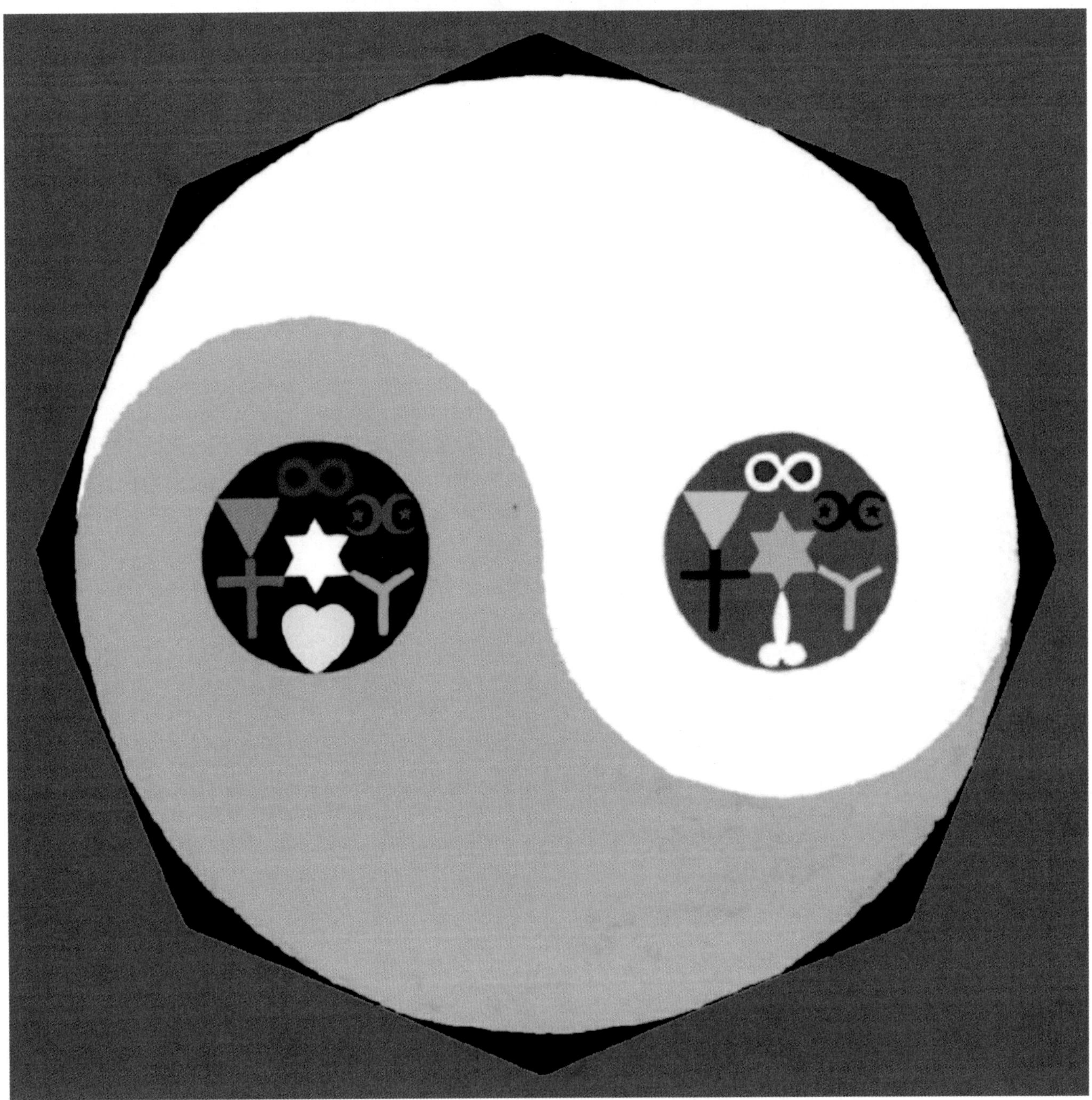

We value certain ideas. These certain ideas are our values. We use our values. We build within our minds. We build our models of the totality. A Mandala is a graphic representation of a model of the totality. Here is my Mandala. With my Mandala, I further externalize my model of the totality.

My model of the totality is my House of Ideology. An ideology is a body of values. Ideology fashions reality. My House of Ideology is my reality. Reality is the way. Things appear to be. Actuality is the way. Things actually are. I am the High Ideologue of my House of Ideology. For that reason, I can change my reality to what. I would like my reality to be.

With my Mandala, I represent a competition within the global culture. The competition is between dissonant and harmonious ways of expressing the four motivations. The four motivations are. The seed creates. The body survives. The soul perfects. The spirit revives. Dissonant ways of expressing the four motivations follow from the act of building pessimistic models of the totality. Harmonious ways of expressing the four motivations follow from the act of building optimistic models of the totality.

The most optimistic model of the totality includes the most optimistic myths. The most optimistic myths include. The totality is an infinite divine eternal being. The infinite divine eternal being enjoys entertainment. The drama of life and death entertains. For that reason, the infinite divine eternal being manifests as an infinite four. The infinite four are an infinite seed, an infinite body, an infinite soul, and an infinite spirit.

I use a variation on the yin-yang symbol as the foundation of my Mandala. I make changes in the color design of the yin-yang symbol. Instead of the traditional yin yang symbol with a two-color design, I use a modified yin yang symbol with a four-color design. The colors white, red, black, and gray, represent the infinite seed, the infinite body, the infinite soul, and the infinite spirit respectively. The colors white, red, black, and gray, also represent the motivations of the seed, body, soul, and spirit.

To this modified yin yang symbol, I add combinations of symbols. Some of these symbols make reference to various social movements. Some of these symbols make reference to various religious movements. The various movements were prominent within our global culture during my lifetime. I place these symbols in an unfamiliar configuration. I communicate a new and unfamiliar message.

Let us suppose. Religious authority figures wrote words down in a set of sacred scrolls. In that event, the words would be subject to interpretation. For that reason, two different communities of faithful believers could adopt the same set of sacred scrolls. The two different communities of faithful believers could interpret the words in two different ways. One community of faithful believers could interpret the words in a dissonant way. Another community of faithful believers could interpret the words in a harmonious way. The dissonant way and the harmonious way are two different ways of interpreting the words.

Our values act as forces upon our emotions. Our emotions act as forces upon our behaviors. For those reasons, the act of building a pessimistic model of the totality leads to a dissonant way of interpreting the words. A dissonant way of interpreting the words leads to a dissonant way of expressing the four motivations. The act of building an optimistic model of the totality leads to a harmonious way of interpreting the words. A harmonious way of interpreting the words leads to a harmonious way of expressing the four motivations.

The interpretation of the words is changeable. With a change of the interpretation of the words, can come changes in the way communities of faithful believers express the four motivations. The changes can lead communities of faithful believers away from a hatred. The hatred follows from Fascist Atheistic Perfectionistic Nationalistic Negativism. The changes can lead communities of faithful believers towards a love. The love follows from Healthy Agnostic Positivistic Nationalistic Spiritization.

I include a black circle within my design of my Mandela. The black circle represents the infinite soul. The infinite soul consists of the soul-spirit of self and the soul-spirits of all of the other living infernal fractal entities.

I place a configuration of seven symbols within the black circle. I call the configuration of symbols within the black circle; the emblem of the soul-spirit. The emblem of the soul-spirit represents harmonious ways of interpreting words. The harmonious ways of interpreting words express a love. This love follows from Healthy Agnostic Positivistic Nationalistic Spiritization.

I include a red circle within my design of my Mandela. The red circle represents the infinite body. The infinite body consists of the seed-body of self and the seed-bodies of all of the other living infernal fractal entities.

I place a configuration of seven symbols within the red circle. I call the configuration of symbols within the red circle; the emblem of the seed-body. The emblem of the seed body represents dissonant ways of interpreting words. The dissonant ways of interpreting words express a hatred. The hatred follows from Fascist Atheistic Perfectionistic Nationalistic Negativism.

Three symbols represent discovery religions. Discovery religions are built upon a lie. The lie is. These pessimistic myths are truths. The lie is represented by words. Words are subject to interpretation. The interpretation is changeable. For that reason, people can transform these discovery religions into mystery religions. Mystery religions are built upon a truth. The truth is. These pessimistic myths are myths.

Our global culture is confronted by fortunes and circumstances of our times. People may act in accord with either yin principle or yang principle given fortunes and circumstances of our times. For that reason, these three symbols appear in both the emblem of the seed-body and the emblem of the soul-spirit. At one point in energy, space, and time, an ideological tradition might be relatively aggressive, and at another point in energy, space, and time, the same ideological tradition might be relatively passive. We fashion our realities. Fashions change.

CHAPTER 89. EMBLEM OF THE SOUL-SPIRIT

I include a black circle within the design of my Mandala. The black circle represents the infinite soul. The infinite soul consists of the soul-spirit of self and the soul-spirits of all of the other living infernal fractal entities. I call the configuration of symbols within the black circle; the emblem of the soul-spirit.

The motivations of the seed, body, soul, and spirit are. Create, survive, perfect, and revive. People express the motivations of the seed, body, soul, and spirit. The harmonious way is one of two different and opposing ways of expressing the motivations of the seed, body, soul, and spirit. The harmonious way is in harmony with the most optimistic model of the totality. The most optimistic myths include. The totality is an infinite divine eternal being.

Let us suppose. Communities of faithful believers self-organize around a love. The love follows from Healthy Agnostic Positivistic Nationalistic Spiritization of self and world. In that event, these are harmonious communities of faithful believers.

The emblem of soul-spirit represents harmonious communities of faithful believers. These harmonious communities of faithful believers have members. These members have seed-bodies. These seed-bodies progress through stages of a life cycle. The six outer symbols represent stages in the lifecycle. These stages are infancy, childhood, adolescence, reproductive adult, supportive adult, and old age.

I know the rainbow as a symbol of compassion, forgiveness, freedom, grace, peace, joy, and divinity. For that reason, I assign the colors of the rainbow to the seven symbols. The colors indicate the chronological order of the stages of their life cycles. Their life cycles begin with red and finish with purple. Red twin crescent stars represent infancy. The orange triangle represents childhood. The yellow gender symbol represents adolescence. The yellow gender symbol also represents the feminine gender identity of the passive yin principle. Harmonious communities of faithful believers self-organize around this passive yin principle. The green Y shaped tree of life represents reproductive adult. The blue Latin cross represents supportive adult. The purple infinity symbol represents old age. The arrangement of the symbols communicates the societal status of individuals. Those at the top of the arrangement are of the highest status and those at the bottom are of the lowest status.

The red twin crescent stars, orange triangle, and yellow gender symbols represent infancy, childhood, and adolescence. These three symbols share points of a triangle. The triangle is on the central star. The triangle points towards the earth. During these stages of their life cycles, members, tend to be more focused on their seed-bodies than on their soul-spirits. These members tend to be more concerned with self than with others.

The green tree of life, blue Latin cross, and indigo infinity symbols represent the reproductive adult role, supportive adult role, and old age. These three symbols share points of a triangle. The triangle is on the central star. The triangle points towards the heavens. During these stages of their life cycles, members, tend to be more focused on their soul-spirits than on their seed-bodies. These members tend to be more concerned with others than with self.

The central star is white. I use the color white to represent the seed-body of the world. I associate the seed-body of the world with emotional forces of inhibition to love. I use the color white to represent the emotional forces of inhibition to love.

I value truths. Scientists say. It appears. Universal laws of cause and effect exist. Our knowledge of these universal laws of cause and effect enables us. We can predict the behavior and fate of matter and energy in the known universe. The known universe is part of the seed-body of the world. For that reason, I use the color white to represent the universal laws of cause and effect.

Let us suppose. Communities of faithful believers accept the infinite soul-spirit as a passive yin principle. In that event, members would exhibit a love. The love would follow from Healthy Agnostic Positivistic Nationalistic Spiritization of self and world. Members would take this Healthy Agnostic Positivistic Nationalistic Spiritization to its logical extreme. They would evaluate the form and function of their own seed-bodies. They would peacefully advance the global culture towards ever higher levels of conscious awareness.

A swirling tear drop shape surrounds the black circle. The color of the swirling tear drop shape is gray. The gray color reveals. The origins of the emblem of soul-spirit are the motivations of the soul-spirit. The act of perfecting is the motivation of the soul. The act of reviving is the motivation of the spirit.

CHAPTER 90. EMBLEM OF THE SEED-BODY

I include a red circle within the design of my Mandala. The red circle represents the infinite body. The infinite body consists of the seed-body of self and the seed-bodies of all of the other living infernal fractal entities. I call the configuration of symbols within the red circle; the emblem of the seed-body.

The motivations of the seed, body, soul, and spirit are. Create, survive, perfect, and revive. People express the motivations of the seed, body, soul, and spirit. The dissonant way is one of two different and opposing ways of expressing the motivations of the seed, body, soul, and spirit. The dissonant way is dissonant to the most optimistic model of the totality.

Let us suppose. Communities of faithful believers self-organize around a hatred. This hatred follows from Fascist Atheistic Perfectionistic Nationalistic Negativism. In that event, these are dissonant communities of faithful believers. The emblem of the seed-body represents dissonant communities of faithful believers.

I assign colors to each of these symbols. The colors are white, pink, black, and gray. I associate these colors with emotional forces of sorrow, fear, anger, and joy. These symbols and their colors indicate. Alpha status members and omega status members are in conflict.

The central star is gray. I associate the color gray with the soul-spirit of the world. I associate the soul-spirit of the world with spiritual laws of love and freedom. I use the color gray to represent the spiritual laws of love and freedom. The gray color of the central star indicates. Members feel a joy. They direct the joy towards the world. They express a freedom to love.

The central star is made up of two equilateral triangles. One equilateral triangle points up to the sky and up to the heavens. At the top of this equilateral triangle is an infinity symbol. Alpha status members exist within the dissonant communities of faithful believers. The infinity symbol represents reproductive functions and roles of the alpha status members. The infinity symbol represents an idealized infinite reproduction of the seed by the alpha status members. The infinity symbol represents the alpha status members and their attitude towards self. The color of the infinity symbol is white. The white color indicates. Alpha status members feel a sorrow. They direct the sorrow towards self. They express an inhibition to love.

The central star is made up of two equilateral triangles. One equilateral triangle points down to Earth and down to hell. At the bottom of this equilateral triangle is a phallus symbol. Omega status members exist within the dissonant communities of faithful believers. The phallus symbol represents non-reproductive functions and roles of the omega status members. The phallus symbol represents termination of the seed by the omega status members. The phallus symbol represents the omega status members and their attitude towards the self. The color of the phallus symbol is white. The white color indicates. Omega status members feel a sorrow. They direct the sorrow towards self. They express an inhibition to love.

The symbols on the right side of the emblem are the tree of infernal life and twin crescent stars. I arrange these symbols to create an abstract female figure. The abstract female figure represents the archetypal heterosexual companion. Alpha and omega status members have their attitudes towards potential heterosexual mates. The two symbols on the right side of the emblem represent their attitudes towards potential heterosexual mates.

The tree of infernal life is located on the corner of an equilateral triangle. The equilateral triangle points up to the sky and up to the heavens. Accordingly, the tree of infernal life represents an attitude towards potential heterosexual mates. Alpha status members express the attitude. Heterosexual members are alpha status members. The color of the tree of infernal life is pink. The pink color indicates. Heterosexual members feel a fear. They direct the fear towards potential heterosexual mates. They express an inhibition to hate.

The twin crescent stars occupy a corner of an equilateral triangle. The equilateral triangle points down to the Earth and down to hell. Accordingly, the two crescent stars represent an attitude towards potential heterosexual mates. Omega status members express the attitude. Homosexual members are omega status members. The color of the twin crescent stars is black. The black color indicates. Homosexual members feel an anger. They direct the anger towards potential heterosexual mates. They express a freedom to hate.

The symbols on the left side of the emblem are the Latin cross and triangle. I arrange these two symbols to create an abstract male figure. The abstract male figure represents the archetypal homosexual companion. Alpha and omega status members have their attitudes towards potential homosexual mates. The two symbols on the left side of the emblem represent their attitudes towards potential homosexual mates.

The Latin cross is located on the corner of an equilateral triangle. The equilateral triangle points up to the sky, and up to the heavens. Accordingly, the Latin cross represents an attitude towards potential homosexual mates. Alpha status members express the attitude. Heterosexual members are alpha status members. The color of the Latin cross is black. The black color indicates. Heterosexual members feel an anger. They direct the anger towards potential homosexual mates. They express a freedom to hate.

The triangle is located on the corner of an equilateral triangle. The equilateral triangle points down to the Earth, and down to hell. Accordingly, the triangle represents an attitude towards potential homosexual mates. Omega status members express the attitude. Homosexual members are omega status members. The color of the triangle is pink. The pink color indicates. Homosexual members feel a fear. They direct the fear towards potential homosexual mates. They express an inhibition to hate.

Dissonant communities of faithful believers are free in the love of Mother God. Members are Soul Children even if they do not believe themselves to be Soul Children. Mother God bestows infinite love, divine forgiveness, eternal freedom, and unifying grace upon all of her Soul Children. The infinite love, divine forgiveness, eternal freedom, and unifying grace enables dissonant communities of faithful believers. Dissonant communities of faithful believers are able to do as they wish with spiritual impunity.

A swirling tear drop shape surrounds the red circle. The color of the swirling tear drop shape is white. The white color reveals. The true origins of the emblem of the seed-body are the motivations of the seed-body. The act of creating is the motivation of the seed. The act of surviving is the motivation of the body.

CHAPTER 91. CYCLICAL CHANGE

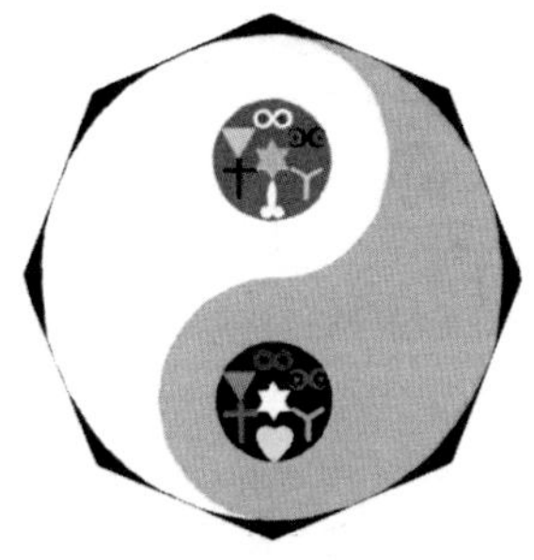 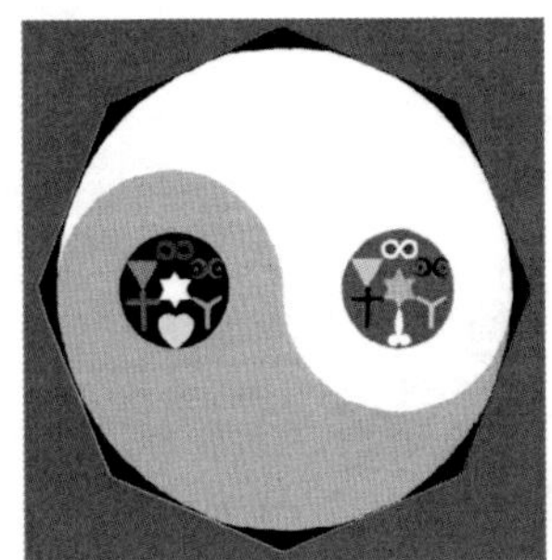 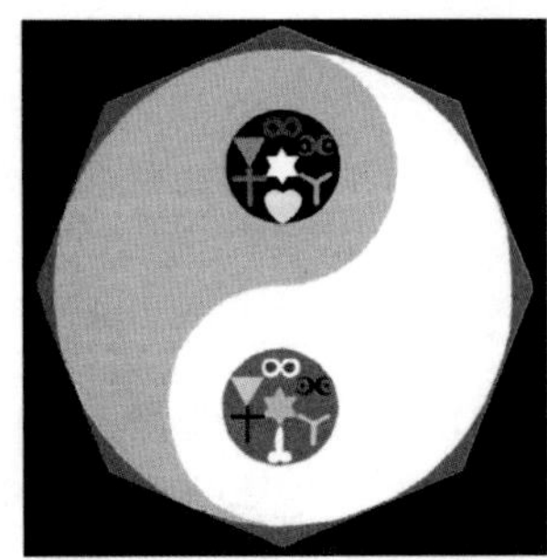 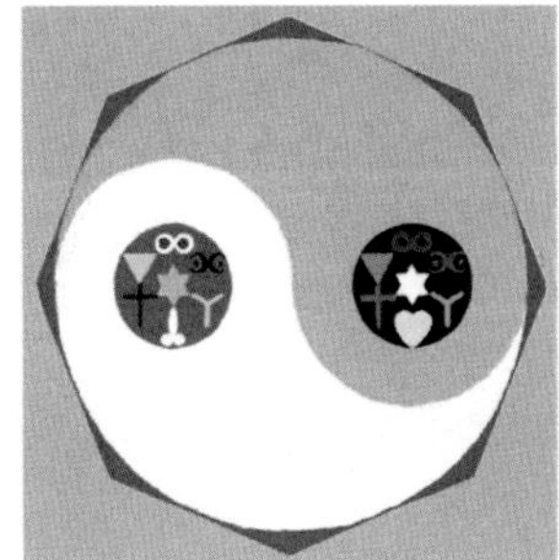

Taoists say. The yin-yang symbol represents cyclical change. Taoists rotate the symbol into any number of positions. Rotating the symbol into any number of positions illustrates cyclical change. Likewise, I rotate my Mandala into a number of possible positions. Rotating my Mandala into a number of possible positions illustrates points within a cycle of change.

Watch hands rotate around the face of a clock in a clock-wise direction. I rotate my Mandala in a clock-wise direction. Rotating my Mandala in a clock-wise direction suggests the passage of time.

The global culture is a complex chaotic dynamic system. Let us suppose. The complex chaotic dynamic system is strangely attracted to progression through phases of a cycle of change. In that event, I depict the cycle of change. I rotate my Mandala in a clock wise direction.

The four major elements of my Mandala are the white element, red element, the black element, and the gray element. I use the four colors white, red, black, and gray. I represent the infinite seed, infinite body, infinite soul, and infinite spirit respectively. The colors white, red, black, and gray, also represent the motivations of the seed, body, soul, and spirit.

The cycle of change has phases. My interpretation of the phases follows from the relative position of each of the four major elements. My interpretation of the phases follows from the meaning of the formation of seven symbols.

At a point within the cycle of change, the red circle rotates into its' highest position. The black circle rotates into its' lowest position. I rotate my Mandala into this position. I depict the symbolic dominance of the yang principle. At this point, the motivation of the seed dominates over all other motivations. The act of creating is the motivation of the seed. From the dominance of the motivation of the seed comes the dominance of the worldview of the creators.

Let us suppose. People devote energy, space, and time to the worldview of the creators. These people affirm. They have an ability to know. They possess knowledge about the existence of at least one deity. These people claim. Their ability to know leads to a belief. In that event, these people are gnostic theists.

Let us suppose. A few paranoid oppressive violent people gain influence over religious authority figures. These religious authority figures gain influence over communities of faithful believers. These communities of faithful believers gain influence over members. These members affirm. They have an ability to know. A good entity rules in Heaven. The good entity issued commands to the faithful. These commands are. The faithful must channel all sexual energy into sex for procreative purposes. The faithful must prohibit sex for occupational, recreational, and homosexual purposes. Sex education could make these practices safer. The faithful must protest against sex education. The faithful must fight against anybody who is not doing the same thing. The faithful must fight against anybody who is not believing in the same way. In that event, these members attribute a will to this good entity. The will of this good entity follows from the motivation of the seed. The act of creating is the motivation of the seed. The net result is. The number of members grows exponentially over time.

The cycle of change continues to progress. The black circle rises to its leftmost position. The red circle falls to its rightmost position. Balance occurs between this rising black circle and this falling red circle. A balance of power occurs between the yin principle and the yang principle. At this point, the motivation of the body dominates over all other motivations. The act of surviving is the motivation of the body. From the dominance of the motivation of the body comes the dominance of the worldview of the survivors.

Let us suppose. People devote energy, space, and time to the worldview of the survivors. These people affirm. They have an inability to know. They can not possess knowledge about the existence of deities. They can not possess knowledge about the nonexistence of deities. These people claim. This inability to know leads to a disbelief. In that event, these people are agnostic atheists.

The reason for this progression in the cycle of change is simple. The act of creating is the motivation of the seed. The dimensions of the body consuming biosphere are limited. The limited dimensions confront the motivation of the seed. The act of creating requires resources. These resources become scarce and hard to come by. For that reason, focus now turns to the survival of the body. The body consumes the body. The strain upon the non-renewable resources of the body-consuming biosphere becomes evident. Human activity causes pollution, deforestation, desertification, and desolation. This pollution, deforestation, desertification, and desolation outpaces the renewal of resources. Subsistence level existence becomes a way of life for many people. Thousands of timid and harmless infants and young children begin to die on a daily basis of starvation and disease.

The cycle of change continues to progress. The black circle rises to its highest position. The red circle falls to its lowest position. The black circle is directly over top of the red circle. The yin principle comes to dominate the global culture. At this point, the motivation of the soul dominates over all other motivations. The act of perfecting is the motivation of the soul. From dominance of the motivation of the soul comes dominance of the worldview of the perfectionists.

Let us suppose. People devote energy, space, and time to the worldview of perfectionists. These people affirm. They have an ability to know. They possess knowledge about the nonexistence of deities. These people claim. This ability to know leads to a disbelief. In that event, these people are gnostic atheists.

The reason for this progression in the cycle of change might be. Qualities of space and longevities of time are inherent in seed-bodies. Gradual environmental degradation and or genetic degradation causes the qualities of space and the longevities of time to diminish. Another reason for this progression in the cycle of change might be. Sudden catastrophic change causes civilization to collapse. Inhibition to hate is an attribute of the motivation of the body. Freedom to hate is an attribute of the motivation of the soul. This progression in the cycle of change marks a triumph. The triumph is. Freedom to hate triumphs over inhibition to hate.

Various species of life exist on planet Earth. A delicate balance of conditions supports the various species of life. It appears. The various species of life evolve. Evolution has progressed at times in a gradual steady manner. At other times, sudden catastrophic change disturbs the delicate balance of conditions. The disturbance of the delicate balance of conditions precipitates mass extinctions.

Let us suppose. An alliance developed between capitalists and fundamentalists. Let us suppose further. Sudden catastrophic change occurs. Maybe a global nuclear war is fought. Maybe a super volcano erupts. Maybe a massive body from outer space falls to Earth. Let us suppose finally. The climate abruptly changes. Human habitat is subsequently lost. In that event, the lives of many people would be lost. Most if not all the many people of our global culture would be incapable of functioning effectively. A global culture of sufficient technological sophistication would cease to exist. As a result, any alliance between capitalists and fundamentalists would be dissolved. Ideological change would occur.

The cycle of change continues to progress. The red circle rises to its leftmost position. The black circle falls to its rightmost position. Balance occurs between this rising red circle and this falling black circle. Another balance of power between yin and yang occurs. At this point, the motivation of the Spirit dominates over all other motivations. The act of reviving is the motivation of the Spirit. From dominance of the motivation of the Spirit comes dominance of the worldview of the revivers. From the infinite spirit comes spiritual laws of love and freedom.

Let us suppose. People devote energy, space, and time to the worldview of the revivers. These people affirm. They have an inability to know. They can not possess knowledge about the existence of deities. They can not possess knowledge about the nonexistence of deities. These people claim. This inability to know leads to a belief. In that event, these people are agnostic theists.

The totality makes possible an infinite number, diversity, and variety of myths. Some agnostic theists value the most optimistic myths. Thereby, some agnostic theists produce emotional balance in their minds. Emotional balance in our minds is conducive to happiness and good health in our lives. Happiness and good health in our lives is conducive to success and prosperity in business.

The reason for this progression in the cycle is. Qualities of space and longevities of time are inherent within seed-bodies. The act of perfecting is the motivation of the soul. This motivation of the soul is effective at improving qualities of space and longevities of time. Above a certain threshold level, the many people of our global culture are capable. They function effectively within a civilization. This civilization has sufficient technological sophistication. This sufficient technological sophistication supports their survival. Human population grows. This leads to the fall of the yin principle and the rise of the yang principle. Eventually, yin and yang reach parity of influence. The global culture is characterized by respect, tolerance, and freedom.

The cycle of change continues to progress. The red circle rises to its highest position. The black circle falls to its lowest position. The red circle is directly over top of the black circle. The yang principle comes to dominate the global culture. The motivation of the seed again dominates over all other motivations.

The reason for the progression in the cycle of change is. This civilization of sufficient technological sophistication makes possible a resurgence of the motivation of the seed. Eventually, the motivation of the seed dominates over all other motivations. From this dominance of the motivation of the seed comes the dominance of the worldview of the creators. From here, a repetition of the cycle may begin.

Four things combine to make up my model of the totality. These four things are the seed-body of the world, the seed-body of self, the soul-spirit of self, and the soul-spirit of the world. From the thought of these four things comes my experience of four basic families of emotion. I experience these four basic families of emotion as sadness, fear, anger, and joy.

All of this leads me to the following questions: "Presently, where is our global culture at in this cycle of change?" The answer is. Just as each of us makes up our own mind about the totality so each of us envisions a world, wherein; one or more of the four motivations dominate over others. Societies combine to make up our global culture.

Let us suppose. The motivation of the body dominates in most if not all societies. In that event, the global culture would be in the phase, wherein; the worldview of the survivors dominates. The global culture would be headed into the phase, wherein; the worldview of the perfectionists comes to dominate.

CHAPTER 92. COSMIC GAME

A passive infinite seed produces combinations and permutations of energy, space, and time. An active infinite spirit evaluates all possible combinations and permutations of energy, space, and time. Some combinations and permutations of energy, space, and time produce large universes of the correct kind to support living infernal fractal entities. At will, our infinite spirit transforms those combinations and permutations, from possibility into energy, space, and time. Those combinations and permutations of energy, space, and time, become part of an active infinite seed-body. The spirit becomes passive, hidden, and mysterious. Soul children become active participants in the cosmic game.

The infinite divine eternal being; wants to play a game. The infinite divine eternal being; wants to enjoy. To enjoy is to experience joy. To experience joy is to be enveloped by joy. To be enveloped by joy is to be surrounded by joy. Joy is bliss and bliss is existence. The infinite divine eternal being enjoys entertainment. The drama of life and death entertains. For that reason, the universe happens spontaneously. The universe is part of the natural movement of existence in the direction of enjoyment. The universe is part of the natural movement of existence in the direction of self-relation.

Existence moves by its nature to enjoy existence. Maybe existences' own infinity and singularity limit enjoyment. Have you ever tried to play monopoly by yourself or any other game? Let us suppose. A person plays a game of hide and seek. Let us suppose further. The person always knows where the other players are hiding. In that event, what fun is hide and seek? The infinite divine eternal being; is in a similar situation.

Let us suppose. The infinite divine eternal being is the only player. In that event, how can the infinite divine eternal being; play a game and enjoy? The infinite divine eternal being must create the illusion of teams of players. These players must be individuals. How does the infinite divine eternal being enable one player to separate from another player? The stages in the evolution of existence into an experience are analogous to the steps necessary to play a game.

The first step in playing a game is. Have more than one player. Existence must exist in a relationship to existence. Let us suppose. Existence does exist in a relationship to existence. In that event, existing in a relationship to existence enables existence. Existence creates enough players to play a game.

The next step in playing a game is. Players must first agree on the game. Let us suppose. The players do agree on the game. In that event, the players will play the game. Before the game begins the players cooperate with their eventual opponents. In this stage in the evolution of existence, existence exists in a relationship to itself. The relational aspects remain aware of their inseparability and connection. The relational aspects of existence lose sight of their connection to the whole in the context of experience, specifically in the context of the experience of seed-bodies.

The next steps in playing a game are. Set up the game board or playing field. Define the boundaries of play. Determine the rules of the game. Existence accomplishes these steps for us. Existence creates our universe. Participants in the game split up into opposing teams, or into opposing players. We become life forms in a body consuming biosphere. A primal conflict between predator and prey divides the body consuming biosphere. Our body consuming biosphere is on a crusted magma globe with a sun and a moon. The sun and moon are reproducible in a galaxy of stars and a universe of galaxies. The universe of galaxies is one of an infinite seed-body of large universes of the correct kind to support living infernal fractal entities. As life forms, we lose sight of our connection to the infinite divine eternal being.

Existence does these things on purpose. Existence enables us. We can have fun playing a game. We can have fun interacting with our friends.

What game is it? To me, it seems to be almost like a game of "hide and seek". Existence wishes to find existence. For that reason, existence hides from existence. In the process of looking and finding, existence enjoys existence.

Our seed-bodies live and die. Our seed-bodies create our unconscious minds. Our souls order the sub-atomic chaos of our unconscious minds. Our souls generate our conscious minds. Our souls confine our conscious awareness of the totality to our conscious minds.

Existence conceals its' joy from itself. Concealing its' joy from itself enables existence. Existence reveals its' joy to itself. All the other games are side-games. We play the side-games within the context of the larger game of "hide and seek".

Why do children love to play hide and seek? Why do infants love peek-a-boo? These activities are an extension of an activity. The activity has brought them here. The activity is. The cosmic game. The cosmic game is. "Hide and seek". The cosmic game is. "Now you see it. Now you don't".

The first step in playing hide and seek is. Existence says to itself. "You turn around and close your eyes. I'll go hide. You come and find me". To turn around and close my eyes means turning away from my soul-spirit. I turn away by directing my attention and thus my awareness into the experience of my seed-body. I experience myself in the context of the defining boundaries of my seed-body. In this way, I experientially wall off my awareness from the rest of existence. I literally close my "I".

I am part of the existence of an infinite divine eternal being. The infinite divine eternal being is in the process of enjoying itself. The infinite divine eternal being is in the process of playing a game with itself. The division of self from world is the motivation for the first movement of my awareness into my seed-body. This first movement of my awareness into my seed-body is a necessary part of the game. For those reasons, I come here. I do this.

> The best athlete wants his opponent at his best.
>
> The best general enters the mind of his enemy.
>
> The best businessman serves the communal good.
>
> The best leader follows the will of the people.
>
> All of them embody the virtue of non-competition.
>
> Not that they do not love to compete.
>
> However, they do it in the spirit of play.
>
> In this, they are like children.
>
> And in harmony with the Tao.
>
> Lao Tzu

A game is something done for enjoyment. Who wins? Who loses? In a true game, the outcome does not matter. One plays for the sake of enjoying the interaction with the other players. In the case of existence, only one player really exists. Existence plays the game for the sake of enjoying itself. Existence plays the game for the sake of experiencing the bliss of its own existence. The process itself is important. The game provides the enjoyment of interaction.

Let us suppose. A person becomes attached to a particular outcome. The person plays the game in question for the sole purpose of obtaining some tangible reward at the conclusion of the game like money, a trophy, the status of being 'number one'. In that event, winning by definition becomes the only reason for playing. For that reason, playing the game becomes less enjoyable for the player.

Let us suppose. The goal of a game is. Enjoy playing the game. In that event, the outcome becomes irrelevant. The game is nothing more than a game. Some people simply enjoy playing the game. Those people are the winners.

CHAPTER 93. I AM AN OPTI-MYSTIC

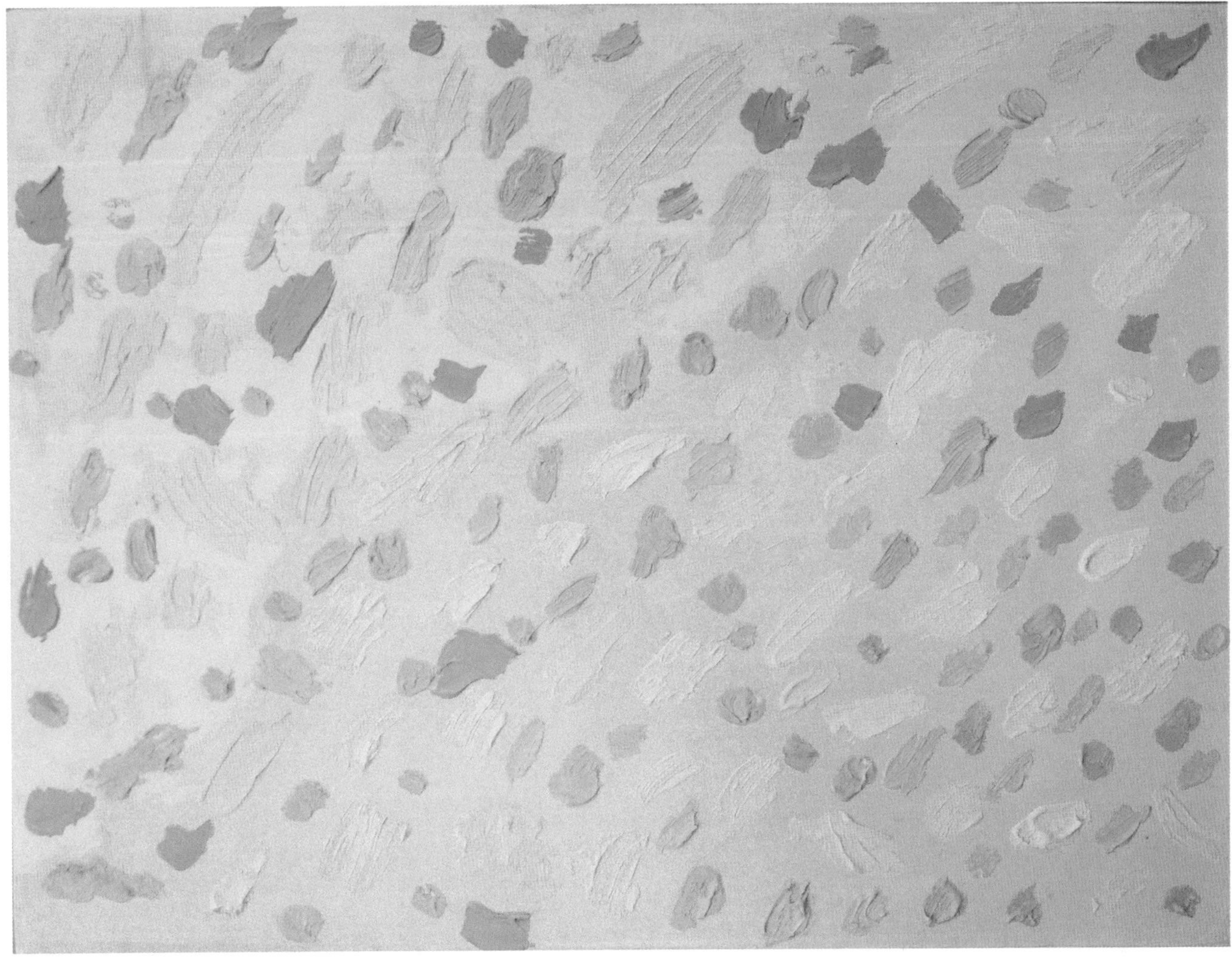

I value the most optimistic myths. Our seed-bodies create our unconscious minds. Our unconscious minds make available a finite number, diversity, and variety of possibilities for thought, feeling, and action. Our souls evaluate these possibilities. Our souls select possibilities. Our souls construct our models of the totality.

We make up our minds in a number, diversity, and variety of ways. Only our creative abilities and powers of imagination limit the number, diversity, and variety of ways. The number, diversity, and variety of ways make the global culture an entertaining place. Let us suppose. Everyone made up their minds about the totality in exactly the same way. In that event, the global culture would be a far less entertaining place.

People have different life experiences. People have differing points of view. People construct differing models of the totality. People believe differently about the totality. I say. Infinity Divinity Eternally One Love Our Gods Your way. Do as you please.

Mother God bestows infinite love, divine forgiveness, eternal freedom, and unifying grace upon all of her Soul Children. The infinite love, divine forgiveness, eternal freedom, and unifying grace permits us. We can do as we wish with spiritual impunity.

I am an Agnostic Theist. I affirm an inability to know. I can not possess knowledge of the non-existence of deities. I claim. Optimism correlates with happiness, good health, and prosperity. I desire happiness, good health, and prosperity. For that reason, my inability to know leads to my belief. My belief is. The totality is an infinite divine eternal being. An infinite divine eternal being is everything, everywhere, at all times.

I am an Opti-Mystic. I value my most optimistic myths. My belief in the value of my most optimistic myths enables me. I have the highest esteem of the totality. I balance the emotional forces of my mind. I am happy. Being happy gives me the best chance. I use my truths and my theories. I achieve and maintain good health. Happiness and good health in my life is conducive to success and prosperity in my business.

CHAPTER 94. THANK YOU FOR YOUR GENEROSITY

Love is hard work. Thank you for sharing your love with the world. You have been generous with your time and energy. Your generosity is an inspiration. You inspire me. I wish us happiness, good health, and prosperity. I offer you my best regards.

My words and my images represent my House of Ideology. My words and my images enable people. People can interpret my words and my images. People can translate my words and my images back into meaningful ideas.

Whether we realize it or not, our souls are in temporal communion with our seed-bodies. Our souls are in continuous communion with our spirit. Let us suppose. People are reading from this book. In that event, continuous spiritual communion enables the people. The people can communicate feedback to me.

Let us suppose. People use their words. Use their voices. Use their writing skills. Devote energy, space, and time to a task. The task is. Offer me feedback. In that event, their words enable them. Their voices enable them. Their writing skills enable them. Their devotion to the task enables them. They can communicate feedback to me.

Let us suppose. People feed me. Shelter me. Clothe me. Tend my garden. Give me their pardon. In that event, the people are generous. The generosity of the people enables me. I can work hard for the people. Love is hard work. I can share my love with the world.

I have my plan. My plan is. Add value to people. Change behaviors with nothing more serious than the simple communication of ideas. Save humanity by changing behaviors. Save humanity from extinction. I am given this hero's journey to take. I have the ability. I am grateful.

Let us suppose. I build a bridge. We can cross my bridge. My bridge enables us. We can avoid a whole bunch of pitfalls. We can align our values with our common needs and aspirations. In that event, I would think, believe, and predict. We would believe in the value the most optimistic myths. We would believe in the value of truths. These would be our values. Our values would act as forces upon our emotions. We would balance the emotional forces of our minds. We would be happy. Our emotions would act as forces upon our behaviors. We would exhibit glad behaviors. Truth telling, sharing, playing well with others, liberating, emancipating, and nurturing are glad behaviors. Friendly tolerant peacemaking behaviors are glad behaviors. Our glad behaviors would be conducive to a state of good health in our bodies. Our glad behaviors would be conducive to a state of good health in our habitats. We would be generous with our time and energy. We would work hard together. We would bring about healing. We would raise our energies to a higher vibration. We would have each other. Emotional balance in our minds would be conducive to happiness and good health in our lives. Happiness and good health in our lives would be conducive to success and prosperity in business.

AFTERWORD

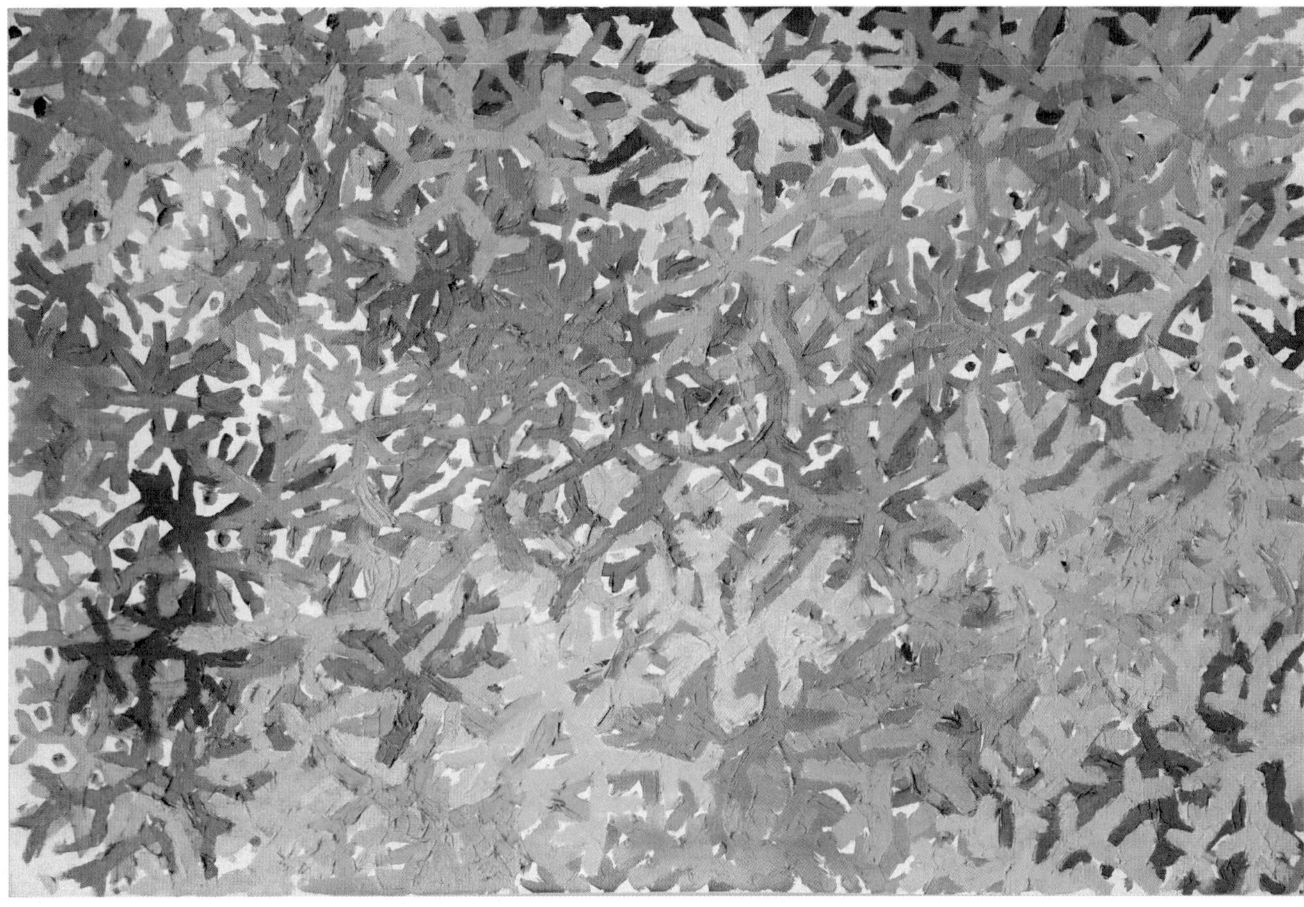

The totality makes possible an infinite number, diversity, and variety of myths. The placebo and nocebo effects suggest to me the following. Optimism correlates with happiness and good health. Pessimism correlates with sorrow, fear, anger, and disease.

Let us suppose. We want to choose happiness and good health. In that event, we need to choose optimism. It is only a matter of time before. We awaken to a freedom of choice. The freedom of choice follows from a truth. The truth is. A myth is a myth. It is only a matter of time before. Optimism self-organizes into spiritual association. It is only a matter of time before. We liberate each other from a spiritual slavery. The spiritual slavery follows from a lie. The lie is. A myth is a truth. It is only a matter of time before. A few paranoid oppressive violent people give up their Institutions of Spiritual Slavery. It is only a matter of time before. Almost all people have the highest esteem of self. Almost all people have the highest esteem of the world. It is only a matter of time before. We celebrate each other with a love of self and world. The love of self and world is taken to its highest esteem. It is only a matter of time before. We acknowledge. We are the authorities. We decide how. We make up our own minds. We are the architects. We build within our minds. We build models of the totality. Our models are our realities. Our realities are our houses of ideologies. It is only a matter of time before. We identify ourselves as the high ideologues of our houses of ideologies. It is only a matter of time before. Nearly everyone is consciously aware of continuous communion between soul and spirit. It is only a matter of time before. Continuous spiritual communion yield inspiration, intuition, and good judgment. It is only a matter of time before. People persevere, overcome obstacles, and progress towards victory.

I believe in the value of truths. The truth is. It appears. The human species may be in danger of going extinct. However, I believe in the value of the most optimistic myths. The most optimistic myths are all about the existence of infinite abundance. One species more or less is not going to mean anything in the grand scheme of things. For that reason, I feel no urgency or give importance to this negativity. However, I enjoy being human. For that selfish reason, I made my plan. I follow my plan. My plan is. Add value to people. Change behaviors with nothing more serious than the simple communication of ideas. Save humanity by changing behaviors. Save humanity from extinction.

Let us suppose. We continue to be pessimistic. In that event, yes all systems will eventually fail including capitalism. The root of our problems is not our politics. The root of our problems is our values. Our values act as forces upon our emotions. We believe in the value truths. The most powerful emotional forces of sorrow, fear, and anger follow from the discovery of a truth. The truth is. It appears. One day, the seed-body of self will die. Some people believe in the value pessimistic myths. The three most commonly valued pessimistic myths are. Self is only a seed and a body. Self has only one life to live. Self has only one body to give. Belief in the value of these pessimistic myths does not enable these people. These people are unable to balance the emotional forces of their minds. These people are unwilling. They will not abandon their beliefs in the value of these pessimistic myths. A few of these people accumulate wealth, income, and power into their own hands. They think, believe, and predict. The accumulation of wealth, income, and power into their own hands will enable them. They will be able to balance the emotional forces of their minds. However, no amount of wealth, income, and power will ever be great enough to compensate them for their discovery of the truth. The truth is. It appears. One day, the seed-body of self will die. They can not find relief from the powerful emotional responses of sorrow, fear, and anger. For that reason, they suffer from a severe emotional imbalance of their minds. Our emotions act as forces upon our behaviors. For that reason, they exhibit sad, mad, and bad behaviors.

These people are making a choice. One totality exists. For that reason, we are part of the existence of one totality. Ideas are thoughts, beliefs, and expectations about the existence of one totality. We value certain ideas. These certain ideas are our values. We know next to nothing about almost everything. For that reason, the existence of one totality makes possible an infinite number diversity and variety of myths. These people choose to believe in the value of pessimistic myths.

So what needs to happen for all systems to succeed? People need to choose to believe in the most optimistic myths. And at the same time, we need to stop lying to ourselves. Stop lying to each other. Start telling the truth. And start behaving in a logical manner. We need to start by being humble. We know of the truth by use of our senses and perceptions. Our senses and perceptions are limited by the attributes of our seed-bodies. Our senses and perceptions are limited by our occupation of specific points in energy, space, and time. For that reason, admit it. We know next to nothing about almost everything. We need to start believing in the value of the most optimistic myths. Belief in the value of the most optimistic myths produces emotional balance in our minds. Emotional balance in our minds is conducive to happiness and good health in our lives.

What are the most optimistic myths? The most optimistic myths are myths about the existence of infinite abundance. An infinite divine eternal being exists. The infinite divine eternal being is in everything, everywhere, at all times. The infinite divine eternal being enjoys entertainment. The drama of life and death entertains. For that reason, the infinite divine eternal being manifests as an infinite four. The four infinity consist of an infinite seed, an infinite body, an infinite soul, and an infinite spirit. The infinite seed consists of an infinite number, diversity, and variety of large universes of the correct kind to support living infernal fractal entities. The infinite body consists of the seed bodies of all of the living infernal fractal entities within all of the infinite number, diversity, and variety, of large universes of the correct kind to support living infernal fractal entities. The infinite soul consists of all of the souls within all the living infernal fractal entities. The infinite spirt consist of an infinite divine eternal being. Mother God is the infinite soul-spirit. Father Love is the infinite seed-body. The union of Mother God and Father Love creates life. We are Soul Children. We are seed, body, soul, and spirit. Each of us has an infinite number, diversity, and variety of lives to live. Each of us has an infinite number, diversity, and variety of bodies to give. Mother God bestows infinite love, divine forgiveness, eternal freedom, and unifying grace upon all of her Soul Children. We are saved. We have been saved. We always will be saved.

ACKNOWLEDGEMENT

Gratitude is a beacon. Appreciation shines bright in the human heart. Thankfulness guides us. We acknowledge countless hands. These innumerable hands lift us up along our journey.

In my tale of transformation, I find. People have paved the path before me. I am enveloped in a symphony of gratitude. Each note echoes the influence of those people.

Individuals provided support. Their support ignited the flame of my potential. First and foremost, I extend my sincerest thanks to these individuals. Their encouragement and belief enabled me. I found the courage to reach for the stars. Their unwavering faith illuminated the path ahead. Their resolute belief propelled me forward with each step.

As I acquired the tools of my trade, from computers to software applications, I realized. These instruments held the immense power. These contraptions unlocked my creativity. With their assistance, I sculpted documents, crafted records, and formatted manuscripts for publication. These devices were not merely tools. These machines were enablers of my vision. These implements enabled me. I manifested my ideas into reality.

With each addition to my creations, whether it be photos capturing moments in time or AI-generated art pushing the boundaries of imagination, I remained humbled by the support of those around me. My family showed me steadfast love and guidance. They witnessed my growth into the person I am today. My mother was an artist in her own right. She cultivated a nurturing home. She provided the fertile ground for my dreams to flourish. My father was a pillar of strength and resilience. He instilled within me the values of hard work and determination.

To my husband, I owe a debt of gratitude. His selflessness knows no bounds. His devotion has been unwavering. He has had a profound impact on my life. His act of saving me was a testament to the depth of his love and the power of human connection.

And to my friends, my companions on this journey called life, I extend my heartfelt appreciation for their camaraderie and companionship. Together, we navigate the complexities of existence. We find solace in the shared experience of being human.

I am indebted to the taxpayers. Our society is built upon an infrastructure. Their contributions sustain the infrastructure. We stand upon a foundation. Their investment in the common good provides the foundation. They offer us the space and resources. We contemplate the totality of our existence.

Doctors, nurses, and medical professionals intervened in my time of need. They are the unsung heroes of our society. Their tireless efforts ensure the preservation of life and the alleviation of suffering.

Teachers imparted knowledge and wisdom. I owe a debt of gratitude. They illuminated the path of learning and enlightenment. The world is often shrouded in darkness. Their dedication to education is a beacon of hope.

Property owners and landlords provided shelter in my time of need. I offer my sincerest thanks for their generosity and compassion. Their kindness was a lifeline in moments of uncertainty. The world is fraught with peril. They provided sanctuary.

The men and women of the armed forces defend our country with valor and honor. They are the guardians of our freedom and the protectors of our way of life. Their sacrifice ensures our safety and security. They enable us. We live in peace and harmony.

Everyday heroes brighten the world around us with their simple acts of kindness and compassion. I offer my deepest gratitude. Their generosity and goodwill are a testament to the inherent goodness of humanity. They remind us. Even in the darkest of times, light can always be found.

In the tapestry of life, each thread represents a person, a moment, a connection. These threads shape us into who we are and who we aspire to be. I recognize the beauty of this interconnectedness through the lens of gratitude. I acknowledge the profound impact of each individual on the fabric of our existence.

ABOUT THE AUTHOR

Mo Go Fa Lo

Mo Go Fa Lo is an accomplished writer whose journey is as inspiring as the words he pens on paper.

Born with a passion for both music and writing, Mo Go Fa Lo's early years were marked by a pursuit of artistic expression. He honed his craft at UCLA, where he earned a Bachelor's degree in Music Composition. He immersed himself in the harmonies of melody and the symphony of words.

However, fate had other plans for Mo Go Fa Lo. A virus swept across the globe. The virus left a trail of devastation in its wake. Afflicted by the disease it caused, Mo Go Fa Lo found. He faced a stark reality. A doctor declared him permanently disabled. His dreams of a career were dashed, replaced by a new reality of uncertainty and hardship.

Yet, in the face of adversity, Mo Go Fa Lo refused to succumb to despair. Instead, he embraced the challenges before him as an opportunity for growth and transformation. With the support of monthly Social Security Disability payments, he found solace in low-income housing. A humble abode became the canvas upon which he would paint his redemption.

Over time, Mo Go Fa Lo embarked on a journey of self-discovery, delving deep into the recesses of his being to confront his values, emotions, behaviors, health, and habitat. Through the act of introspection and self-improvement, he unearthed a newfound sense of purpose and resilience. He gradually reclaimed his path to happiness, good health, and prosperity.

It was amidst this journey of self-realization that Mo Go Fa Lo found the inspiration to share his story with the world. Turning his mess into his message, he poured his heart and soul into a book. Clear, relatable, and practical, his words resonate with readers of all walks of life, offering guidance and wisdom to those who seek it.

Through his book, Mo Go Fa Lo transforms theory into practice and practice into results, empowering readers to navigate life's challenges with courage and conviction. His journey serves as a testament to the resilience of the human spirit and the transformative power of self-discovery.

In the tapestry of his life, Mo Go Fa Lo has woven a story of redemption and hope, reminding us that even in our darkest moments, there is always a glimmer of light waiting to guide us home.

DESCRIPTION OF ILLUSTRATIONS

Chapter 2: Neural.love AI Art Generator Depiction of a Carbon Atom.

Chapter 3: Stock photo showing various facial expressions.

Chapter 4: Stock Design Elements depicting Physical Stress, Psychological Stress, and Psychosocial Stress

Chapter 4: Stock Design Elements depicting work, school and family life.

Chapter 5: Stock Design Elements depicting ethics, scientific research, and commerce.

Chapter 6: Stock Design Elements depicting happiness, good health, and prosperity

Chapter 7: "Blurry Sky" oil painting on canvas by Mo Go Fa Lo

Chapter 10: Neural.love AI Art Generator rendering of we can find things, scientists can find things, and scientists can predict things.

Chapter 12: Neural.love AI Art Generator rendering of truth telling, sharing, and playing well with others

Chapter 14: Neural.love AI Art Generator rendering of some people have declared god dead, a dying institution, the wave of the future.

Chapter 15: Stock photo of a single-cell organism.

Chapter 15: Neural.love AI Art Generator rendering of a microscopic Tardigrade.

Chapter 15: Stock photo showing a magnifying glass hovering over a person's mouth. Cartoon bacteria are added.

Chapter 15: Stock photo of a man's torso. The outline of a digestive system is added.

Chapter 15: Neural Love AI Art Generator rendering of fruits, vegetables, greens, herbs, seeds, roots, nuts, and berries.

Chapter 15: Stock photo of the planet Earth.

Chapter 15: Stock photo of a prescription medicine bottle. Tipped over. Tablets spill out on to a white surface. A stethoscope is visible.

Chapter 17: Stock Photos representing balance, complements, and synthesis

Chapter 18: Neural.love AI Art Generator rendering of God rules in Heaven, God is at war with an evil entity and the evil entity rules over the Earth.

Chapter 18: Neural.love AI Art Generator rendering of a few paranoid oppressive violent people are at war with outsiders.

Chapter 18: Neural.love AI Art Generator rendering of a good entity chose messengers, a set of sacred scrolls, and religious authority figures

Chapter 19: Neural.love AI Art Generator rendering of continuous spiritual communion

Chapter 20: Neural.love AI Art Generator rendering of a head of cauliflower, a river, a coastline, and leaf of a fern.

Chapter 20: Neural.love AI Art Generator rendering of Seventeenth-century astronomer and mathematician Johannes Kepler

Chapter 20: Neural.love AI Art Generator renderings of self gazing up at the night sky, a fault line, and a winding coastline

Chapter 20: Neural.love AI Art Generator renderings of a frond of a fern, a frozen lake, plumes of pollution emanating from industry

Chapter 20: Neural.love AI Art Generator rendering of snowflakes falling from the sky.

Chapter 20: Neural.love AI Art Generator rendering of convincing alien landscapes

Chapter 21: Neural.love AI Art Generator rendering of confession, sacrifice, petition, pilgrimage, prayer, chanting, dance, meditation, and stewardship

Chapter 22: Neural.love AI Art Generator rendering of a body-consuming biosphere, crusted magma globe, sun, moon, galaxy, and universe.

Chapter 23: Neural.love AI Art Generator rendering of water flows, fruit in trees and on vines, vegetables in soil, grains cultivated and harvested

Chapter 24: Blurry Horizon oil painting on canvas by Mo Go Fa Lo

Chapter 25: Stock Photo of Points of Divine Intervention

Chapter 27: Neural.love AI Art Generator rendering of truth telling, sharing, and playing well with others

Chapter 27: Stock design elements depicting happiness, good health, and prosperity.

Chapter 31: "Microcosmos" oil painting on canvas by Mo Go Fa Lo

Chapter 34: Stock Photos of the solar system, stars, and galaxies

Chapter 35: Stock Photos of a sunset, the lunar cycle, and the four seasons.

Chapter 36: Stock photo of a background appears. On the background, text appears. The text reads. Quotient = Numerator ÷ Denominator.

Chapter 36: Stock photo of a background appears. On the background, text appears. The text reads. Self = The Totality ÷ Infinity

Chapter 36: Stock photo of a background appears. On the background, text appears. The text reads. World = The Totality ÷ One

Chapter 37: Infinite Four computer generated imagery by Mo Go Fa Lo.

Chapter 39: Cosmology, Acrylic on canvas painted by Mo Go Fa Lo

Chapter 40: Neural.love AI Art Generator rendering of Unicorns, Dragons, and Fairies.

Chapter 40: Neural,love AI Art Generator rendering of Unicorns are blue, single-horned, horse-like creatures.

Chapter 40: Neural.love AI Art Generator rendering of an invisible dragon living in a garage space meant for a car.

Chapter 40: Neural.love AI Art Generator rendering of Pink Fairies

Chapter 40: Neural.love AI Art Generator rendering of Unicorns, Dragons, and Fairies.

Chapter 41: Neural.love AI Art Generator rendering of we can find things, scientists can find things, and scientists can predict things.

Chapter 42: Neural.love AI Art Generator rendering of people were isolated in their ancestral homelands and developed their own standards of beauty.

Chapter 42: Neural.love AI Art Generator rendering of population overshoot, resource depletion, climate change, habitat loss, war, and extinction.

Chapter 42: Stock Photos of human faces of various complexions.

Chapter 44: Stock design elements depicting, birth, DNA, and baby steps

Chapter 45: "Blurry Landscape" oil painting on canvas by Mo Go Fa Lo

Chapter 47: Stock design elements depicting happiness, good health, and prosperity.

Chapter 48: Stock design elements representing literature, film, poetry, song, theatre, and opera

Chapter 50: Neural.love AI Art Generator rendering of we can find things, scientists can find things, and scientists can predict things.

Chapter 50: Stock design elements depicting happiness, good health, and prosperity

Chapter 53: "Four Motivations", acrylic on canvas by Mo Go Fa Lo

Chapter 58: "Earthy Texture" oil painting on canvas by Mo Go Fa Lo

Chapter 59: Neural.love AI Art Generator rendering of the projection of the moon, world, and sun into imagination as deities.

Chapter 60: Neural.love AI Art Generator rendering of an evil entity tempted our ancestors, sin entered the world, and with sin came death.

Chapter 60: Neural.love AI Art Generator rendering of an evil entity rules in hell, self lives on planet earth, and a good entity rules in Heaven.

Chapter 61: Neural.love AI Art Generator rendering of famine in a desolate war zone, war against humanity, and ruins of modern civilization.

Chapter 62: Neural.love AI Art Generator rendering of a body-consuming biosphere on a crusted magma globe.

Chapter 62: Neural.love AI Art Generator rendering of population overshoot, logging, factory farms, mining, pollution, and melting glaciers

Chapter 62: Neural.love AI Art Generator rendering of amber waves of grain, rice fields, and population over shoot.

Chapter 63: Neural.love AI Art Generator rendering of radical clerics, militant extremists, and a few paranoid oppressive violent people.

Chapter 65: Neural.love AI Art Generator rendering of war against humanity, and concentration camps.

Chapter 67: Neural.love AI Art Generator rendering of a good entity revealed prophecies, a set of sacred scrolls, and religious authority figures

Chapter 67: Neural.love AI Art Generator rendering of an antichrist will rise to power, a final necessary horrible war, and god will have final victory.

Chapter 68: Neural.love AI Art Generator rendering of the good entity chose messengers, a set of sacred scrolls, and religious authority figures.

Chapter 68: Neural.love AI Art Generator rendering of our ancestors sinned, sin entered the world, and with sin came death.

Chapter 68: Neural.love AI Art Generator rendering of people raptured up to Heaven, Jesus returns as a warrior, and Armageddon unfolds on sinners.

Chapter 70: Neural.love AI Art Generator rendering of an evil entity rules over the Earth, we are sinners, and these are the end times.

Chapter 71: Neural.love AI Art Generator rendering of a few paranoid oppressive violent people, a central bank building, and war against humanity.

Chapter 72: Neural.love AI Art Generator rendering of an imperial megacity, fiat currency, and oil well

Chapter 73: Stock design elements representing happiness, good health, and prosperity

Chapter 74: Stock photo of a crowd of people

Chapter 76: Neural.love AI Art Generator rendering of we feed, clothe, house, nurture, educate, and care for each other.

Chapter 77: Dynamic Influence Diagram in its simplest form, computer generated imagery, by Mo Go Fa Lo.

Chapter 77: Dynamic Influence Diagram with 4 circles shown in four colors, computer generated imagery by Mo Go Fa Lo

Chapter 77: Dynamic Influence Diagram with 13 circles shown in four colors, computer generated imagery by Mo Go Fa Lo

Chapter 77: Dynamic Influence Diagram with 40 circles shown in four colors, computer generated imagery by Mo Go Fa Lo

Chapter 77: Dynamic Influence Diagram with 47 circles shown, computer generated imagery by Mo Go Fa Lo

Chapter 80: Neural.love AI Art Generator rendering of population overshoot, pollution, lack of resources, climate change, habitat loss, and extinction

Chapter 80: Neural Love AI Art Generator rendering of a virus

Chapter 82: Neural.love AI Art Generator rendering of earthquake, volcano eruption, lightning, tornado, hurricane, flood, famine, plague, and astronomy.

Chapter 83: Neural.love AI Art Generator rendering of a portrait of Xenophanes.

Chapter 85: Neural.love AI Art Generator rendering of the universe theatre, all the world is a stage, and we are actors in the drama of life and death.

Chapter 86: Stock Photo of Yin Yang Symbol

Chapter 87: Neural.love AI Art Generator rendering of a portrait of Lao Tzu.

Chapter 88: Mandala of the House of Ideology, computer generated imagery by Mo Go Fa Lo

Chapter 88: Modified yin yang symbol with a four-color design oil paint on canvas by Mo Go Fa Lo

Chapter 88: Two Emblems, computer generated imagery by Mo Go Fa Lo

Chapter 89: Emblem of the Soul-Spirit, oil paint on canvas, by Mo Go Fa Lo

Chapter 90: Emblem of the Seed-Body, oil paint on canvas by Mo Go Fa Lo

Chapter 91: Cyclical Nature, computer generated imagery by Mo Go Fa Lo

Chapter 92: Neural.love AI Art Generator rendering of Seed Body Soul Spirit Living Infernal Fractal Entity

Chapter 93: Inspiration Celebration oil painting on canvas by Mo Go Fa Lo

Chapter 94: Leonardo.ai AI Art Generator rendering of Happiness, Good Health, and Prosperity

Chapter 94: Neural.love AI Art Generator rendering of a bridge between Earth and Heaven.

Afterward: "Coral Bed" oil painting on wood panel by Mo Go Fa Lo

Made in the USA
Columbia, SC
27 August 2024

e884082e-e53e-4518-b8ee-122f42a84c5bR01